THE KABBALAH OF TIME

The Kabbalah of Time

Revelation of Hidden Light
Through the Jewish Calendar

Rabbi Daniel Kahane

and

Ann Helen Wainer

iUniverse LLC
Bloomington

The Kabbalah of Time
Revelation of Hidden Light Through the Jewish Calendar

iUniverse books may be ordered through booksellers or by contacting:

iUniverse LLC
1663 Liberty Drive
Bloomington, IN 47403
www.iuniverse.com
1-800-Authors (1-800-288-4677)

ISBN: 978-1-4759-9658-6 (sc)
ISBN: 978-1-4759-9659-3 (ebk)

Printed in the United States of America

iUniverse rev. date: 07/23/2013

CONTENTS

ACKNOWLEDGEMENTS

First of all, we praise and thank G-d for the privilege to spread His wisdom. We are very grateful to be able to see the fruits of this project, a life-long pursuit in which we always felt guided by Him.

We would like to thank our parents Michael Abraham Z"L and Iliana Cooper, Allan Kahane and Sandra Felzenszwalbe. We also thank husband and father-in-law, Raul Wainer and daughter and wife, Danielle Kahane, for all their support during this journey.

We are very grateful to the Rebbe and his emissaries, and the entire Chabad-Lubavitch community. We always have in mind the blessing that came with the dollar that Ann Helen received from the Rebbe "for writing books." We are thankful for the great care and affection we always receive from so many rabbis and rebbetzins, be they in Rio de Janeiro, Miami, Sudbury, and so many other places around the world. We also wanted to thank Rabbi Aryeh Citron for his time and assistance, as well as Rabbi Pinchas Ellovitch for his words of encouragement and support.

To the Philanthropic Institute Vicky and Joseph Safra, who made possible the first publication of this book, originally in Portuguese. May they and their future generations be forever blessed, and may they be able to continue the beautiful work of preserving our Jewish heritage through the "Revista Morasha" as well as through so many other media. In the eternal words of *Birkat Kohanim*, the priestly blessing: "May the Lord bless you and keep you; May the Lord shine His countenance upon you and be gracious unto you; May the Lord lift His countenance toward you and grant you peace."

Finally, thank you also dear reader. As mentioned in the introduction, today's life is so hectic that is difficult to find time to sit down and read a book. We are honored by your time and trust, and we look forward to sharing with you this beautiful journey. We are at your disposal if you have any questions or comments, as we hope to build on this new relationship. Our email is: cabaladotempo@gmail.com.

The book is dedicated to our ancestors and siblings, as well as to our children and grandchildren: David and Hanith Wainer, Danielle, Jacob, Olivia, Benjamin and Ariella Kahane, and all future descendants. May G-d always protect them, and may they always follow in His ways, connected to the Torah, the People, and the Land of Israel, with much health, happiness and peace.

Ann Helen Wainer and Rabbi Daniel Kahane
28th of *Sivan*, 5772, Week of the 3rd of *Tammuz*

Letter of Blessing

From the desk of Rabbi Aryeh Citron
Dean of Yeshivah LeSmicha, Aventura, Florida
8910 Carlyle Ave., Surfside, FL 33154
www.yeshivahcollege.org
rabbicitron@yeshivahcollege.org

Erev Rosh Chodesh Tammuz, 5773

To Whom It May Concern,

I have known and studied with Rabbi Daniel Kahane for many years and hold him in high regard.

The book he has written together with his mother-in-law, Ann Helen Wainer, presents deep Kabbalistic concepts in a straightforward and readable manner. The parallels it draws between the Jewish calendar, the Divine Attributes, the Songs of the Animals and the teachings of the Ethics of the Fathers are original insights and are quite remarkable. I'm sure that readers will gain inspiration and knowledge from this well-written work.

I wish them both continued success in their personal lives and in their further literary works.

Sincerely,

Rabbi Aryeh Citron

INTRODUCTION

> *"For everything there is a season and for
> every time there is a purpose under Heaven."*
> (Ecclesiastes 3:1)

We spend much of our life in spiritual darkness. We often
go about our lives with great uncertainty, without the
benefit of sage advice or guidance. Yet somehow we just
keep going, attaching ourselves to values that confuse our
minds and our hearts, and ignoring the real needs and
wants of our soul.

We become so busy with our own personal affairs and so
distracted by the avalanche of superfluous information
directed at us, that we blind ourselves to the signs all
around, the lessons and warnings G-d presents to us at
every moment. Certain instances, however, awaken us
from this darkness. In those times, which are like lightning
bolts of clarity, we realize that there is something greater,
something beyond this physical plane and our worldly
concerns.

The reality is that our soul needs to sing! Yet what are we
to do if we do not know the melody and the lyrics of the
song? The Ba'al Shem Tov, the founder of the Chassidic
movement, explains that this is the feeling behind the
shofar blast on *Rosh Hashanah*. The *shofar* is the most basic
and primal expression of the soul, and it is with this cry
that the Jewish people awaken spiritually at the start of
every year.

This book's objective is to bring us closer to our song. The song of the soul: of the individual, of the Jewish people, of humanity, and of nature.[1] This "four-fold song"[2] is directed towards G-d, and the Jewish calendar itself is its sheet music.

In an effort to promote more harmony in our lives, we will study Jewish values and techniques for spiritual enhancement that will make ourselves attuned to the energy of each week of the year. This book will give access to unknown tools, which allow for an open channel of dialogue with G-d. These teachings are not new. They are already found in the Torah itself. They are within everyone's reach, close to the mouth and to the heart.[3]

Through continuous effort, an individual who is committed to change can obtain personal as well as collective transformation: in the family, the local community, the city, and beyond. As the prophet Isaiah exclaims, the Earth was not created to be chaos.[4] We desperately need to live in a better world, and leave it more peaceful for future generations.

Rabbi Schneur Zalman of Liadi, the Alter Rebbe, teaches that one should "live with the times."[5] By connecting Jewish lessons to fixed times in the Jewish calendar, the book is meant to serve as a tool for self-reflection and

---

[1] *Orot HaKodesh II*, p. 444

[2] *Id.*

[3] Deuteronomy 30:11; *Tanya*-Introduction

[4] Chapter 45:18

[5] *Hayom Yom*, 2nd of *Cheshvan*, p. 101

spiritual development through the songs of the animals in *Perek Shirah*, the teachings of the rabbis in *Pirkei Avot*, as well as the kabbalistic meaning behind the numbers and divine attributes (*sefirot*) related to each day of the Counting of the *Omer*.

The Counting of the *Omer*

The Counting of the *Omer*, known in Hebrew as *Sefirat Ha'Omer*, is a Torah commandment to count the weeks and days from which the *omer* sacrifice was offered in the Temple. This sacrifice was made of barley, which in those days was primarily an animal food, and had the Biblical measurement of one *omer*. The counting takes place every year during the 49 days between the holidays of Passover and *Shavuot* (Pentecost).

The Counting of the *Omer* has always been used by the Jewish People as a basis for spiritual development. In Egypt, the Jewish People had reached the 49th level of spiritual impurity. During the first 49 days that followed their escape from Egypt, the Jewish people gradually purified itself, until it reached the 49th level of purity. Within but seven weeks, upon reaching Mount Sinai, the Jewish people had become so spiritually and emotionally refined that the entire nation was able to encamp there in complete harmony, peace, and unity: "as one person with one heart."[6] It was only in this way that they merited to receive the Torah.

---

[6]   Exodus 19:2, *Rashi*

During the *omer* count performed every year between Passover and *Shavuot*, there is a custom to spend each day concentrating on a different combination of *sefirot*. *Sefirot*, as further explained below, are Divine attributes which are also found within every individual. By doing so, it is possible to obtain a level of spiritual and emotional improvement similar to what the Jewish people achieved after leaving Egypt.

The Counting of the *Omer* takes places mostly during the Jewish month of *Iyar*, a month known for its healing powers. A hint of *Iyar's* connection to healing is found within the letters of its name, *alef, yud* and *reish*, an acronym from the biblical verse *Ani Hashem Rofechah*, "I am G-d your Healer."[7]

Besides from being a time of great spiritual elevation and healing, unfortunately the *omer* is also a reminder of a sad period in the history of the Jewish people. Twenty-four thousand students of Rabbi Akiva passed away during these days. They suffered from a plague inflicted due to their lack of unity and respect for one another, the very opposite of what characterized the Children of Israel at Mount Sinai.

---

[7] Exodus 15:26; The Rebbe in his Chassidic Discourse for *Tu B'Shvat*, 5741 states that the *Arizal* and previous rebbes note that the Hebrew word for ill, *choleh* has the numerical value of of forty-nine, a reference to the Forty-Nine Gates of Understanding, which in turn are related to the forty-nine days of the *omer*. (*Available at:* http://www.sichosinenglish. org/books/sichos-in-english/8/21.htm)

The plague ended on the 33rd day of the *omer*, known as *Lag Ba'Omer*. This is one of the reasons why this date is so commemorated. Another reason for celebrating *Lag Ba'Omer* is because it is the *yahrzeit*—the anniversary of the passing—of the great *tzadik* Rabbi Shimon Bar Yochai, who died many years after the plague. Rabbi Shimon Bar Yochai, himself a student of Rabbi Akiva, is the author of the *Zohar*, the basic and most important text of the Kabbalah.[8]

The order in which the combination of *sefirot* takes place for each day of the *omer* follows a very simple principle. As further explained below, there are seven emotional *sefirot*, and since the Counting of the *Omer* occurs over seven weeks, each week represents one *sefirah*. The first week represents the first *sefirah*, *chesed* (kindness), while the second week represents the second *sefirah*, *gevurah* (discipline), and so forth. Furthermore, each day within each week represents a subdivision of one of the seven emotional *sefirot* within that *sefirah*. For example, the first day of the *omer* represents the attribute of *chesed* within *chesed* (*chesed shebechesed*), as

---

[8] "Kabbalah" is a general term used to describe the inner most spiritual dimension of the Torah. The term "Kabbalah" literally means that which was "received," passed down from master to teacher since the giving of the Torah at Mount Sinai. At one point in Jewish history, Kabbalah was studied only by a relatively small group of saintly individuals, and this remains true for the more esoteric teachings. Nonetheless, since the times of the Holy Ari, Rabbi Isaac Luria, the Lion of Safed, as well as the later rise of the Ba'al Shem Tov and Chassidism, the fundamental principles of Kabbalah are now not only widespread, but their study by the general population is encouraged.

it is the first day of the first week. The second day of the first week represents the attribute of *gevurah* within *chesed* (*gevurah shebechesed*). *Lag Ba'Omer* is the fifth day of the fifth week. The fifth *sefirah* is *hod*, and therefore *Lag Ba'Omer* represents *hod shebehod*. The *sefirot* combinations of each day of the *omer* are found in most prayerbooks.

Furthermore, the most basic element in the commandment of the Counting of the *Omer* is to give each day a specific number. Numbers in Judaism have tremendous meaning that goes much beyond their day-to-day usage. Each number has kabbalistic significance, and each letter in the Jewish calendar has a numerical value.

Incredibly, just as *Lag Ba'Omer* takes place on the thirty-third day of the *omer*, two thirds into the counting between Passover and *Shavuot*, so too—and this is quite remarkable—the week of *Lag Ba'Omer* falls two thirds into the Jewish year, exactly on the thirty-third week! Each week of the year therefore parallels each day of the Counting of the *Omer*, and each week is connected to the *sefirah* combination for that day. It is therefore possible to work on oneself through the *sefirot* and the numbers related to the *omer* during the entire year.[9] (*See* Calendar)

---

[9]   At the time of the writing of this book, the authors had not come across the idea of expanding the Counting of the *Omer* to the entire year in any earlier source. Recently however, the authors became aware of a book by Brazilian rabbi Nilton Bonder called Exercícios D'Alma (Soul Exercises), which has a similar premise, although the counting itself is done differently, based on the Torah readings for each week instead of on *Lag Ba'omer*.

Pirkei Avot and Perek Shirah

In addition, from Passover to *Shavuot*, in most religious Jewish communities there is a custom to study the *Pirkei Avot*, also as a mechanism of self-improvement. *Pirkei Avot*, which literally means "Chapters of the Fathers," is part of the *Mishnah* (the Oral Torah) compiled by Rabbi Yehudah HaNassi. In these chapters, each of the main rabbis of the generation writes in concise form what he considers to be most important in order to live ethically and in accordance with the principles of the Torah. *Pirkei Avot* can also be understood as "Father Chapters," since these chapters include the fundamental principles for the study and fulfillment of the rest of the Torah. In this sense, the teachings of *Pirkei Avot* are like "parents," and the rest of the Torah's teachings are like their children.[10]

This book shows how the teachings of rabbis found within the first four chapters of *Pirkei Avot* are organized in such a way that each rabbi corresponds to a week of the year. Similarly, this book will show how this weekly method of self-improvement is also related to each animal of *Perek Shirah*.[11]

---

[10] Marcus, p. 12

[11] No authoritative source has been found for the idea of connecting the weeks of the Jewish calendar to *Perek Shirah* and *Pirkei Avot*, but the authors strongly feel that these connections are not only present, but become increasingly apparent with each coming week. In any event, there is certainly much to be learned from these sources regardless of any specific connection.

Perek Shirah, which means Chapter of Song, is an ancient text that is not very well known, as it has been published only in a handful of prayerbooks around the world. While the authorship of this work is not certain, many attribute it to King David. *Perek Shirah* itself hints to David's authorship as it describes his interaction with a frog immediately following the completion of the Book of Psalms. In this conversation, the frog exclaims, "David! Do not become proud, for I recite more songs and praises than you."

Among sacred Jewish texts, *Perek Shirah* is a groundbreaking work, relevant to our current concerns about the environment. It is a work of enormous lyricism and exaltation of the Creator, including songs from the sun and the moon, Heaven and Earth, as well as from various members of the plant and animal kingdoms. The praises found in this book are like a great orchestra in which, instead of musicians, each element and living being contributes to a beautiful and emotional masterpiece. That result is the best possible exclamation of G-d's greatness by all of His Creation.

It is extraordinary that of all the different elements and creatures listed in *Perek Shirah* that glorify the Creator, there are exactly fifty-two animals in *Perek Shirah*, one for each week of the solar year.[12]

---

[12] The solar calendar of fifty-two weeks is used in Judaism on various occasions. For example, it is used to calculate the blessing over the sun, *Birchat Hachamah*, as well as to calculate the time to switch part of the prayer in the *Amidah* connected to the harvest and the rain (this change is always

In Judaism, as well as in many other cultures, it is well known that humans can learn many important lessons on how to behave by observing animals and nature. The Book of Job, for example, teaches that we should learn how to glorify G-d by observing birds.[13] The Talmud teaches that "Had the Torah not been given, we would have learned to be modest from cats, to avoid theft from ants, to avoid promiscuity from doves, and *derech eretz* (proper conduct) from roosters."[14] The Book of Proverbs advises those that are lazy to observe the ant. Despite the fact that this animal has no supervisor, it collects its food in the summer and stores it during the harvest season.[15] In a similar vein, in *Pirkei Avot*, Rabbi Yehuda Ben Teima tell us to be "bold like the leopard, swift like the eagle, fast like the deer, and courageous like the lion, in order to fulfill the will of your Father in Heaven."[16]

It is quite often easier for a person to learn character traits from animals because human beings are full of paradoxes and internal conflicts, while animals have emotional attributes that are strong and clear, without room for human subtleties. The fact that during the *omer* we work on our emotional characteristics (our animal qualities) is reflected in the *omer* offering itself, which was made out

---

made on the 5th or 6th day of December). The number 365 is also used in Judaism in order to calculate the stockpiling of incense, *ketoret*, in the Temple, and in order to remember the number of biblical prohibitions in the Torah, 365 in all.

13   Chapter 35:11
14   Talmud, *Eruvin* 100b
15   Chapter 6:6.
16   Chapter 5:23

of barley, an animal food. The Lubavitcher Rebbe explains that the process of self-analysis which begins on Passover and runs through the Counting of the *Omer*, culminating on *Shavuot*, is parallel to the kind of food related to each of these days. On Passover we eat *matzah*, which involves total nullification of the ego; the *omer*, made of animal food, reflects our struggle to improve our emotional/ animal characteristics; on *Shavuot*, once our character traits have been refined, leavened bread is brought into the Temple for the first time.[17]

When reading *Perek Shirah*, it is fascinating to observe how the animals so gracefully praise and acknowledge G-d's actions. If animals glorify G-d in such a way, how much more so should we! Furthermore, through each animal and its respective song, we extract examples and lessons on how to help us heal and combat sadness.

How to Read this Book

The pages of this book will show the link between each week of the year and 1) the animals of *Perek Shirah*, 2) the rabbis of *Pirkei Avot*, as well as 3) the number and *sefirah*

---

[17]   Touger, Eliyahu, <u>Timeless Patterns in Time</u>, *available at*: http://www.sichosinenglish.org/books/timeless-patterns/37. htm (Chassidism also explains that working on our "inner animal" is also one of the main purposes of animal sacrifices in the Temple, as explained in the Chassidic discourse *Kuntres U'Ma'ayan*, by Rabbi Shalom Dovber of Lubavitch, the fifth Rebbe of Chabad).

combination of each day of the *omer*. This book can be read from beginning to end all at once, but its main purpose is to be *experienced* during each week. Along with the meaning of every Jewish month and the important dates of the Jewish calendar, the idea is to connect with the spiritual energy of the week through these three paradigms: *Perek Shirah*, *Pirkei Avot*, and the Counting of the *Omer*. While doing so, one should try to absorb and internalize the teachings found in them, in order to improve one's daily conduct.

The book can also be experienced during each day of the actual *omer* count, from Passover until *Shavuot* (using one week for each day), given that the *omer* count is itself a microcosm of the whole year. The fifty-two weeks of the year are also reflected in the rituals and times connected to each day. (*See* Appendix and Table I)

The weeks of this book can even technically be applied on a yearly basis, with each week representing a different year. This may have both an individual application, with each week representing a year in a person's life, but could even be applied to history as a whole, which would more or less parallel the cycles of Sabbatical and Jubilee years. (*See* Table II)

For the individual, the cycle would start at birth, and then restart at age 52. Examples of this would be King Solomon and Shmuel *HaNavi*, who both lived 52 years. This may also apply to more than one reincarnation. In the Passover *Hagaddah*, Rabbi Elazar Ben Azariah states that he "was like a man of 70." The Vilna Gaon teaches that Rabbi Elazar, who was only 18, knew that he was a reincarnation of Shmuel *HaNavi*, and so therefore, he saw himself as being 18 plus 52, which equals 70.[18]

For those seeking a daily connection throughout the year, this can be done simply by subdividing each week, using a different *sefirah* for each day. In this way, a person would perform seven separate "*omer* counts." The first day of the year is *chesed shebechesed shebechesed* (the first day of the first week of the first series of seven weeks), and *Lag Ba'Omer* will represent not only *hod shebehod* but, *hod shebehod shebehod* (the 5th day of the 5th week of the 5th series of seven weeks).[19]

---

[18] Perhaps one can also say that there is an even bigger connection between 70 and 18. Perhaps the 70th year is really like the 18th year of the second cycle, and that everyone who is 18 is really like 70, and vice-versa. The very word *Ben* in the phrase, "*Harei Ani keBen Shivim Shanah*" equals 52. There *keBen* is 20, 2, and 50. If the 2 is subtracted from the 20 and added to the 50, you have 18+52 =70. Rabbi Shmelke of Nicholsberg also said that he had the soul of Shmuel, and he also alluded to Shmuel's age of 52, his age when he made this statement upon his deathbed. The Ba'al Shem Tov's life can also be considered to be 52 in total; 26 years before Achiah *haShiloni* revealed himself to him, and then 26 years after he revealed himself to the world (the ten years in which Achiah *haShiloni* taught him Torah would not count, as they are more parallel to the World to Come; some *Chassidim*, however, count it doubly). (*See Likutei Diburim*)

[19] All "33rd days" for each cycle of seven weeks are connected to important days in the Chassidic calendar: the 29th of *Tishrei-yahrzeit* of Shimon HaTzadik, which

In order to succeed in this journey, the reader will benefit from one more ingredient: *emunah*. *Emunah* means faith in G-d. The *Midrash* states that the Sea of Reeds only split, allowing the Jewish people to cross, after Nachshon ben Aminadav threw himself into the water.[20] At that time, we know that the Jewish People was completely cornered, seeing the Egyptian army approach on one side, and facing the deep waters of sea on the other. What was the way out? The Jewish people hesitated, and somewhat panicked, despite the great number of Divine miracles they saw upon being freed from Egypt. At this moment, without having second thoughts and believing firmly that everything would work out for the best, Nachshon jumped into the sea. When the waters were already entering his nostrils, the Sea of Reeds split and all of the Jewish people followed him. The *Midrash* explains that G-d wanted His people to act based on *emunah*.

Thus, it is through Nachshon's example that we learn how to conduct our lives. *Emunah* is a process we develop (it is etymologically linked to the Hebrew word for craft, *omanut*), but to begin, a person needs a certain amount

---

is commemorated by *Chassidim* in many of the same ways as *Lag Ba'Omer*, including giving three-year-olds their first haircut by his grave. In fact, many those in Jerusalem that cannot go to Shimon Bar Yochai's grave on *Lag Ba'Omer* go to Shimon HaTzadik's instead; *Yud Tes Kislev*; *Yud Shvat*; the 27th of *Adar* (date of the Rebbe's two strokes); *Lag Ba'Omer*; the 8th of *Tammuz* (halfway between the 3rd and the 12th/13th of *Tammuz*); and the 29th of *Av* (day the Alter Rebbe flees Liadi, which led directly to his passing)

[20] *Bamidbar Rabbah* 13:7; Talmud *Sotah* 37A

of faith, to just jump in like Nachshon. The obstacles in Nachshon's way were removed because he was determined to bring G-d's will into reality. After all, nothing is impossible or even difficult for the Eternal One, Who took His people out of the land of Egypt.[21] G-d took His dear people out of slavery; He did not do so through an angel or a messenger, but did it Himself, through His strong hand and outstretched arm.[22] For this reason, besides celebrating Passover annually, the Jewish people also remember its freedom from Egypt in its daily prayers, despite the fact that this liberation took place a few millennia ago.

In conclusion, filled with *emunah,* one can march onward with ease in this beautiful spiritual journey. It is with this strong sense of faith, truth and hope that we present the tools for Jewish wisdom, understanding and knowledge contained in the pages to follow.

---

[21] Exodus 20:2; Psalm 78

[22] Deuteronomy 4:34

THE SEFIROT

> *"And G-d said: Let us make man in Our image
> and likeness"* (Genesis 1:26)

It is expressly written in the Book of Genesis that
G-d created humankind in His image. According to
Maimonides, one of the greatest Jewish philosophers and
legal authorities of all time, men and women resemble
G-d in that they received from Him divine attributes, such
as the capacity for ethical behavior, rational thought, and
free will. We resemble G-d intellectually, emotionally and
spiritually—not physically. Maimonides teaches that our
purpose in this world is to emulate G-d's ways. Just as G-d
is merciful, so should we be merciful. Just as He is holy, so
should we be holy.[23]

In addition, the Kabbalah explains that G-d's attributes
manifest themselves in heavenly spheres known as
sefirot. *Sefirah* (*sefirot* in the plural) can be translated as
emanation, characteristic, quality or divine attribute. We
also have a reflection of these *sefirot* within us, which are
also known as *middot*. By focusing on perfecting our own
sefirot, we are able to emulate G-d and to better relate
to Him. That is why it is so important to acquire a clear
understanding of what the *sefirot* are and represent.[24]

---

[23]   Maimonides, *Mishna Torah*, *Hilchot De'ot*, Chapter 1:6

[24]   One of the authors once dreamt with the title of this book.
In the dream, the book was entitled, "All of these are like
G-d, none of these are G-d," a reference to the *sefirot*.

One of the easiest ways to comprehend the meaning of the *sefirot* is through a better understanding of the "Seven Shepherds," the seven *tzadikim* (righteous men) that the Jewish people has the privilege of "receiving" in the *sukkah* during the Jewish festival of *Sukkot*.

The Jewish People have three patriarchs: Abraham, Isaac and Jacob. On the first night of *Sukkot*, the Jewish people have the honor of receiving Abraham. This patriarch is characterized by his tremendous kindness and generosity, represented by the *sefirah* of *chesed*. So imbued was the *sefirah* of *chesed* in Abraham that the kabbalistic work *Sefer HaBahir* states that the *sefirah* of *chesed* itself "complained" to G-d of its lack of purpose during the life of our patriarch.[25] Because Abraham was *chesed* personified, the attribute felt that it had nothing left to do. Abraham was extremely hospitable, always receiving guests at his home in an exceptional manner—even when those guests were completely idolatrous. Furthermore, Abraham went to war to rescue his nephew Lot, even though Abraham was well aware of his flaws. All of this demonstrates that our father had a very strong inclination towards *chesed*.

Next is the *sefirah* of *gevurah*, which signifies strength, discipline, and self-control. Isaac, Abraham's son, visits the *sukkah* on the second night of the holiday. *Pirkei Avot* tells us that the one who is a *gibbor* (strong, literally one that has *gevurah*) is the one who dominates his or her physical impulses. This *sefirah* is connected with Isaac, who controlled his impulses to such an extent that he even allowed Abraham to offer him as a sacrifice. *Gevurah* also

---

[25] *Hayom Yom*, 22nd of *Cheshvan*, p. 106

represents strength and the ability to restrain oneself and not to give to another when such giving may cause harm to the receiver, or when the receiver is simply undeserving. An example of this occurred when Isaac gave no additional blessings to his son Esau. Isaac loved Esau very much, yet he had just given all the blessings he had in store to Jacob. Isaac also appears to have finally understood that Esau himself was not deserving of those blessings.

Following this chronology, it is Jacob who comes to the *sukkah* meal on the third night. This patriarch is connected to the *sefirah* of *tiferet*, a balance between *chesed* and *gevurah*. Jacob, who later had his name changed to Israel, represents such harmony. He started his life more connected with the sefirah of *chesed* (he was his mother Rebecca's favorite, and Rebecca, like Abraham also represents *chesed*). Later in life, Jacob had to wear the clothes of Esau, who is linked to the evil part of *gevurah*, in order to receive his father's blessings. From that moment on, Jacob faced extreme challenges with tremendous courage and discipline, such as working for Laban, facing Esau's angel, and then facing Esau himself, before returning to the Land of Israel. The *sefirah* of *tiferet* is also known as *rachamim*, mercy. *Rachamim,* mercy is not pure kindness like *chesed*. It contains an element of *gevurah* in that it provides for a certain leniency in the context of a judgment, *din*. *Din* and *gevurah* are also kabbalistic terms that are often interchangeable.

After the presence of the three patriarchs, on the fourth night of *Sukkot*, the Jewish people receive in their *sukkah* a new guest: Moses. This great leader is characterized by his humility, perseverance, redemption and victory, symbolized by *sefirah* of *netzach*. Moses, the humblest man on Earth, firmly persevered against Pharaoh in Egypt, who represented the pinnacle of arrogance. It was through Moses that G-d redeemed the Jewish people from Egypt and gave them the Torah.

During the fifth night of *Sukkot*, Aaron, the brother of Moses, visits the *sukkah*. On this night, the focus is on the *sefirah* of *hod*. *Hod* can be understood by gratitude, acknowledgement and glory, but also as devotion and self-sacrifice in divine service, as well as nullification before G-d. This *sefirah* is connected to Aaron, who was the first High Priest, serving, thanking and glorifying G-d with his whole being, totally nullifying himself before Him. Aaron served the Jewish people in a similar manner, always seeking harmony and peace for those around him.

On the sixth night, Joseph comes to the *sukkah*. Joseph is connected to the *sefirah* of *yesod*, which means foundation, firmness and uprightness. Joseph stood firm and resisted the seductions of Potiphar's wife, and preserved his Jewish identity even after many years alone in Egypt. It is noteworthy that of all Seven Shepherds, Joseph is the one known as *Yosef Hatzadik*, "Joseph the Righteous." The *tzadik* is the foundation of the world,[26] and is characterized by the *sefirah* of *yesod*, representing the source of spiritual and material sustenance for the whole world, as was Joseph.

Finally, on the last night of the festival of *Sukkot*, the Jewish people receive a visit from King David, who

---

[26] As in the Hebrew phrase, "*Tzadik Yesod Olam*."

is linked to the *sefirah* of *malchut*. This *sefirah* can be translated as kingship or royalty, and represents the ability to make an impact on this material world. *Malchut* absorbs the qualities of all the other *sefirot*, and puts them into practice. The *sefirah* of *malchut* is also linked to the attribute of speech, as it is mainly through speech that a king wields power. King David represents well this *sefirah* given that his reign, as well as that of his son Solomon, is the greatest example of the manifestation of the Kingdom of G-d in this material world. It was Solomon who built the Temple, G-d's home on Earth, after King David had laid its physical and spiritual foundations. King David also instituted the reading of the Psalms (again, connected to the attribute of speech), and taught the world of the great power of repentance and return to G-d, *teshuvah*. Moreover, *malchut* is the only emotional *sefirah* that is feminine. Therefore, in addition to King David, *malchut* often is symbolized by our matriarch Rachel. The *Shechinah*, the Divine Presence in this world, which is also female, is represented by the divine attribute of *malchut* as well.

There are ten *sefirot* in total, three intellectual and seven emotional. However, it should be noted that during the Counting of the *Omer*, the three intellectual *sefirot* are not worked on simultaneously with the emotional *sefirot*. This is because on Passover, G-d provides us with a higher level of these three *sefirot*: *chochmah*, *binah* and *da'at* (or *keter*), respectively: wisdom, understanding, and knowledge (or crown). *Chochmah* represents the first contact with wisdom; that initial "*eureka*" feeling when an idea lights up in our minds. *Binah* represents the development of a concept after it is first conceived. *Da'at* is the application of that knowledge to the reality of everyday life. Endowed with these qualities, we now have the ability to further develop his emotional attributes during the Counting of the *Omer*. After this task is completed, as a reward, on *Shavuot*, G-d gives us an even higher level of these intellectual *sefirot*, in a way that is completely above physical limitations.[27]

---

[27] Heard from Rabbi Casriel Brusowankin, the Rebbe's emissary at Chabad of Aventura, FL. Rebbe Nachman of Breslov explains that the forty-nine days of the *omer* correspond to the Forty-Nine Gates of Repentance, which in turn correspond to the forty-nine Hebrew letters of the names of Jacob's twelve sons. (Likutei Moharan II, 73; *available at* http://www.azamra.org/Advice/omer.html) Interestingly, three of those names are oftened spelled with an additional letter: *Binyamin* often is spelled with two *yuds*; *Zevulun* with two *vavs*; and *Yosef* sometimes is spelled with a *heh*. These three additional letters are those of G-d's name, bringing the total number of letters to 52.

The Structure of the Sefirot

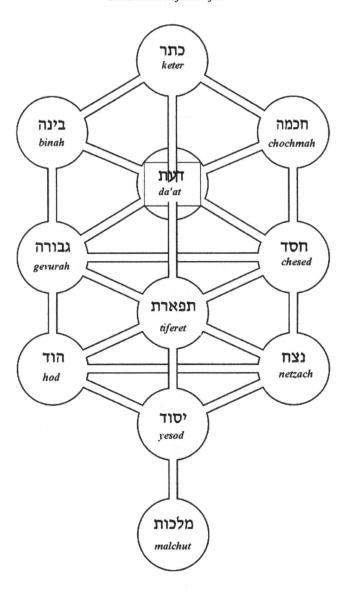

The Order of the Ten Sefirot

כתר
keter

חכמה
chochmah

בינה
binah

חסד
chesed

גבורה
gevurah

תפארת
tiferet

נצח
netzach

הוד
hod

יסוד
yesod

מלכות
malchut

WEEK 1: TO RAISE OUR HEADS, CHOOSE A MASTER, AND RECOGNIZE G-D'S ONENESS

Each week will begin by quoting the week's animal in *Perek Shirah*, rabbi in *Pirkei Avot*, and *sefirah* combination. The program begins on the week of *Rosh Hashanah*, coinciding with all or part of *selichot*, the days of repentance leading up to the holiday. The exact day of the week in which counting starts is the same as the day the Counting of the *Omer* starts, the second day of the Passover holiday.

The rooster is saying, "When the Holy One, blessed be He, comes to the righteous in the Garden of Eden, all the trees in the Garden of Eden scatter their spices, and they rejoice and praise, and then He, too, is aroused and praises." (Zohar, Vayakhel 195b)

In its first call it says, "Lift up your heads, O gates! And be lifted up, O everlasting doors! And the King of glory shall come in! Who is this King of glory? G-d strong and mighty, G-d mighty in battle!" (Psalms 24:7-8)

In its second call it says, "Lift up your heads, O gates! Lift them up, O everlasting doors! And the King of glory shall come in! Who is this King of glory? G-d of hosts, He is the King of glory, Selah!" (Psalms 24:9-10)

In its third call it says, "Stand, O righteous ones, and busy yourselves with Torah, so that your reward will be double in the World-to-Come."

In its fourth call it says, "I have hoped for Your salvation, O G-d." (Genesis 49:18)

In its fifth call, it is saying, "How long will you sleep, O sluggard? When will you arise from your sleep?" (Proverbs 6:9)

In its sixth call, it is saying, "Do not love sleep, lest you come to poverty; open your eyes and you shall be satisfied with bread." (Proverbs 20:13)

In its seventh call, it is saying: "It is time to act for G-d; for they have made void Your Torah." (Psalms 119:126)

Moses received the Torah from Sinai and gave it over to Joshua. Joshua gave it over to the Elders, the Elders to the Prophets, and the Prophets gave it over to the Men of the Great Assembly.

They [the Men of the Great Assembly] would always say these three things: Be cautious in judgment. Establish many pupils. And make a safety fence around the Torah.

Shimon the Righteous was among the last surviving members of the Great assembly. He would say: The world stands on three things: Torah, the service of G-d, and deeds of kindness.

Antignos of Socho received the tradition from Shimon the Righteous. He would say: Do not be as slaves, who serve their master for the sake of reward. Rather, be as slaves who serve their master not for the sake of reward. And the fear of Heaven should be upon you.

Yossi the son of Yoezer of Tzreidah, and Yossi the son of Yochanan of Jerusalem, received the tradition from them. **Yossi the son of Yoezer of Tzreidah would say:** Let your home be a meeting place for the wise; dust yourself in the soil of their feet, and drink thirstily of their words.

Yossi the son of Yochanan of Jerusalem would say: Let your home be wide open, and let the poor be members of your household. And do not engage in excessive conversation with a woman. This is said even regarding one's own wife—how much more so regarding the wife of another. Hence, the sages said: One who excessively converses with a woman causes evil to himself, neglects the study of Torah, and, in the end, inherits purgatory.

Joshua the son of Perachia and Nitai the Arbelite received from them. **Joshua the son of Perachia would say:** Assume for yourself a master, acquire for yourself a friend, and judge every man to the side of merit.

Nitai the Arbelite would say: Distance yourself from a bad neighbor, do not cleave to a wicked person, and do not abandon belief in retribution.

Judah the son of Tabbai and Shimon the son of Shotach received from them. **Judah the son of Tabbai would say:** When sitting in judgment, do not act as a counselor-at-law. When the litigants stand before you, consider them both guilty; and when they leave your courtroom, having accepted the judgment, regard them as equally righteous.

Shimon the son of Shotach would say: Increasingly cross-examine the witnesses. Be careful with your words, lest they learn from them how to lie.

Shmaayah and Avtalyon received from them. **Shmaayah would say:** Love work, loath mastery over others, and avoid intimacy with the government.

Avtalyon would say: Scholars, be careful with your words. For you may be exiled to a place inhabited by evil elements [who will distort your words to suit their negative purposes]. The disciples who come after you will then drink of these evil waters and be destroyed, and the Name of Heaven will be desecrated.

Hillel and Shammai received from them. **Hillel would say:** Be of the disciples of Aaron—a lover of peace, a pursuer of peace, one who loves the creatures and draws them close to Torah.

He would also say: One who advances his name, destroys his name. One who does not increase, diminishes. One who does not learn is deserving of death. And one who make personal use of the crown of Torah shall perish.

He would also say: If I am not for myself, who is for me? And if I am only for myself, what am I? And if not now, when?

Shammai would say: Make your Torah study a permanent fixture of your life. Say little and do much. And receive every man with a pleasant countenance.

> **Rabban Gamliel would say:** Assume for yourself a master; stay away from doubt; and do not accustom yourself to tithe by estimation.
>
> ***Chesed shebeChesed*** (kindness within the context of kindness)

The month of *Tishrei* is represented by the tribe of Ephraim, and is almost entirely devoted to spiritual pursuits. It is replete with Jewish holidays, full of joy from beginning to end. Ephraim, the son of Joseph, studied Torah under his grandfather Jacob and led a life that was almost completely devoted to spiritual concerns.

The first week of the Jewish calendar is the week of *Rosh Hashanah*, which literally means "the head of the year." The first animal in *Perek Shirah* is the rooster, who awakens us by singing an introductory verse followed by seven songs, one for each day of the week. Similarly, on *Rosh Hashanah*, the Jewish people experience a spiritual awakening through the blowing of the *shofar*. Each of the songs of the rooster parallel the meaning behind the *shofar* blows that take place on *Rosh Hashanah*. The *shofar* is blown 100 times, and the rooster's verses contain 100 words.

The first week also contains the days leading up to *Rosh Hashanah*, which are called *selichot*. On these days, like the rooster, we arise early in the morning in order to ask forgiveness for our sins and begin the year with a clean slate.

The rooster, the majestic animal that heads the list of animals in *Perek Shirah*, represents the concept of G-d's kingship. It is exactly on *Rosh Hashanah* that the Jewish people acknowledge G-d as King.

The number one represents G-d's unity as the Master and Creator of the universe. This is the fundamental belief of the Jewish faith.

In *Pirkei Avot*, the first set of sayings found in Chapter I repeat the idea of receiving guidance from a single teacher/ spiritual guide (*rav*). In order to grow as a person, it is important to have a life coach; someone that knows us well and can therefore guide, answer questions, and be objective about what aspects of our life need improvement.

These verses of *Pirkei Avot* include an introduction followed by seven pairs of rabbis, which is parallel to the introduction followed by the seven songs of the rooster. Upon careful review, one will find that each of these lessons is intimately connected to *Rosh Hashanah*, in which we acquire G-d as our ultimate Master.

The first week is associated with the *sefirah* combination of *chesed shebechesed*. *Chesed* means loving kindness, and on *Rosh Hashanah* we feel that G-d pours his kindness upon His children.[28] The Ba'al Shem Tov explains that the

---

28 It is worth noting that *Rosh Hashanah* is also known as *"Yom HaDin,"* the "Day of Judgment," which is more associated with *gevurah* than with *chesed*. That is because *Rosh Hashanah* is associated with the judgment of our actions during the *previous* year (*See* Week 52), although it is also the day in which all the blessings of the coming year are determined. Perhaps that is another reason why *Rosh*

blowing of the shofar is like the cry of a prince who spent years away from home and forgot his mother tongue. Seeing his father, the King, from a distance, the son screams to Him in order to be recognized.

It was exactly on *Rosh Hashanah* that G-d showed enormous kindness to Sarah, the first of the four matriarchs of the Jewish people. During this festival, Sarah, an elderly woman who had been unable to become pregnant her entire life, received the news that she would give birth to a son, Isaac. It was also on *Rosh Hashanah* that Chanah was told of the extraordinary news that she would give birth to a son, the prophet Samuel. Chanah was also barren and advanced in years. It is worth noting that the rooster is mentioned in our prayer book as an animal that recognizes the kindness of its Creator. Every day, in our morning prayers, we thank G-d for giving the rooster the understanding to distinguish between day and night.

We can also learn a very important lesson in self-improvement from the rooster. It tells us to stop sleeping, to get up, and to move forward. Getting out of bed is an important first step in fighting sadness. The act of arising in the morning is a daily miracle, as well as an essential action in facing the joys and the challenges of every new day. By tapping into the song of the rooster and the call of the *shofar*, our physical and spiritual alarm clocks, we acknowledge G-d's oneness, and take an important first step towards a harmonious, spiritually aware, and productive new year.

Hashanah is called "*kesseh*," the hidden holiday, for G-d's tremendous *chesed* on this day is somewhat hidden.

WEEK 2: TO RELATE WELL TO OTHERS AND TO OUR OWN BODY

> **The hen is saying**, "He gives bread to all flesh, for His kindness endures forever." (Psalms 136:25)
>
> **[Rabban Gamliel's] son, Shimon, would say:** All my life I have been raised among the wise, and I have found nothing better for the body than silence. The essential thing is not study, but deed. And one who speaks excessively brings on sin.
>
> **Gevurah shebeChesed** (discipline and judgment within the context of kindness)

In the second week of the Jewish year, the week of *Yom Kippur*[29] (the "Day of Atonement"), it is the turn of the hen in *Perek Shirah* to sing of G-d's eternal kindness, for providing food for every living being. It is during this time of the year that G-d determines specifically how much sustenance each being will receive, but also who will live and who will not. Many people may not know this, but eating well on the eve of *Yom Kippur* is considered to be as meritorious as the fast itself.

There is also an important parallel here: It is exactly in this second week, on the eve of *Yom Kippur*, when we are busy

---

[29] *Erev Yom Kippur* always falls on the second week of the year, but in certain years, the day of *Yom Kippur* itself falls on the first day of Week Three. This is the only exception for all dates described in this book.

asking each other for forgiveness, that the Jewish people make *Kapparot*, an ancient custom where each individual symbolically atones for one's sins before G-d through the means of a hen! After the ritual is performed, each chicken is slaughtered and given to families in need. Nowadays, many have the custom to use charity money in order to fulfill this ritual. Before *Yom Kippur*, we also have the custom to ask each other for forgiveness.

The number one is somewhat lonely, but once another one is added they make a pair, just like the rooster and the hen. The number two also represents the two tablets containing the Ten Commandments (*Luchot HaBrit*). While one tablet contains laws regarding our relationship with G-d, the other tablet contains laws regarding relationships between human beings. It was precisely on *Yom Kippur* that the tablets were given for the second time for the Jewish People. The number two represents the concept of relationship, as well as the idea of giving and receiving.

The *Pirkei Avot* of this week contains the recommendation of Shimon ben Rabban Gamliel: "All my life I grew up among the Sages, and found nothing better for the person [literally, the body] than silence; it is not to study, but rather action which is of the essence . . . one who talks too much brings forth sin" (I:17). In order to properly receive and absorb the words of others, one must first be silent.

Furthermore, the "silencing" of the body, appears to be a clear reference to the fasting that takes place on *Yom Kippur*, as well as other actions such as not wearing leather shoes, anointing ourselves (using perfumes or lotions), having sexual relations—preventing all these things on

Yom Kippur is a way to distance ourselves from physicality and be very close to G-d, like angels, even if only for a single day. *Yom Kippur* is also a day of reflection and introspection, for which silence is an important virtue.

We saw that the *Pirkei Avot* of week number one focuses on acquiring a single main teacher. In this week, we speak about learning from "sages," in the plural. While the number one relates to unity, two represents the concept of multiplicity. These two concepts are not contradictory—they complement each other. One can still have a single main teacher, while still learning from every person. In fact, as we will see in week 30 of *Pirkei Avot*, that Ben Zoma states that to do so is a sign of true wisdom.[30]

On *Yom Kippur*, we also focus on fact that the main thing that G-d values is our actions. One of the high points of this holy day is the reading of the Book of Jonah, which in turn has as its climax the following verse: "And G-d saw their actions . . . and G-d reconsidered the evil which He had spoken to perform against them, and He did not perform it."[31]

In the second week, the *sefirah* combination is *gevurah shebechesed*, discipline and judgment within the context of kindness. During the fast of *Yom Kippur*, the Jewish people act with discipline, willpower, and self-control. We

---

[30] Chapter IV:1

[31] Chapter 3:10. Jonah in Hebrew means "dove," the animal in *Perek Shirah* for Week Three.

do so while begging our Creator for mercy and protection, knowing that G-d is just and kind.

This week, a lesson in self-improvement we draw from *Perek Shirah* is that even the hen recognizes that G-d nourishes all living beings. After getting out of bed, as we learned from the rooster, the next step in combating sadness is to take proper care of ourselves, eating properly and exercising.

WEEK 3: TO BE HAPPY, BALANCED, AND SECURE IN G-D

> **The dove is saying**: "Like a swift or crane, so do I chatter; I moan like a dove, my eyes fail with looking upward; O G-d, I am oppressed, be my security." (Isaiah 38:14) The dove says before The Holy One, Blessed be He, "Master of the World! May my sustenance be as bitter as an olive in Your hands, rather than it being sweet as honey through flesh and blood." (Talmud, *Eruvin* 18b).
>
> **Rabbi Shimon the son of Gamliel would say:** By three things is the world sustained: law, truth and peace. As is stated (Zachariah 8:16), "Truth, and a judgment of peace, you should administer at your [city] gates."
>
> *Tiferet shebeChesed* (beauty and balance within the context of kindness)

In the third week of the Jewish year, when we celebrate *Sukkot*, the dove is the next animal to sing in *Perek Shirah*. It calls to G-d to be its source of protection, and states that it prefers that its sustenance be as bitter as an olive branch but come directly from Him, than it be as sweet as honey from the hands of humans. This week also usually marks the *yahrzeit* of the fourth Lubavitcher Rebbe, Rabbi Shmuel, the Rebbe Maharash, on the 13th of *Tishrei*.

Throughout these days we eat apple and honey and dip our challah in honey, yet we live under the branches of the *Sukkah*. The dove asks for protection by using the word "*Arveni*," which means "be my Guarantor"—but also can be understood as "be sweet to me." *Arveni* is also reminiscent of the phrase "*Kol Israel Arevim Zeh LaZeh*," which means every Jew is responsible for, mixed together with, and/or sweet to one another, one of the main themes of *Sukkot*.[32]

On *Sukkot*, the Jewish people remember how G-d protected them in the desert, and celebrate how that protection continues until today. We live as in an everlasting *sukkah*, which is fragile and vulnerable to changes in weather conditions. While we must do our part to protect ourselves, we also realize that ultimately we all depend entirely on G-d for our sustenance and safety.

The dove is also characterized by faithfulness and loyalty. The Torah compares the Jewish people to a dove, and *Tefillin* to its wings: just as the wings protect the dove, so too the *mitzvot*, the commandments, protect the Jewish people.[33] Just as we are loyal to G-d, He too shows loyalty to us and protects us.

The dove is also considered a bearer of good news and symbolizes peace and tranquility: when Noah wanted to make sure that the flood waters had already receded, he

---

[32] *Arveni* comes the word *Aravah*, the "poorest" of the four species used for the *mitzvah* of shaking the *lulav*, in that it represents the Jew that has no Torah or *mitzvot*. Nevertheless this Jew is equally important and essential to this *mitzvah*.

[33] Talmud, *Shabbat* 49

sent the dove, which came back with an olive branch in its mouth, indicating that the Flood had subsided.[34]

In this third week, the dove mentions two birds aside from itself: the crane and the swallow—three animals in total. The number three is related to the three patriarchs, and also represents balance and stability. While the number two brings tension, three creates harmony. It is well known that on the second day of creation, G-d did not say "it was good." On the third day, however, G-d said "it was good" twice.

The Torah itself is a third and balancing force in the relationship between the Jewish people and G-d. The Talmud states that the Torah, which has three parts (*Torah*, *Nevi'im* and *Ketuvim*) was given to the three-part Jewish people (*Kohanim*, *Levi'im* and *Israelim*), by the third son (Moses, the younger brother of Aaron and Miriam), on the third day of separation, in the third month (*Sivan*, counting from the month of *Nissan*).[35]

One of the first statements in *Pirkei Avot* is that the world stands on three pillars: *Torah*, *Avodah* (Divine service), and *Gemilut Chassadim* (acts of kindness). These three pillars are also represented by the patriarchs themselves: Abraham represents acts of kindness, Isaac represents Divine service, and Jacob represents the Torah.

As explained in the beginning of this book, Jacob, the third patriarch, represents *tiferet*, the balance between

---

[34]   Genesis 8:11

[35]   Talmud, *Shabbat* 88a

Abraham's *chesed* and Isaac's *gevurah*. Jacob is also strongly associated with *Sukkot* itself. This is a verse in the Torah that explicitly refers to this: after parting from Esau, Jacob goes to [a place called] *Sukkot*![36]

Jacob is also connected to the concept of truth. In our morning prayers, we recite "*Titen Emet L'Ya'akov, Chesed l'Avraham*," give truth to Jacob, mercy to Abraham. In Jewish law, three also represents the concept of *chazakah*, a legal basis for assuming that statement is true. Furthermore, if a certain occurrence happens three times, there is a *chazakah* (a legal assumption) that it will happen again.

The number three also plays an important role in the *Pirkei Avot* lesson for the third week. Rabbi Shimon the son of Gamliel teaches that the world endures because of three things: justice, truth and peace. (I:18) Without these three things there would be no balance and security in the world. This teaching is closely related to the above mentioned teaching in *Pirkei Avot*, about the three pillars in which the world stands.

The three things mentioned by Rabbi Shimon are directly related to the three holidays in the weeks mentioned so far: *Rosh Hashanah*, *Yom Kippur* and *Sukkot*: *Rosh Hashanah* is also known as *Yom HaDin* (Day of Judgment). *Din* means justice, the exact word used in this teaching. *Yom Kippur* is the day in which individual Jews are sealed in the Book of Life (our sages explain that "G-d's seal is truth"). *Sukkot* is strongly tied to peace, as can be seen in the blessing

---

[36] Genesis 33:17

HaPoress Sukkat Shalom Aleinu (the One who extends a *Sukkah* of peace over us), which is part of *Ma'ariv*, the night time prayer.[37]

During this week, the combination of *sefirot* is *tiferet shebechesed*. As mentioned above, Jacob represents the *sefirah* of *tiferet*. The Rebbe Maharash also represents this *sefirah*. He was born on the 17th day of the *omer*, *tiferet shebetiferet*, and his father would sometimes even refer to him by this combination.[38] The Rebbe Maharash's *yahrzeit* falls on or close to the 17th day of the year, which, if one were to attribute a *sefirah* to each day of the year, would be equivalent to *tiferet shebetiferet shebechesed*. (*See* Calendar at the end of the book)

During these days, the Jewish community receives blessings of spiritual and physical assistance, under the fragile construction of their *sukkot*. Furthermore, during these days we are *commanded* to be happy, as stated in the verse "*veSamachta beChagechah Vehaitem Ach Sameach*, you shall rejoice in your festival and you shall be very happy."[39]

In general, *Sukkot* are spiritually as well as visually quite beautiful. The actual building, decorating, and preparing

---

[37] From the Rebbe's *Sichos*

[38] *Hayom Yom*, 2nd of Iyar, p. 50

[39] Deuteronomy 16: 14. One may ask, "How can a certain emotion be *commanded*?" The *Tanya*, the Alter Rebbe's seminal work, explains that ultimately it must be the mind that controls the heart. By meditating on G-d's greatness and kindness, we are able to inspire the love for Him in our hearts as well. The same can be said for happiness.

meals in the *sukkah*, are all activities that can be very inspiring. The beauty of the *sukkah* in the context of the blessings we receive are a great example of *tiferet shebechesed*.

In this week, we learn from the dove not to be worried or anxious, but instead to have full faith in G-d, Who is All Powerful, and Who provides for all our needs. That said, it is also important to create a vessel to receive G-d's blessings. It is very important to be grateful for what we have. Furthermore, besides from taking care of the body, it is crucial to be in an environment that is organized, balanced and pleasant, just like a *sukkah*.

The eagle[40] **is saying,** "And You, G-d, Lord of Hosts, Lord of Israel, awake to punish all the nations; do not be gracious to any wicked traitors, sela!" (Psalms 59:6)

Rabbi [Yehudah HaNassi] would say: Which is the right path for man to choose for himself? Whatever is harmonious for the one who does it, and harmonious for mankind.

Be as careful with a minor mitzvah as with a major one, for you do not know the rewards of the mitzvot. Consider the cost of a mitzvah against its rewards, and the rewards of a transgression against its cost.

Contemplate three things, and you will not come to the hands of transgression: Know what is above from you: a seeing eye, a listening ear, and all your deeds being inscribed in a book.

Netzach shebeChesed (victory and endurance within the context of kindness)

On the fourth week of the year, which encompasses the end of *Sukkot* (including *Hoshanah Rabbah*), as well as *Shemini Atzeret* and *Simchat Torah*, the eagle sings. During

---

[40] Rabbi Slifkin translates *Nesher* as vulture. Other translations have it as an eagle.

this week, as soon as each community completes the annual reading of the entire Torah, we immediately start our studies anew, just like the eagle renews its feathers from year to year.[41] It is also worth noting that during these days, both for *hoshanot* and *hakafot*, we spend a large portion of our service circling the *bimah*,[42] just like the eagle.

Rebbe Nachman's *yahrzeit*, the 18th of *Tishrei*, often falls on this week of the year, the week of *Simchat Torah*. Two of Rebbe Nachman's main teachings are relate to the concept of always being happy and of always starting anew.[43] That is exactly what *Simchat Torah* is all about. As Rebbe Nachman said himself, his "main day" is *Rosh Hashanah*, and as further explained below, *Simchat Torah* is the culmination of the judgment that took place from *Rosh Hashanah* to *Hoshanah Rabbah*.

The eagle is the greatest of birds, flying higher than the rest. It therefore has an extremely broad and potent view and perspective on all Creation. Unlike other birds, which carry their young between their talons, the eagle carries them on their wings because no other animal can reach that high. So is our relationship with G-d: "You have seen

---

[41]   Psalm 103:5; *Rashi*

[42]   The *bimah* is the platform in the middle of the synagogue, which parallels the altar (*mizbeach*) in the Temple.

[43]   Rebbe Nachman stated, "*Mitzvah Gedolah Lihyot B'Simchah Tamid!* (It is a great mitzvah to be happy always!)" (*Likutei Moharan* II, 24). He also would say, "Start serving God as if you had never started in your whole life. This is one of the most basic principles of serving God. We must literally begin all over again every day." (*Likutei Moharan* I, 261).

what I did unto the Egyptians, and how I took them on eagles' wings and brought them to Me."[44]

The eagle requests that G-d remember the nations (Psalms 59:6). The word "remember" can have both a positive (remember for good) as well as a negative connotation (remember in order to punish). The continuation of the eagle's song appears to be more connected to the latter, as it states, "do not be gracious to any wicked traitors, selah." Throughout *Sukkot*, the Jewish people have been bringing sacrifices on behalf of all nations. However, on *Shemini Atzeret*, we stop bringing sacrifices for others, and place them aside for the time being, so that the Jewish people can be alone with G-d.

The number four represents stability and strength more than the number three, just as a table with four legs is firmer than a tripod. The number four also refers to the matriarchs of the Jewish People: Sarah, Rebecca, Rachel and Leah. The Torah itself is quite explicit about how the matriarchs were more firm than the patriarchs when it came to protecting their family and their lineage from bad influences and from veering off to wrong paths. Sarah made sure that Yishmael was sent away in order not to be a bad influence for Isaac. When Abraham became apprehensive about this, G-d told him to listen to Sarah. Similarly, Rivkah made sure that Jacob would receive the proper blessings from Isaac, instead of Esau. She also insisted that Jacob not intermarry with the local tribes.

---

[44] Exodus 19:4

The stability of the number four is reflected in various aspects of the world itself. There are four basic elements in the world: fire, water, air, and earth. There are also four spiritual worlds, or dimensions, mentioned in the Kabbalah: *Atzilut*, *Beriah*, *Yetzirah*, and *Assiyah*. There are also four rivers that flow from the Garden of Eden, and four levels of Torah knowledge, also known as *Pardes*. Pardes literally means "orchard," and stands for: *Peshat* (simple/meaning), *Remez* (implied/hinted), *Derush* (interpreted), and *Sod* (secret). All of the above concepts are deeply related.

In *Pirkei Avot*, Rabbi Yehudah HaNassi discusses how to stay on the right path, and be laudable in their own eyes and in the eyes of his fellow man. The word used by Rabbi Yehudah to describe this state of equilibrium is *tiferet*, the *sefirah* connected to *Sukkot*.

As part of his teaching, he states that different *mitzvot* should not be compared. Some think that dancing with the Torah on the day of *Simchat Torah* is somehow less important than the prayers recited on *Rosh Hashanah* and *Yom Kippur*, or even that this *mitzvah* is somehow smaller compared with the daily study of the Torah. In fact, in the eyes of G-d, dancing with the Torah is very important.

Continuing the transition from Week Three to Week Four, Rabbi Yehudah HaNassi tells us to reflect upon three things, which are actually four: "(1) Know what is above you: (2) an Eye that sees, (3) an Ear that hears, and (4) all your deeds are recorded in a Book." This lesson describes the four Jewish holidays of the first four weeks: On *Rosh Hashanah*, we acknowledge that G-d is above us (the Hebrew word is *lada'at*, "to know," and *Rosh Hashanah* is connected with *da'at*, as explained in Week 52); on *Yom Kippur*, G-d sees our *teshuvah* (our repentance), as stated in the *Haftorah* of Jonah read on *Yom Kippur*;[45] the festival of *Sukkot* is connected to the ear; and *Hoshanah Rabbah*, *Shemini Atzeret* and *Simchat Torah* all reflect the idea that our actions are written in a book, the Book of Life, because it is precisely on *Hoshanah Rabbah* that the judgment is concluded.

On this week, the *sefirah* combination is *netzach shebechesed*. In it, we complete the reading of the entire Torah, which ends with *Vezot haBrachah*, when Moses blesses each one of the twelve tribes of Israel. As explained in the beginning of the book, Moses is associated with the *sefirah* of *netzach*. *Netzach* means victory and endurance, which we feel as we reach the completion of the Torah's reading. Moses' blessings are linked to *chesed*.

As mentioned above, the number four, associated with *netzach*, is connected to Sarah, Rebecca, Rachel and Leah. As a leader, Moses displays maternal characteristics, drawing a striking parallel with our matriarchs. In a particularly difficult time of his journey, Moses desperately please with G-d: "Was it I who gave birth to this entire people, that You ask me to carry them in my bosom as one who carries a nursing [baby], to the land You promised their ancestors?"[46]

---

45 The Book of Jonah states, "And G-d *saw* their actions . . . and G-d reconsidered the evil which He had spoken to perform against them, and He did not perform it." (3:10, emphasis added)

46 Numbers 11:12

It is also worth noting that the Rambam, Rabbi Moshe Ben Maimon, whose known for the phrase, that "from Moshe to Moshe there was no one like Moshe," was known as the "Great Eagle."

Rebbe Nachman also always said about himself that his *sefirah* was *netzach*. Rebbe Nachman also stated, "I have been victorious (*nitzachti*) and I will be victorious (*v'anatzeach*); I have finished and I will finish."

The lesson of self-improvement that can be derived from the song of the eagle is that we should show care and concern for all others, not just ourselves. In fact, caring about others besides oneself is a great way to fight sadness. The eagle shows concern for the community and for all nations, not just for itself.

WEEK 5: TO USE ALL TOOLS AVAILABLE IN ORDER TO ELEVATE THE WORLD

The crane is saying, "Give thanks to G-d with the lyre; make music for Him with the ten-stringed harp." (Psalms 33:2)

Rabban Gamliel the son of Rabbi Yehudah HaNassi would say: Beautiful is the study of Torah with the way of the world, for the toil of them both causes sin to be forgotten. Ultimately, all Torah study that is not accompanied with work is destined to cease and to cause sin.

Those who work for the community should do so for the sake of Heaven; for then the merit of their ancestors shall aid them, and their righteousness shall endure forever. And you, [says G-d,] I shall credit you with great reward as if you have achieved it.

Be careful with the government, for they befriend a person only for their own needs. They appear to be friends when it is beneficial to them, but they do not stand by a person at the time of *his* distress.

He would also say: Make that His will should be your will, so that He should make your will to be as His will. Nullify your will before His will, so that He should nullify the will of others before your will.

Hillel would say: Do not separate yourself from the community. Do not believe in yourself until the day you die. Do not judge your fellow until you have stood in his place. Do not say something that is not readily understood in the belief that it will ultimately be understood [or: Do not say something that ought not to be heard even in the strictest confidence, for ultimately it will be heard]. And do not say "When I free myself of my concerns, I will study," for perhaps you will never free yourself.

He would also say: A boor cannot be sin-fearing, an ignoramus cannot be pious, a bashful one cannot learn, a short-tempered person cannot teach, nor does anyone who does much business grow wise. In a place where there are no men, strive to be a man.

He also saw a skull floating upon the water. Said he to it: Because you drowned others, you were drowned; and those who drowned you, will themselves be drowned.

He would also say: One who increases flesh, increases worms; one who increases possessions, increases worry; one who increases wives, increases witchcraft; one who increases maidservants, increases promiscuity; one who increases man-servants, increases thievery; one who increases Torah, increases life; one who increases study, increases wisdom; one who increases counsel, increases understanding; one who increases charity, increases peace. One who acquires a good name, acquired it for himself; one who acquires the words of Torah, has acquired life in the World to Come.

Hod shebeChesed (glory and gratefulness within the context of kindness)

On the fifth week of the Jewish calendar, we celebrate *Rosh Chodesh Cheshvan*. The month of *Cheshvan* is represented by the tribe of Menashe. Menashe, the firstborn son of Joseph, assisted his father in managing the entire Egyptian empire at the time. In *Cheshvan*, we bring all the holiness that we acquired in *Tishrei*, and use it in our day-to-day spiritual and physical endeavors to elevate the world. After the introspection and delving into the treasures of the Torah that took place in *Tishrei*, we must put our new resolutions into practice in this physical world. In this service, we use all powers, tools, and technologies available to us. In *Perek Shirah*, the crane sings to G-d with joy, asking that we use musical instruments such as the lyre and the ten-stringed harp to thank *Hashem*.[47] With instruments, our music to Him will be even more beautiful.

The number five represents the five books of Moses, the Torah. At Mount Sinai, Moses brought the Torah down from heaven into this physical world, transforming it forever. Five is also one more than the number four, which as mentioned in the previous week, reflects the basic structure of the world(s).

In *Pirkei Avot*, the words of Rabban Gamliel the son of Rabbi Yehudah HaNassi are also related to the above description of the month of *Cheshvan*. Rabban Gamliel states that the study of Torah should be combined with making a living. Rabban Gamliel explains that it is

---

[47]   *See* Genesis 4:21, on how musical instruments, specifically the lyre is described in the Torah as one of the first technologies developed by human beings.

specifically through the combination of Torah and work that one is able to stay away from sin. The subsequent sayings of Rabban Gamliel are also related to the concept of being active in the world. He describes how one should go about work on behalf of the community, as well as how to interact with the government. The additional sayings of Rabban Gamliel, as well as the words of Hillel, included in this section, also discuss how to interact with others and how to balance the need to engage with the material world, and yet not lose focus on what is truly important.

Hillel specifically talks about a situation of someone who was drowned in the water, which is very appropriate for the beginning of the month of *Cheshvan*, the month of the Flood. As will be further explained in week twenty-four, the Flood and its mighty waters are often used as a reference to material concerns, which threaten to drown us.

This week's sefirah is *hod shebechesed*, which, as mentioned above, is closely connected with Aaron, and the service of the *Kohanim* (priests). As also mentioned, *Cheshvan* will be the month in which the future Third Temple will be inaugurated, and that is where the *Kohanim* will elevate the material world through their sacrifices.

A lesson in self-improvement that we can learn from the crane is the power of music. After all, music and the sound of instruments is one of the most powerful and ancient forms of fighting sadness. David would play the harp in order to gladden King Saul, who was tormented by depression. The Levites would also sing beautiful songs as the *Kohanim* performed their tasks.

The songbird is saying, "The songbird has also found her home, and the sparrow a nest for herself, where she may lay her young—Your altars, G-d of Hosts—my King and my Lord." (Psalms 84:4)

Rabban Yochanan the son of Zakkai received the tradition from Hillel and Shammai. He would say: If you have learned much Torah, do not take credit for yourself—it is for this that you have been formed.

Rabban Yochanan the son of Zakkai had five disciples: Rabbi Eliezer the son of Hurkenus, Rabbi Yehoshua the son of Chananya, Rabbi Yossi the Kohen, Rabbi Shimon the son of Nethanel, and Rabbi Elazar the son of Arach. He would recount their praises: Rabbi Eliezer the son of Hurkenus is a cemented cistern that loses not a drop; Rabbi Yehoshua the son of Chananya—fortunate is she who gave birth to him; Rabbi Yossi the Kohen—a *chassid* (pious one); Rabbi Shimon the son of Nethanel fears sin; Rabbi Elazar ben Arach is as an ever-increasing wellspring.

[Rabban Yochanan] used to say: If all the sages of Israel were to be in one cup of a balance-scale, and Eliezer the son of Hurkenus were in the other, he would outweigh them all. Abba Shaul said in his name: If all the sages of Israel were to be in one cup of a balance-scale, Eliezer the son of Hurkenus included, and Elazar the son of Arach were in the other, he would outweigh them all.

[Rabban Yochanan] said to them: Go and see which is the best trait for a person to acquire. Said Rabbi Eliezer: A good eye. Said Rabbi Yehoshua: A good friend. Said Rabbi Yossi: A good neighbor. Said Rabbi Shimon: To see what is born [out of one's actions]. Said Rabbi Elazar: A good heart. Said He to them: I prefer the words of Elazar the son of Arach to yours, for his words include all of yours.

He said to them: Go and see which is the worst trait, the one that a person should most distance himself from. Said Rabbi Eliezer: An evil eye. Said Rabbi Yehoshua: An evil friend. Said Rabbi Yossi: An evil neighbor. Said Rabbi Shimon: To borrow and not to repay; for one who borrows from man is as one who borrows from the Almighty, as is stated, ``The wicked man borrows and does not repay; but the righteous one is benevolent and gives" (Psalms 37:21). Said Rabbi Elazar: An evil heart. Said He to them: I prefer the word of Elazar the son of Arach to yours, for his words include all of yours.

Yesod shebeChesed (foundation and firmness within the context of kindness)

On the sixth week of the Jewish year, during the month of *Cheshvan*, the songbird in *Perek Shirah* praises G-d for providing it a home, and for providing a nest for the sparrow to lay its young. The songbird's verse also speaks of the altars of G-d. As mentioned above, it is during this month that the Third Temple, G-d's home and the location of His altars, will be dedicated, perhaps even in this sixth week. (*See* Table I)

The number six represents the six orders of the *Mishnah*, of which the Oral Torah is comprised. Like much of the Written Torah, most of the *Mishnah* is about transmitting G-dly concepts in a manner that deeply involves the physical realm, monetary damages, and criminal punishments. What happens when an ox destroys neighboring property? What happens when two people claim to have rights over the same piece of property? The Oral Torah goes a step further than the Written Torah, giving specific examples and rulings, and analyzing such cases with great minutiae.

In *Pirkei Avot*, Rabban Yochanan the son of Zakkai, who received the oral tradition from Hillel and Shammai used to say that those who have learned much Torah should not want special recognition, since they were created exactly for this purpose. (II:8) As further noted below, this week is connected to the *sefirah* of *Yesod* and Joseph. In fact, the special recognition that Joseph received, and which he himself felt he merited, created great problems for him in his relationship with this brothers.

Rabban Yochanan the son of Zakkai perfectly represents the Oral Torah, as well as the number six. His teaching is clearly related to the learning the Oral Torah. Furthermore, he is portrayed in *Pirkei Avot* with five additional students, making six in total. The praises he gives to his students are closely related to their ability to receive the oral tradition from him. Finally, Rabban Yochanan's entire life story is about complete dedication to the Oral Torah. He managed to escape the Roman siege of Jerusalem right before its destruction, and set foot on a journey to establish a center for Jewish scholars in *Yavneh*. There, he and other sages transmitted the Oral Torah and ensured the survival of Judaism as a whole.

Rabban Yochanan son of Zakkai's journey is also connected to the month of *Cheshvan*, when we leave our introspective and purely spiritual pursuits and delve into the material world in order to elevate it and to ensure our survival. Similarly, he asks his students to "go out" and see which is the proper path to way to take and which should be avoided. This request is also connected with concept of going out of our state of introspection during the month of *Tishrei* in order to engage in the material world and ensure our livelihood.

This week's *sefirah* combination is *yesod shebechesed*. This combination, as well as the song of the songbird, reminds us of Joseph, who provided sustenance for his entire family and for the rest of the world. He was the viceroy of Egypt, in charge of all of the provisions of the empire. It was his interpretation of Pharaoh's dream that allowed for Egypt to stockpile its food supplies, preempting a seven-year period of extreme famine that greatly impacted the entire region. Joseph was the foundation of the good that all others received, both physically and spiritually.

We can draw a precious lesson in self-improvement from the songbird. As explained in the fourth week, we have an obligation to care for others besides ourselves. The songbird teaches us that we must work to create a solid foundation for our children and for all future generations, including one's students. This can serve as a great motivation for a person who is overwhelmed by his or her own challenges.

WEEK 7: TO RECOGNIZE AND REVEAL THE DIVINE PRESENCE WITHIN US AND THE WORLD

The swallow is saying, "So that my soul shall praise You, and shall not be silent, G-d my Lord—I shall give thanks to You forever." (Psalms 30:13)

They would each say three things. **Rabbi Eliezer would say:** The honor of your fellow should be as precious to you as your own, and do not be easy to anger. Repent one day before your death. Warm yourself by the fire of the sages, but be beware lest you be burned by its embers; for their bite is the bite of a fox, their sting is the sting of a scorpion, their hiss is the hiss a serpent, and all their words are like fiery coals.

Malchut shebeChesed (kingship within the context of kindness)

On the seventh week of the year, still in the month of *Cheshvan*, the swallow sings in *Perek Shirah* of how it cannot be silent, but rather must sing to Him of His glory and thank Him forever (Psalm 30: 13).

The Hebrew word for forever is *l'olam*, which contains the word *olam*, which means world. *Olam* comes from the word *ehelem*, which means "mask" or "hidden." It is through our involvement with the world during this month that we reveal G-d's presence in the world, which until that point had been hidden.

The number seven has many meanings. Our sages tell us that "*Kol haShvi'im Chavivim*," every seventh is precious/ beloved. Seven represents the seven days of the week, and particularly the beloved seventh day, the Sabbath. The number seven and the Sabbath are both connected with the idea of returning to G-d. There are seven emotional *sefirot*, and the number seven is represented by *sefirah* of *malchut*.

As mentioned previously, King David represents *malchut*, and is connected to the idea of repentance and return to G-d. As also mentioned, *Malchut* is associated with the power of speech, like swallow which that cannot be silent.

The Alter Rebbe explains that *malchut*, which means kingship, is closely related to the concept of *kavod*, honor or glory, a word also used in the song of the swallow. The connection between *malchut* and *kavod* can be gleaned from the phrase we say right after reciting the *Shemah*: "*Baruch Shem Kvod Malchuto L'Olam Va'ed*," "Blessed be the Name of the Honor of His kingdom forever and ever." *Cheshvan* is also a month that is closely related to the Temple, where the glory, *kavod* of *Hashem* rests.

In *Pirkei Avot*, Rabbi Eliezer teaches that the honor [*kavod*] of your neighbor must be so precious [*chaviv*] to you as if it were your own, and that one should not become easily angered. (II:10). Rabbi Eliezer also teaches that one must repent one day before death. However, as no one knows when he or she will die, everyone must repent daily. Rabbi Eliezer further cautions us regarding our behavior in front of sages in order not to be harmed by their reactions.

We know that the Flood began on the seventeenth of the month of *Cheshvan*, which falls either during Week 7 or Week 8. This unfortunate phenomenon would not have taken place had the people of the time repented one day before their death and properly treated their neighbors and sages. The Torah also holds Noah accountable for the Flood, because he did not pray for the rest of the people. In this sense, the honor of his neighbors was not precious to him—he thought only of himself.

For Rabbi Eliezer, in order to follow a just path, it is very important to have a "good eye," and to avoid an "evil eye" at all costs. We also know that one of the main causes of the Flood was stealing. Such criminal actions usually begin by looking at someone else's possessions with an evil, jealous eye.

The *sefirah* combination for this week is *malchut shebechesed*. This week marks the *yahrzeit* (anniversary of passing) of our matriarch Rachel, who represents *malchut*. Aside from *malchut*, she also displayed a strong attribute of *chesed,* and perfectly exemplified the abovementioned teaching in *Pirkei Avot*: she helped her sister Leah secretly marry her beloved Jacob, just so that her sister would not be publically embarrassed. Jacob agreed with Rachel's father, Laban, that Jacob would work seven years to marry Rachel. After seven years passed, Laban placed Leah under the canopy instead. The *Talmud* teaches that Jacob foresaw the possibility that Laban would try to trick him, and so he had given Rachel certain signs so that he would be able to recognize her on their wedding night. When Rachel saw

Leah under the canopy, she could not bear to see her sister be so humiliated and gave her the signs.[48]

We extract from the swallow a very important lesson in self-improvement and daily living: to always recognize and thank G-d. The swallow recognizes the greatness of G-d and constantly shows its gratitude. The swallow also teaches us that when praising G-d it is not enough to simply use instruments (as in Week 6); it is also important to sing using our own voice.

[48] *Bava Batra*, 123a.

WEEK 8: NOT TO LOSE FOCUS ON OUR SPIRITUALITY AND RELATIONSHIP WITH G-D

> **The swift is saying,** "My help is from G-d, Maker of Heaven and Earth." (Psalms 121:2)
>
> **Rabbi Yehoshua would say:** An evil eye, the evil inclination, and the hatred of one's fellows, drive a person from the world.
>
> **Chesed shebeGevurah** (kindness within the context of discipline and judgment)

In the eighth week of the year, as we approach the end of the month of *Cheshvan*, the swift sings of its recognition that all help comes from G-d, Creator of Heaven and Earth (Psalm 102:2).

The swift's verse is closely connected with *Cheshvan*. As we go deeper into this month, we feel increasingly immersed (and sometimes even sinking) in the various material concerns and tasks we need to accomplish. Therefore, we need *Hashem*'s help in order to keep us afloat, and not to lose focus on our spiritual objectives.

The number eight represents the concept of that which is extraordinary and above nature. Eight is one more than seven, which represents nature, such as the seven days of the week. Eight is associated primarily with the concept of *Mashiach*, in that when *Mashiach* comes, our whole existence will be one that is above nature as we know it today. While King David's harp had seven strings, the harp of *Mashiach* will have eight.[49] The number eight is also a reference to the unique relationship of the Jew with G-d (a relationship that is above nature). A concrete example of this relationship is the fact that circumcision is performed exactly on the eighth day of life of a newborn.

Eight is also related to the eight garments of the *Kohen Gadol*, the High Priest of the Temple, whose service to G-d was above this world. The *Kohen Gadol*'s garments, as well as the service he performed, were particularly aimed at rectifying the sins of the Jewish people.

This week, the teaching of *Pirkei Avot* is in the words of Rabbi Yehoshua, who teaches about sin: "The evil eye, the evil inclination and hatred towards [G-d's] creations take a person out of this world" (II:11). Sin takes us out of this world. However, this phrase can be understood in a positive way: repentance after sin takes a person to much higher levels, beyond the limitations of this physical and material world.

There is a strong connection between the teaching of Rabbi Yehoshua in *Pirkei Avot* and the month of *Cheshvan*. The evil inclination and hatred prevailed upon the land at that time. The Torah teaches that theft was particularly prevalent at that time—theft—act on the desire of the evil eye and desire for that which is not yours. People of the time were so materialistic that they downplayed the importance of ethics and spirituality.

---

[49]   "The Month of Cheshvan According to the Book of Formation," *available at: http://www.inner.org/times/cheshvan/cheshvan.htm*

For Rabbi Yehoshua, in order to follow the right path, it is very important to have a "good friend," and avoid a "bad friend" at all costs. The Flood was caused because people did not behave as good friends; much to the contrary.

The combination of the *sefirot* for this week results in *Chesed shebeGevurah*. The Flood began slowly, giving people ample opportunity to repent, even after the rain began.[50] The truth is that the flood was not all bad—it served to cleanse the world, and to allow for a fresh start. The flood, which lasted for 40 days and 40 nights, parallels the 40 cubits necessary for a kosher *mikvah*, the purifying ritual bath that cleanses a person of impurity. (This week would also represent the "eighth week," of "*Shavuot*" of the cycle of *Chesed* and the seven days in which *Shavuot* sacrifices were brought, known as "*Shivah Yemei Miluim*")

In this week, we see that the swift is fully aware of G-d's kindness, His justice, and His omnipotence. We must strive to follow suit, and direct ourselves always to Him. We learn from the swift that we need G-d in everything and for everything. Thus, if we are feeling alone and helpless, we should follow the example of this bird and pray to G-d for help.

---

[50] Genesis 7:12, *Rashi*

WEEK 9: TO BEHAVE PROPERLY, FIGHTING DARKNESS WITH LIGHT

> **The stormy petrel is saying,** "Light is sown for the righteous, and joy for the straight-hearted." (Psalms 97:11)
>
> **Rabbi Yossi would say:** The property of your fellow should be as precious to you as your own. Perfect yourself for the study of Torah, for it is not an inheritance to you. And all your deeds should be for the sake of Heaven.
>
> *Gevurah shebeGevurah* (discipline and judgment within the context of discipline and judgment)

In the ninth week of *Perek Shirah,* the stormy petrel announces that, "Light is sown for the *tzadik* (righteous) and joy for the upright of heart." (Psalm 97:11) In some years, this week falls entirely in the month of *Cheshvan,* while in other years it already includes the first day of *Kislev,* the month of *Chanukah.* Even in years when *Rosh Chodesh Kislev* does not take place this week, there is another date in it closely linked to the Maccabees: the 23rd day of *Cheshvan.* In the era of the Talmud, this date was quite celebrated, as it marked the removal of the stones of the Temple's altar that had been rendered impure by the Greeks. The stormy petrel's verse, which mentions light, seed, and protection for the righteous, is very connected to the Maccabees and to the events that took place during *Chanukah,* which is called the "Festival of Lights." Miraculously, G-d made it so that the Maccabees, righteous warriors of the seed of Aaron, defeated Greece, the greatest empire of the time.

The number nine is associated with the nine months of pregnancy. It is also connected to truth. If one adds the digits in the *gematria* of the Hebrew word for truth, *emet*, the total is nine. The total of the sum of the digits (also known as *gematria ketanah*) in all of G-d's names is also nine, because G-d's "seal" is truth.[51] Nine is also three times three, a "double *chazakah*," as explained in Week 3.

In *Pirkei Avot*, Rabbi Yossi states: "The money of your neighbor should be precious to you as if it were your own. Ready yourself for the study of Torah, as it does not come to you as an inheritance, and may all your actions be for the sake of Heaven." (II:12)

This teaching in *Pirkei Avot* is deeply connected with the month of *Kislev* and to the struggle of the Maccabees. While the Greeks admired the Torah as a philosophy, with highly practical concepts (like the idea of respecting other people's money), they tried to break our link to the Torah, as well as our personal connection with G-d. The *Midrash* tells us that "darkness symbolizes Greece, which darkened the eyes of Israel with its decrees, ordering Israel to, 'Write on the horn of an ox that you have no inheritance in the G-d of Israel.'"[52]

It is also worth noting that Rabbi Yossi was himself a *kohen*, just like the Maccabbees. Also like the Maccabbees, Rabbi Yossi is called a "chassid"—extremely pious, going beyond the letter of the law to do the will of G-d.

---

[51] From the writings of the Rebbe's father, HaRav Levi Yitzchak Schneerson.

[52] Genesis Rabba 2:4

For Rabbi Yossi, in order to follow a righteous path, it is very important to have a "good neighbor," and avoid a "bad neighbor" at all costs. Here, a good neighbor, *Shachen Tov*, may be a reference to the *Shechinah*, which dwells among the Jewish people and in the Temple. A bad neighbor, is likely a reference to the Greeks, which tried so hard to make us assimilate and to take us away from our roots.

The combination of *sefirot* for this week is *gevurah shebegevurah*. Note that for those that are part of the Lubavitch Chassidic movement, *Rosh Chodesh Kislev*'s connection with *gevurah shebegevurah* is quite clear. The first is an openly positive one: with great strength and courage, Rabbi Menachem Mendel Schneerson, the Seventh Lubavitcher Rebbe, miraculously survived a heart attack, and returned to his home on *Rosh Chodesh Kislev*. On the other hand, with much sorrow, it is on *Rosh Chodesh Kislev* that we commemorate the day that the Chabad-Lubavitch emissaries of Mumbai, India, were killed.

The stormy petrel tells us that one of the most important steps in achieving happiness is to be a good, honest and fair person. Rebbe Nachman of Breslov teaches that one should always take note and focus of such good qualities and actions in others and in oneself. Even if these good points are small, imperfect and incomplete, they are nonetheless a cause for great joy.[53]

---

[53]   *Likutei Moharan* I:282

Week 10: To Trust in G-d's Mercy

> **The bat is saying,** "Comfort My people, comfort them, says your Lord." (Isaiah 1:40)
>
> **Rabbi Shimon would say:** Be meticulous with the reading of the *Shemah* and with prayer. When you pray, do not make your prayers routine, but [an entreaty of] mercy and a supplication before the Almighty, as is stated ``For He is benevolent and merciful, slow to anger and abundant in loving kindness, and relenting of the evil decree" (Joel 2:13). And do not be wicked in your own eyes.
>
> *Tiferet shebeGevurah* (balance and beauty within the context of discipline and judgment)

On the tenth week, the bat reiterates G-d's words, asking that His people be comforted. (Isaiah 40:1) In this week, we fully enter into the month of *Kislev*, which is represented by the tribe of Benjamin. Benjamin is known for its ability to preserve Jewish values for future generations and for its great capacity for self-sacrifice.[54] The bat has the ability to see in the dark, an important trait in this month of long and cold nights. Yet it is also on this month, during *Chanukah*, that we feel that G-d does indeed comfort us. On *Chanukah*, the Jews defeat the spiritual darkness of the Greeks, and the light of the Temple is restored.

---

[54] Ryzman, pp. 64, 232.

The number ten represents a complete unit, an intensification of the concept of unity reflected in the number one. Ten represents the Ten Commandments, the ten *sefirot*, as well as the ten Divine expressions.[55] In *Pirkei Avot*, ten is also associated with mercy. G-d waited ten generations from Adam to Noah before punishing humanity. The generations after Noah also sinned, and G-d also mercifully waited ten generations from Noah to Abraham, who then began the process of returning humanity back to the belief in One G-d.[56]

In *Pirkei Avot*, Rabbi Shimon states: "Be careful with the reading of the *Shemah* and with prayer. When you pray, do not act as if this were routine, but rather a plea for mercy and supplication before G-d . . . Do not be evil in your own eyes." The *Shemah* is the greatest expression of monotheism and of the acceptance by the Jewish people of G-d as One, and as the King of the Universe. Similarly, the prayer shows our intimacy with our Creator. These concepts are exactly what the Greeks wanted to destroy. They had a problem with the people's monotheism. They even accepted the concept of a Cosmos—cold and indifferent to human behavior—but not of a G-d that was a Merciful Father and King.

For Rabbi Shimon, in order to follow a righteous path, it is very important to see what lies ahead, and to avoid not paying back loans. He states that one who borrows from his friend is as if he borrows from G-d. To be able to see what is about to happen (literally, "seeing what is

---

[55] *Pirkei Avot*, 5:1.

[56] *Pirkei Avot*, 5:2-6

being born") is one of the Talmudic definitions of being truly wise, and achieving *Chochmah*. The Greeks were known for their wisdom. However, wisdom it and of itself, is not sufficient. Wisdom must be tied to the ethics of monotheism and to a firm relationship with a Merciful G-d. Not paying back loans, for example, is not only unethical, it is a rejection of the great mercy someone had towards us, an ultimate reflection of G-d's mercy. Giving interest-free loans to our neighbors is a Divine commandment from the Torah.

The *sefirah* combination for this week is *tiferet shebegevurah*: beauty and balance within strength and discipline. As explained above, *tiferet* also is known as *rachamim*, mercy. While we are more distanced from *Tishrei*, we still remember the beauty of our Torah, we ask *Hashem* for mercy, in order for us to maintain our strong our dedication to the spiritual resolutions we had made on *Rosh Hashanah* and *Yom Kippur*.

An important teaching of self-improvement to be drawn from the words of the bat is to always pray for mercy, and to remember to support our fellow, especially the needy and the oppressed.

Week 11: To Have a Heart: Fighting Evil and Heresy, Yet Knowing How to Forgive

The stork is saying, "Speak to the heart of Jerusalem, and call to her, for her time has arrived, for her sins have been pardoned, for she has taken double from G-d's hand for all her sins." (Isaiah 40:2)

Rabbi Elazar would say: Be diligent in the study of Torah. Know what to answer a heretic. And know before whom you toil, and who is your employer who will repay you the reward of your labors.

Netzach shebeGevurah (victory and endurance within the context of discipline and judgment)

In the eleventh week, in *Perek Shirah*, the stork sings to the heart of Jerusalem, repeating G-d's words that the time of punishment has ended, and that the city will be rescued from iniquity: the city has received a double punishment for its sins (Isaiah 40:2). This week marks the Chassidic holiday of *Yud Kislev*, when the second Rebbe of Lubavitch, the Mitteler Rebbe, was released from imprisonment. He had been briefly arrested on purely fabricated charges of seeking a rebellion against the government, which were strikingly similar to the accusations made against his father (discussed in Week 12). The life of the Mitteler Rebbe was a great example of purity, righteousness, and wonders—the prevailing characteristics of this month.

The verse of the stork is the continuation of the verses of the bat, and is also closely connected with *Chanukah* and the month of *Kislev*. The stork sings to the heart of Jerusalem. However, we must first ask ourselves, what is the heart of Jerusalem? As noted in Week 32, Jerusalem itself is called a heart. The heart of Jerusalem is most likely none other than the Temple itself, the *Beit haMikdash*. It was on *Chanukah* that the Temple in Jerusalem was liberated, cleansed of impurity, and rededicated to the service of G-d. The word *Chanukah* itself means "dedication."

The number eleven is also associated with *kelipah*, impurity, which consists of eleven attributes, known also as *sefirot* or crowns. In the Temple, that incense (*ketoret*), which consisted of eleven ingredients, was used in order to cleanse the people of Israel of their sins. Additionally, the incense functioned as a powerful remedy in the face of death, the greatest source of all impurity. The Torah states that Aaron "placed the *ketoret* [in the pan] and atoned for the people. He stood between the dead and the living, and the plague was halted."[57]

Like the numbers five and eight, eleven is also connected to the idea of being above the natural order, this time represented by the number ten. The power to purify and cleanse from spiritual impurity, and even to prevent certain death, is certainly such an above-nature quality.

One of the basic teachings behind the *ketoret* is that among the required spices used was the *chelbena*, which had a very foul odor. However, when it was mixed with the other ten

---

[57]   Numbers 17:13

elements, the *ketoret*'s aroma was sublime. The same can be said about us: even though individually we may not all be perfect, as a group, we atone for one another, and have a "good smell."

In Joseph's dream, eleven stars (eleven sheaves of wheat in the other dream) bowed down to him, each representing one of his brothers. When Joseph told the brothers about the dream, they were outraged. The idea of his brothers bowing to him appeared to be heretical and presumptuous. However, this was not heretical on Joseph's part—he simply saw things more deeply. Joseph's dreams represented the concept of self-nullification before the *tzadik* (in this case, *Yosef HaTzadik*) both in spiritual matters (stars) as well as material ones (wheat). Through this nullification, the *tzadik* is able to properly bind and blend and bring out the best in all eleven elements, very much like the *ketoret*.

The *Pirkei Avot* lesson for this week is taught by Rabbi Elazar, who states that one must be diligent in Torah study and know how to answer an epicurean (or heretic, *apikores* in Hebrew). This lesson is directly related to *Kislev* and the festival of *Chanukah*, because it is in these days that we celebrate our success in combating aspects of Greek philosophy that run counter to Jewish values. Epicureanism in particular, with its focus on worldly pleasures, is most likely the kind of Greek philosophy that is most antithetical to the Torah, and one that had particular appeal during the time when *Chanukah* took place.

Rabbi Elazar also advises: "Know before Whom you toil, and Who is the Master of your work that will pay your wages." The emphasis again is on our direct connection with G-d, and His involvement in our struggles, a concept the Greeks simply could not fathom or accept.

For Rabbi Elazar, in order follow the righteous path, it is very important to have a "good heart," and avoid a "bad heart" at all costs (this is reminiscent of the song of the stork, which is also about the heart). Rabbi Yochanan Ben Zakai states that within the words of Rabbi Elazar are contained the words of all other disciples.

Rabbi Matis Weinberg points out that the difference between the Hebrew word *Tzion* (Zion, Jerusalem) and *Yavan* (Greece) is just a single letter, the *tzadik*.[58] The difference between Judaism and Greek philosophy is the *tzadik*: the need to act justly before G-d, with a good heart, as well as the ability to be bound to G-d and to the righteous individuals of every generation. (It is no coincidence that the *Midrash* states that the Greeks demanded that a heretical statement be written specifically "on the horn of an ox," a reference to *Yosef HaTzadik*).

This week, the combination of *sefirot* results in *netzach shebegevurah*. Therefore, we should be inspire ourselves in the Mitteler Rebbe, a great *tzadik*, and be disciplined and determined in our pursuit of Torah and *mitzvot*. The first chapter in the Code of Jewish Law, the *Shulchan Aruch*, teaches that the main place of *gevurah* is in the heart, where we can defeat (*lenatzeach*) our internal enemy, the *yetzer harah*, the evil inclination.

---

[58] Matis Weinberg, <u>Patterns in Time Volume 8: Chanukah</u>, Feldheim Publishers, New York, 1992, page 78.

As to a lesson in self-improvement, we should follow the example of the stork. We must learn how to humbly ask for forgiveness, and also to truly forgive. After all, we are only alive due G-d's daily forgiveness.

WEEK 12: REVEALING WARMTH TO THOSE THAT ARE COLD AND INDIFFERENT

The raven is saying, "Who prepares food for the raven, when his young ones cry out to G-d?" (Job 38:41)

Rabbi Tarfon would say: The day is short, the work is much, the workers are lazy, the reward is great, and the Master is pressing.

He would also say: It is not incumbent upon you to finish the task, but neither are you free to absolve yourself from it. If you have learned much Torah, you will be greatly rewarded, and your employer is trustworthy to pay you the reward of your labors. And know, that the reward of the righteous is in the World to Come.

Hod shebeGevurah (glory and gratefulness within the context of discipline and judgment)

During the twelfth week, it is the turn of the raven to exclaim with great humility that it is G-d that provides prey when its young roam in search of food. (Job 38:41) This is the week of *Yud Tes Kislev*, known as the *Rosh Hashanah* of Chassidism, the day in which the Alter Rebbe was released from prison and the *yahrzeit* of the Maggid of Mezeritch.

After being falsely accused of treason by the enemies of Chassidism, to the point of being threatened with the death penalty, the Alter Rebbe, through the help of G-d, emerged victorious. The release of the Alter Rebbe on *Yud Tes Kislev* directly led to a new phase in the history of Chabad philosophy. The Alter Rebbe saw it as not only a vindication of his work in earthly courts, but in the Heavenly Court as well. The Alter Rebbe became much more open and expansive in his teachings.

The redoubled efforts to spread the Alter Rebbe's teachings, celebrated this week, brought Chassidism's warmth and love for Judaism into the coldest and most indifferent part of the Jew: the intellect. Geographically, the capital of "intellectual Judaism" was in Vilna, Lithuania, where the Alter Rebbe was sent as an emissary.

Chassidism has the power to uplift even the animals that are the most distant from *Hashem*. The raven was literally kicked out of Noah's Ark for not obeying its rule of celibacy.[59] The raven is also known for its cruelty and indifference to its offspring. However, even the raven can redeem itself. When Elijah the Prophet fled from the King Ahab and his evil wife, G-d determined that precisely the raven, which does not even provide for its own young, should bring food to Elijah.[60]

At the time Elijah ran away, he was overcome by despair and complained to G-d about the rebellious state of the Jewish people. G-d sought to teach Elijah that, like the raven, we all have the potential for warmth and good; it just needs to be revealed.

---

[59] *Midrash Tanchuma, Noach*

[60] 1 Kings 17:2-7

Interestingly, the very word for raven in Hebrew, *orev*, reveals that potential. *Orev* is related to the word *arev*, which, as explained in Week 3, means "responsible for the other," as well as "sweet" and "mixed together" as in the saying, *Kol Israel Arevim Zeh LaZeh*, which means that "all of Israel is responsible for (sweet to and mixed together with) one another." This saying also encompasses practically the entire basis of Chassidism and the Torah: to love your fellow as yourself.

The number twelve represents the twelve tribes of Israel. Despite our differences, and setbacks, we all are mixed together and responsible for one another and sweet to one another. Upon his deathbed, Jacob was very concerned about the differences among the different tribes. The *Talmud* teaches that his twelve sons responded to his concern by calling out in unison: "Listen O Israel (a reference to Jacob), *Hashem* is our G-d, *Hashem* is One."[61]

The number twelve is also closely associated with Elijah the Prophet himself, "a man whose eyes have seen twelve generations." Bear in Hebrew, *dov*, has the *gematria* of twelve. The *Tanach* teaches us that before Eliyahu rose to Heaven, Elisha asked Elijah to bequeath to him twice Elijah's own power.[62] Shortly thereafter, Elisha purified the waters of a city, and was insulted by a group of youths. When Elisha responded to their insult, two bears immediately appeared and killed them.[63]

---

[61] Talmud, *Pesachim* 56a

[62] 2 Kings 2:9

[63] 2 Kings 2:23-25

Elijah is most likely the biblical figure most associated with the revelation of the hidden and mystical secrets of the Torah. Elijah's own teacher, *Achiah HaShiloni* was also the teacher of the Ba'al Shem Tov. It is therefore quite appropriate that he should be connected to the week of *Yud Tes Kislev*, given that the Alter Rebbe, who was freed on *Yud Tes Kislev*, taught the kabbalistic secrets revealed by the Ba'al Shem Tov.

In *Pirkei Avot*, Rabbi Tarfon reminds us that "the day is short, the work is plenty, the workers are lazy, the reward is great, and the owner insists [urges]." (II: 15) There is also a strong connection between the New Year of Chassidism and the teaching of Rabbi Tarfon. Chassidism came to light up a fire in order to awaken those who were depressed and spiritually asleep. It was like an alarm clock, a spiritual wake-up call: time is short, now is the time to serve G-d![64]

The number twelve is also linked to time: there are twelve months in the year, twelve halachic hours during the day, and twelve halachic hours during the night. In the Jewish calendar, a daytime halachic hour (*shaah zmanit*) is defined as 1/12 of the time it takes from sunrise to sunset. A nighttime *shaah zmanit* is 1/12 of the time between sunset and sunrise. The exact amount of time of each of these hours varies throughout the year. When the days are long, as in the summer, a daytime halachic hour is equivalent to more than sixty minutes. In the winter, when days are shorter, the daytime hour amounts to less than sixty minutes.

---

[64] *Hayom Yom*, 17th of *Av*, 79a

In this week, the *sefirah* combination results in *hod shebegevurah*. This week, we are inspired by the Alter Rebbe, who after facing the *gevurah* of incarceration, reveals even more the hidden secrets of the Torah through the teachings of the Chabad Chassidism. The *sefirah* of *hod* is connected with the inner dimensions of the Torah, the Kabbalah, just as *Lag Ba'Omer*, which is *hod shebehod*. *Lag Ba'Omer* is the *yahrzeit* of Rabbi Shimon Bar Yochai, who wrote down the seminal kabbalistic work, the Zohar.

A lesson for this week is that even the raven and its offspring recognize G-d's kingship and the importance of requesting one's sustenance directly from G-d.[65] We inspire ourselves in the song of the raven, who knows that it is never alone—G-d is always by its side.

---

[65] Psalm 147:9

WEEK 13: TO PUBLICIZE MIRACLES WITH PRIDE AND HUMILITY

The starling is saying, "Their seed shall be known among the nations, and their offspring among the peoples; all who see them shall acknowledge them, that they are the seed that G-d has blessed." (Isaiah 61:9)

Akavia the son of Mahalalel would say: Reflect upon three things and you will not come to the hands of transgression. Know from where you came, where you are going, and before whom you are destined to give a judgment and accounting. From where you came—from a putrid drop; where you are going—to a place of dust, maggots and worms; and before whom you are destined to give a judgment and accounting—before the supreme King of Kings, the Holy One, blessed be He.

Yesod shebeGevurah (foundation and firmness within the context of discipline and judgment)

We now come to the thirteenth week, which includes the beginning of *Chanukah*, when in *Perek Shirah* the starling declares that "Their seeds will be known among the nations and their offspring among the people: all who see them will recognize that they are the seed that *Hashem* blessed" (Isaiah 61:9). During this week, it is actually a *mitzvah* to publicize the miracles of *Chanukah* to the rest of the world, so that all may recognize the blessings bestowed on the Jewish people during the times of the Greeks. This *mitzvah* in Hebrew is called *pirsumei nissa*, to publicize the miracle.

The starling's song's focus on the seed of the Jewish people appears to be an important reference to the *kohanim*, the priestly class, whose lineage, unlike most of Judaism, is actually determined by the physical male seed. There are even DNA tests available to check for a "*kohen* gene," to know with almost complete certainty if someone is or is not a direct descendant of Aaron, the first *kohen*. The Maccabees were *kohanim*, and their miraculous actions during the days of *Chanukah* made the seed of Aaron known among the nations. They ensured that Aaron's offspring would be recognized as the seed *Hashem* blessed.

Chanukah also comes from the word *chinuch*, which means education. The starling also teaches us that just as each of us is a "seed," planted, nurtured and blessed by our parents, teachers, and most importantly, by G-d, so too must we ensure that the same or better is done for our children and students. It is ultimately through education that we will defeat the forces of darkness and assimilation.

The number thirteen represents the thirteen attributes of G-d's mercy, as well as the thirteen principles used in studying and interpreting the Torah. Thirteen is also the *gematria* of the Hebrew word *echad*, one, as well as *ahavah*, love. It is also a reference to the Tribe of Levi, which is the "thirteenth tribe," when counted together with the other twelve. As *kohanim*, the Maccabees come from the Tribe of Levi. Their highly improbable victory over the Greeks was a revelation of *Hashem*'s great mercy and love, as well as of His oneness, and absolute power over creation.

In *Pirkei Avot*, Akavia the son of Mahalalel teaches: "Reflect upon three things and you will not come to sin:

know from where you came, to where you are going, and to Whom, in the future, you are to provide an accounting. From where did you come? From a putrid drop. To where you are going? To a place of dust, maggots and worms. To Whom will you provide an accounting? To the King of kings, the Holy One, Blessed be He." (III: 1) It is interesting to note that this lesson in *Pirkei Avot* also speaks of the human seed, although in a much less flattering way.

Interestingly, there is quite a strong connection between the words of Akavia and *Chanukah*. *Chanukah* celebrates our victory against Hellenistic culture and humanism, which valued mankind, and in particular, the human body above all else. Akavia claims that the human being, or at least the body, comes from a putrid drop, and that its fate is to be consumed by worms. The lowly human being is then judged by G-d Himself. Akavia demonstrates to us that our life should be focused on G-d, not on man.

The thoughts of Akavia help us understand just how merciful G-d is towards His people. Despite our lowly past and lowly future, we nevertheless have a strong and direct relationship with the King of kings, just like children have with their Father. We have a spark of G-d within us, and when He punishes us, it is for our own good. Chassidism teaches us that we have no idea just how precious the body is to G-d, like the seed described in the song of the starling.

The *sefirah* combination for this week results in *yesod shebegevurah*. This could not be more appropriate: *yesod* means foundation, and it is this week that we celebrate *Chanukah*, when the Jewish people, through its deep connection to its religious foundation, as well as courage and strength, was able to resist the forced assimilationist policies of the Greeks.

Regarding self-improvement, we see from the song of the starling that we must not only publicize the miracles that we merit to witness, but also be aware that everything comes from G-d, our Creator, who is ultimately responsible for everyone and everything.

Week 14: To Believe in Our Own Strength, which Comes from G-d

> **The domestic goose is saying,** "Give thanks to G-d and call upon His name, make His works known amongst the peoples, sing to Him, make music to Him, speak of all His wonders!" (Psalms 105: 1-2)
>
> **Rabbi Chanina, deputy high priest would say:** Pray for the integrity of the government; for were it not for the fear of its authority, a man would swallow his neighbor alive.
>
> *Malchut shebeGevurah* (kingship within the context of discipline and judgment)

In the fourteenth week, it is the turn of the domestic goose to sing: "Praise and proclaim the Name of G-d, disseminate His deeds among all nations, sing songs and hymns, narrate all His wonders" (Psalm 105:1-2). In addition to *Chanukah*, this week also marks *Rosh Chodesh Teveth*.

Teveth is considered a difficult month, as it includes the fast of the 10th of *Teveth*, when Jerusalem was besieged. *Teveth* is represented by the tribe of Dan, which is characterized by strength and the ability to be fruitful and multiply. Dan himself had only one child, and was perceived as being at risk of extinction. However, Dan quickly became one of the largest tribes.[66] Samson was from the tribe of Dan,

---

[66]   Ryzman, p. 77.

and he also is associated with the physical strength and the power of procreation.[67]

This week also marks the Chassidic holiday of *Didan Netzach,* "Victory is Ours," on the 5th of *Teveth,* also known as "the day of victory of the books." On *Didan Netzach,* the Lubavitcher Rebbe won a great victory, maintaining the sanctity of the sacred books of the Lubavitch library. He earned the recognition of a non-Jewish secular court, which openly acknowledged the special relationship between a Rebbe and his Chassidim. As will be explained in more detail next week, the month of *Teveth* is very connected to the importance of valuing our sacred writings. *Didan Netzach* is also closely linked with the physical and spiritual victory of the Maccabees.

The song of the domestic goose is related to the *mitzvah* of publicizing the miracle of *Chanukah, pirsumei nissa,* mentioned last week. On *Chanukah,* we sing to Him, praise Him, and thank Him, through various songs.

Fourteen is comprised of the letters *yud* and *dalet,* which spells *yad,* meaning hand or arm. In the widely accepted version of the Order of the Passover Seder, attributed to Rashi or one of the *Tosafot,* fourteen steps are listed. That is because in the Torah it is written that G-d brought His people out of Egypt with a *yad chazakah,* a strong arm.[68] Fourteen is therefore associated with strength and firmness,

---

[67]   Talmud, *Sotah* 10a.
[68]   Ki Yishalcha Bincha, Rabbi Bogomilsky, p. 56.

as well as redemption. Such redemptive qualities are felt on *Chanukah*.

The teaching of *Pirkei Avot* for this week can be found in the words of Rabbi Chaninah, Deputy *Kohen Gadol* (High Priest): "Pray for the welfare of the government, because if it were not for fear of it, men would swallow each other alive." (III:2) Rabbi Chaninah is also speaking metaphorically, that without outside intervention, the strong exploit the weak both physically and economically.[69]

It is amazing that the *Pirkei Avot* teaching of the deputy *kohen gadol* falls exactly during the week of *Chanukah*, when the Jewish people celebrate their liberation from Greek dominance and exploitation, due to the heroic acts of a group of *kohanim*. During these days, we thank G-d for "delivering the strong into the hands of the weak," as can be found in the additions made to the daily prayer (the *Amidah*) inserted during *Chanukah*.

This week, we complete another cycle of seven weeks, and the *sefirot* combination is *malchut shebegevurah*. The Maccabbees were tough and disciplined (*gevurah*) and after their victory even started a dynasty of kings (*malchut*). Like the Maccabees, we must take action within this physical and material world, with discipline and strength, which is also an attribute of the entire month of *Teveth*.

---

[69] Marcus, p. 82, *citing Bartenura*'s commentary on the Talmud, *Avodah Zarah* 4a.

We learn from the domestic goose about the importance of acknowledging the miracles that occur all around us on a daily basis, and of publicizing these miracles as well. To recall and publicize miracles that occur throughout life is a great way to be more grateful in our day-to-day. In fact, it is a great source of blessing and happiness.

WEEK 15: GIVING PROPER VALUE TO TORAH AND TO THE PRESENCE OF THE SHECHINAH

The wild goose flying in the wilderness, when it sees Israel busy with Torah, is saying, "A voice cries, Prepare in the wilderness the way for G-d, make straight in the desert a path for our G-d" (Isaiah 40:3). And upon finding its food in the wilderness, is says: "Cursed is the man who trusts in human beings; Blessed is the man who trusts in G-d, and G-d shall be his assurance." (Jeremiah 17: 5, 7)

Rabbi Chanina son of Tradyon would say: Two who sit and no words of Torah pass between them, this is a session of scorners, as is stated, "And in a session of scorners he did not sit" (Psalms 1:1). But two who sit and exchange words of Torah, the Divine Presence rests amongst them, as is stated, "Then the G-d-fearing conversed with one another, and G-d listened and heard; and it was inscribed before Him in a book of remembrance for those who fear G-d and give thought to His name" (Malachi 3:16). From this, I know only concerning two individuals; how do I know that even a single individual who sits and occupies himself with the Torah, G-d designates reward for him? From the verse, "He sits alone in meditative stillness; indeed, he receives [reward] for it" (Lamentations 3:28).

Chesed shebeTiferet (kindness within the context of beauty and balance)

In the fifteenth week, the wild goose sings two songs: When it sees Israel occupied with the study of Torah, it calls for us to prepare a way for the Lord, to make a straight path for our G-d. Then, after finding food, is blesses the Lord, and curses those that place their trust in man. (Isaiah 40:3; Jeremiah 17:5-7) This week marks the fast of the Tenth of *Teveth*, when Jerusalem was besieged at the time of the First Temple. It was the first step towards its destruction and the exile of the *Shechinah*. The 10th of *Teveth* is also the *yahrzeit* of Rabbi Nathan of Breslov, the main disciple of Rebbe Nachman of Breslov.

Few Jews survived the destruction of the First Temple. Even so, they multiplied and returned to being a numerous people, just like the Tribe of Dan, the symbol of the month of *Teveth*. Similarly, when Rabbi Nathan took the reins of the Breslov movement, it was still very small, and he had to face incredible obstacles and adversities. Nonetheless, not only did the movement survive, but it grew exponentially, and today Rebbe Nachman's fire is more alive than ever.

The *Midrash* states that Jerusalem was besieged and the First Temple later destroyed because the Jewish people did not "recite the blessing over Torah study." In other words, this tragedy took place due to the lack of spiritual importance given to the Torah and other holy texts at that time. There is a strong connection here with *Didan Netzach*, the day of the "victory of the books."

Through the words of the wild goose, we mourn the destruction of the First Temple, when the Jewish people not only was not properly occupied with the study of Torah, but also put inappropriate trust in their alliance with the Kingdom of Egypt at the time. The prophets warned against trusting in Egypt. In a prophecy made on the twelfth of *Teveth*, still prior to the siege, the prophet Ezekiel calls Egypt a "reed-like support for the House of Israel—whenever they held you in their hand you would snap, piercing their every shoulder . . ."[70] When Egypt fell to the Babylonians, the Kingdom of Israel soon followed.

The number fifteen contains the first two letters of *Hashem*'s name, *yud* and *heh*. These two letters also form another name for G-d, *Yah*. This is a feminine name and a reference to the *Shechinah*, the Divine Presence. The moon, which represents the feminine *sefirah* of *malchut*, is always full on the fifteenth of the Jewish month.

The Talmud states that in the Temple, there were fifteen steps from Israelite men's courtyard to the women's courtyard, corresponding to the fifteen Songs of Ascents *(Shir haMaalot)* found in King David's Psalms.[71] The Talmud further explains that it was through the power of composing these fifteen songs that King David saved the entire world from being engulfed by the waters running under the Temple Mount. Here again we see a reference to the Temple and to the power of the written Torah.

In the *Pirkei Avot* lesson for this week, Rabbi Chaninah ben Teradion teaches: "If two [people] are sitting together and do not exchange words of Torah, this is a company of scorners . . . However, if two sit together and exchange words of Torah, the Divine Presence rests between them."

---

[70] Ezekiel 29:6-7
[71] Talmud, *Sukkah* 51a

(III:2) Rabbi Chaninah further explains that even when a person sits alone and is occupied with the Torah, G-d provides him with a reward. The connection with the above concepts is quite clear.

During this week, the *sefirot* combination results in *chesed shebetiferet*. When the siege of Jerusalem began, the situation was not yet so precarious. There was still a chance for the people to repent and avoid the tragedy altogether. This can be regarded as kindness within mercy (*rachamim*), which is another meaning for the term *tiferet*. (This week would also represent the "eighth week," of *Shavuot* and "*Shivah Yemei Miluim*" of the cycle of *Gevurah*)

Regarding self-improvement, we learn that even the wild goose understands the great importance of Torah study, and that its survival and sustenance depends solely on G-d, not on human beings. If we do our part, surely G-d will do His.

Week 16: To Use Adversity as a Way to Grow, Relying on G-d for Support

> **The ducks are saying**: "Trust in G-d forever and ever, for G-d, the Eternal, is the strength of worlds." (Isaiah 26:4)
>
> **Rabbi Shimon [Bar Yochai] would say:** Three who eat at one table and do not speak words of Torah, it is as if they have eaten of idolatrous sacrifices; as is stated, "Indeed, all tables are filled with vomit and filth, devoid of the Omnipresent" (Isaiah 28:8). But three who eat at one table and speak words of Torah, it is as if they have eaten at G-d's table, as is stated, "And he said to me: This is the table that is before G-d" (Ezekiel 41:22).
>
> *Gevurah shebeTiferet* (discipline and judgment within the context of beauty and balance)

We now come to the sixteenth week, when the ducks proclaim their everlasting trust in G-d, the Eternal Rock (Isaiah 26:4). The song can also be understood as praise, that G-d is the strength of all worlds. During this week of the month of *Teveth*, we remain connected with the strength of the tribe of Dan, and to its ability to multiply. The Talmud states that *Teveth* is the coldest month of the year, "when the body takes pleasure in the body."[72]

It is no coincidence that *Perek Shirah* mentions the ducks in the plural. Ducks multiply quickly and have large

---

[72] Talmud, *Megillah* 13a

families; they travel in groups and rely on each other for survival during migration from the cold. After the destruction of the First Temple, the number of Jewish survivors was very small. According to the Book of Jeremiah, 4,600 people were exiled to Babylon *in total*.[73] And yet, in a relatively short period of time, the Jewish community in Babylon thrived, becoming numerous, influential, and wealthy.

The song of the ducks also appears to be a reference to G-d's strength as well as to the fact that He grants us the ability to procreate. The name *Tzur* is a reference to G-d's strength, but can also be translated as Creator or Craftsman. The word *Yotzer*, which as the same root as *Tzur* is used in Tanach specifically as a reference to G-d, Who "fashioned you from the womb."[74]

The song also contains a mixture of both masculine and feminine names of G-d. It contains the name formed by the letters *yud* and *heh*, which is feminine, and *Tzur*, which is masculine. In between, the name *Hashem* is used, which contains both masculine and feminine aspects.

Similarly, while last week's number fifteen contained two letters of *Hashem*'s name, *yud* and *heh*, and was feminine, the number sixteen also contains two letters of *Hashem*'s name, *yud* and *vav*, but is masculine in nature. The *yud* in *Hashem*'s name represents the *sefirah* of *chochmah* (also known as the "father") while the *vav* in His name represents the six masculine emotional *sefirot* from *chesed*

---

[73] Chapter 52:28-30

[74] Isaiah 44:2

to *yesod* (known as *Ze'er Anpin*). These concepts are in line with this week's theme of procreation, as well as contrasting G-d's masculine and feminine qualities.

The number sixteen also contains aspects of strength and support evoked in the song of the ducks. Sixteen is four times four. Just as the number four represents stability, as explained above in the fourth week, so too does the number sixteen express an even higher dimension of such stability.

The teaching of *Pirkei Avot* for this week is found in the lesson of Rabbi Shimon (Bar Yochai): "Three [people] who ate at the same table and did not speak words of Torah, it is as if they had eaten of sacrifices to the lifeless [idols] . . . But three [people] who ate at the same table and spoke words of Torah, it is as if they had eaten from the table of G-d." (III:3)

Rabbi Shimon speaks of the importance of using words of the Torah, so that we are always connected to *Hashem*. This teaching of *Pirkei Avot* is connected to the month of *Teveth* because, as explained earlier, the disregard for the spiritual importance of Torah study was the cause of the destruction of the First Temple. Rabbi Shimon was the greatest expert of the hidden secrets of the Torah. He understood perfectly how by refraining from words of Torah, one can negatively affect the world.

Furthermore, by teaching us about the importance of infusing our meals with words of Torah, Rabbi Shimon Bar Yochai is teaching us how to serve *Hashem* with our bodies. That is the deeper meaning behind the above

Talmudic statement that in this month, "the body takes pleasure in the body." The Lubavitcher Rebbe explains that by serving *Hashem* with our bodies, not just with our minds and souls, we bring forth an even deeper impact, affecting *Hashem*'s "body," His very essence.[75] In this way, we fulfill G-d's ultimate desire, which is to build a dwelling place for Him in this lowly realm. If we follow Rabbi Shimon's advice, our eating a simple meal, becomes as if we were eating from the "table of G-d," in the Temple. The same can be said for marital relations. It can be the most holy of activities, or the most profane, it all depends on the circumstances and the intentions of the couple.

This week, the combination of the *sefirot* results in *gevurah shebetiferet*. We recover from the pain of the destruction of the Temple and use our strength and discipline to connect to the balanced and spiritual beauty of the Torah.

A lesson in self-improvement that we can learn from the ducks' words is that we must have total confidence in G-d, relying on Him always, just as we would rely on a strong and stable rock for support.

---

[75] "*Love in the Ice Age,*" based on the talks of the Rebbe, Shabat *Vayeishev* 5735 and Shabat *Vayigash* 5750, *available at: https://meaningfullife.com/torah/parsha/bereishit/vayigash/ Love_in_the_Ice_Age.php*

WEEK 17: TO PAY ATTENTION TO G-D'S GUIDANCE AND TO TRUST IN OUR REDEMPTION

> **The bee-eater[76] is saying,** "I will whistle to them and gather them, for I have redeemed them, and they shall increase as they have before increased." (Zechariah 10:8)
>
> **Rabbi Chanina the son of Chachina'i would say:** One who stays awake at night, or travels alone on the road, and turns his heart to idleness, has forfeited his life.
>
> *Tiferet shebeTiferet* (beauty and balance within the context of beauty and balance)

In the seventeenth week, still in the month of *Teveth,* in *Perek Shirah,* the bee-eater sings that, "I will whistle [as a Shepherd to his flock] to gather them, because I have redeemed them, and they shall increase as they increased [in the past]. (Zechariah 10:8) The song of the bee-eater has a clear connection with the tribe of Dan, as it explicitly speaks of the power to be fruitful and multiply.

This week also marks the *yahrzeit* of the Alter Rebbe, on the 24th day of *Teveth.* The Alter Rebbe passed away due in great part to the struggles he faced when running away from Napoleon, during the war between Russia and France. The Alter Rebbe supported Russia's efforts in the war, for fear that Napoleon's egalitarian principles would cause assimilation. The Alter Rebbe felt that such spiritual

---

[76] The Bee-Eater is a type of bird.

persecution (similar to the threat of the Greeks in the times of *Chanukah*) was more dangerous than the physical oppression of the Russian government.

During the flight from Napoleon, the Alter Rebbe sat in a carriage that was third in line, and his grandson, Rabbi Nachum, would sit in the first carriage. Whenever they would approach a crossroads, the Alter Rebbe would be asked which road to take. In one of the crossroads, Rabbi Nachum mistook the Alter Rebbe's directions. Much later, when they realized the mistake, "[T]he Alter Rebbe sighed deeply and said: 'How good is it when a grandson follows in the path of his grandfather—and the opposite is true when a grandfather has to follow the path in which his grandson leads him.' . . . The mistake at the crossroads caused all kinds of troublesome detours, and soon after Alter Rebbe passed away in Piena."[77]

The whistle mentioned in the Song of the bee-eater is a metaphor for the various methods that G-d uses guide us and to help a lost Jew return to Him. As further explained in Week 26, and as is well known from Psalm 23, G-d is our Shepherd and we are His flock. Furthermore, the Zohar teaches that Moses was called *Rayah Mehemnah*, a faithful shepherd (also a shepherd of faith), and that the leader of every generation is like the Moses of that generation, as was the Alter Rebbe. It is important that we follow their advice in order not to lose our way in the darkness of exile, as unfortunately occurred in the above story.

---

[77] *Likutei Diburim*, Volume I, Chapter 2a, Section 5, pages 34-35

It is well known that seventeen is the *gematria* of *tov*, which means "good." Yet, it also connected to exile and to the sad events of the seventeenth of *Tammuz*, which led to the destruction of the Temple. The Alter Rebbe's premature and apparently preventable passing presents us with same dilemma. How could G-d have permitted such an occurrence? In fact, the Talmud makes an explicit connection between these two kinds of events, stating that the passing of tzadikim is likened to the burning of the Temple.[78]

The Lubavitcher Rebbe specifically addresses this apparent contradiction, both regarding exile as well as regarding the premature passing of a *tzadik*, in this case, his own father:

> This is a descent for the purpose of ascent. Indeed, the ascent to be achieved through the Messianic redemption will be great enough to make the time we spend in exile worthwhile.
>
> There is no other means for us to reach this high rung. Were we able to make this ascent without going through the pains of exile, G-d surely would not have exposed us to them.
>
> The above concept also helps clarify a difficult problem in regard to the death of Tzadikim. (. . .) The passing of the Tzadik allows us to reach a high level that could not be approached through any other means.

---

[78]   *Rosh Hashana* 18b

Therefore, this ascent compensates for the tremendous loss caused by death.

If the above is true regarding the passing of any Tzadik, it surely applies regarding the passing of a Tzadik who sacrificed his life for the entire people. Indeed, his self-sacrifice caused him to die before his time. Surely, the only reason for such a passing is the ascent achieved through it.

Seventeen is in fact associated with good, although the full extent of that good is hidden for now. Nowadays, seventeen might be associated primarily with the tragedy of destruction and exile, but in the future, when we fully return to *Hashem*, He will gather us and redeem us through *Mashiach*, and we will then understand that everything that happened was genuinely good all along. Seventeen is also the *gematria* of *cheit*, which means sin, which is the only thing that is truly preventing us from entering the messianic era—as we say in our prayers, "*mipnei chateinu galinu m'artzeinu*"—because of our sins we have been exile from our land. Therefore, if we truly repent from our sins, we will be immediately redeemed.[79]

The *Pirkei Avot* of this week can be found in the words of Rabbi Chaninah son of Chachina'i, who states: "Whoever stays up at night or travels alone on the road, and turns his heart to idleness, forfeits his life." (III: 4) Rabbi Chaninah is referring to the night of exile. In exile, we cannot be isolated and concerned only with vain works in our hearts.

---

[79]   From the Rebbe's *Sichot*, Chassidic discourses.

We have to be assembled and attentive to the whistle of G-d, and occupy ourselves with the study of Torah, so that we do not lose our way and endanger our lives. This lesson is reminiscent of the story of the passing of the Alter Rebbe. There is also a strong connection between this teaching and the month of *Teveth,* given that it was negligence regarding proper Torah study that caused the destruction of the Temple.

Rebbe Nachman of Breslov explains the words of Rabbi Chaninah in a completely different light. He explains that travelling alone is in fact a reference to someone who forges his own path in prayer and meditation (*hitbodedut*) and that the Hebrew word for idleness, *batalah*, is in fact a reference to *bitul*, nullification of the self. "Forfeits his life" in Hebrew is *mitchayev et nafshoh*, which Rebbe Nachman interprets as makes his soul worthy that the whole world be obligated (*chayav*) to exist. This is the condition of the *tzadik* of the generation, as was the *Alter Rebbe*.

The combination of the *sefirot* of the seventeenth week results in *tiferet shebetiferet*. To survive these cold days and long nights, we have to temper the darkness of exile with the light and inspiration of *Chanukah*, as well as the Alter Rebbe's *yahrzeit*, connecting ourselves with the beauty and balance of the Torah. We must also trust in G-d's infinite mercy—mercy in Hebrew, *Rachamim* is another meaning for *tiferet*—knowing that He will soon bring us out of this exile. The root of the bee-eater's name in Hebrew, *Rachamah*, is *Rachamim*.

Similarly, the lesson in self-improvement we can derive from the words of the bee-eater is to hold strong to the conviction that G-d is always with us, guiding us through adversity, and that He will ultimately raise us up. We must not only believe that His call will come, but must also be attentive to it, so that when it does come we do not miss it.

WEEK 18: TO LIVE IN HARMONY WITH NATURE IN A MANNER THAT IS ABOVE NATURE

The grasshopper is saying, "I lift my eyes up to the mountains, where shall my help come from?" (Psalms 121:1)

Rabbi Nechunia the son of Hakanah would say: One who accepts upon himself the yoke of Torah is exempted from the yoke of government duties and the yoke of worldly cares; but one who casts off the yoke of Torah is saddled with the yoke of government duties and the yoke of worldly cares.

Netzach shebeTiferet (victory and endurance within the context of beauty and balance)

In the eighteenth week, of *Rosh Chodesh Shevat*, it is the turn of the grasshopper to call out to G-d, stating: "I lift my eyes to the mountains, from whence will my help come?" (Psalm 121:1) The song of the grasshopper is one of prayer and faith.

The song of the grasshopper, the <u>eight</u>eenth animal, is so closely tied to the song of the eighth animal, the swift. The swift's song is the verse that immediately follows the grasshopper's. It answers the grasshopper's question, singing: "My help comes from the Lord, Creator of Heaven and Earth." (Psalm 121:2) As mentioned above, the number eight is connected to that which is extraordinary, beyond nature.

The grasshopper's song seems to always fall in the weeks in which we read the weekly Torah portions of *Vaera* or *Bo*. These portions depict the plagues (including that of locusts) inflicted on the Egyptians, perhaps the ultimate example of help coming directly from G-d, in a manner that is completely beyond nature.

The month of *Shevat* is marked by *Tu B'Shvat*, the New Year of the Trees, which occurs on the fifteenth day of the month of *Shevat*. There is a debate in the *Mishnah* as to whether the New Year of the Trees should be celebrated on *Rosh Chodesh Shevat* or on the fifteenth, as is the custom.

The month of *Shevat* is deeply tied to the concept of faith. We celebrate the *Rosh Hashanah* of the Trees while still in the midst of winter.

Shevat represents the tribe of Asher, and is related to *ta'anug*, "pleasure" or "delight." According to the Sixth Lubavitcher Rebbe, the word *asher* also means delight, from the word *ashruni*.[80] Furthermore, Asher receives a blessing from his father Jacob that he will "bring delicacies to the king." On *Tu B'Shvat*, we drink wine and eat many different kinds of fruit, all of which is very much tied to the above concepts.

However, this month is not only tied to physical delights, but to spiritual and intellectual delights as well. *Shevat*, and particularly *Rosh Chodesh*, is also deeply connected to the Oral Torah. It was on this day that Moses began reviewing the teachings he had taught to the Jewish people

---

[80]   *Likutei Diburim*, Vol. III, p.137

during their forty years in the desert. This review is what comprises the entire Book of Deuteronomy. So connected is *Shevat* to the Oral Torah, that the *Chidushei HaRim* states that all insights one has in developing novel Torah ideas come to a person during the month of *Shevat*.[81]

The transmission and development of the Oral Torah requires a fundamental character trait: humility. Without humility, one cannot teach in a pure and objective way exactly that which he or she learned from the previous generation. Humility is the hallmark characteristic of Moses, the humblest of men, and the first to transmit the Oral Torah, which he received directly from G-d.

Perhaps this emphasis on humility is the reason why in *Perek Shirah*, the insects, the humblest of animals, are the ones to sing during each of the four weeks of *Shevat*. As King David, another great example of humility and an important link in the chain of the Oral Tradition, once said, "*Ani Tola'at Velo Ish*," "I am a worm and not a man."[82]

---

[81] Ryzman, p. 89

[82] Psalms 22:7; In Chapter 12 of Tzava'at Harivash, the Ba'al Shem Tov further expands on this point:

Do not think that by worshipping with *deveikut* you are greater than another. You are like any other creature, created for the sake of His worship, blessed be He. G-d gave a mind to the other just as He gave a mind to you.

What makes you superior to a worm? The worm serves the Creator with all its mind and strength!

It is well known that the number eighteen represents life, which in Hebrew is *chai*. For this reason, it is customary among Jews to make donations in multiples of *chai*. *Rosh Chodesh Shvat* and *Tu B'Shvat* are, in a way, much more than simply a celebration of trees, but a celebration of life in general, and not just human life.

The *chai* of something is not only associated with its life, but also with its essence. The Ba'al Shem Tov and the Alter Rebbe were both born on *Chai Elul*, literally known as the life as well as the essence of *Elul*. The date that marks the death of Rebbe Nachman of Breslov is the eighteenth of the month, *chai* of *Tishrei*. Interestingly, the festival of *Lag Ba'Omer* is also on the eighteenth, *chai* of *Iyar*. Eighteen is also the number of blessings in the *Shmoneh Esreh*, which is also known as the *Amidah*, or simply as *Tefilah*, prayer, because it represents the essence of prayer.

Man, too, is a worm and maggot, as it is written "I am a worm and no man." (Psalms 22:7) If G-d had not given you intelligence you would not be able to worship Him but like a worm. Thus you are no better than a worm, and certainly [no better] than [other] people.

Bear in mind that you, the worm and all other small creatures are considered as equals in the world. For all were created and have but the ability given to them by the blessed Creator.

Always keep this matter in mind.
http://www.chabad.org/library/article_cdo/aid/145438/jewish/12.htm

Prayer is also related to the realization that the life of a Jew is anything but natural. Our life, sustenance, and salvation come from G-d, Who is beyond this world, as expressed in the songs of the grasshopper and the swift.

The *Pirkei Avot* for this week it taught by Rabbi Nechunia son of Hakanah: "whoever takes upon himself the yoke of Torah, the yoke government and the yoke of worldly obligations are withdrawn from him; but whoever casts off the yoke of Torah, the yoke of government and the yoke of worldly obligations are imposed on him." (III: 5) On *Rosh Chodesh Shevat,* Rabbi Nechunia is advising us to take upon ourselves the study and devotion to the Torah, the Tree of Life, *Etz Chayim,* which is above the world. If we do not, we subject ourselves to the world's obligations. By depicting the Torah as a yoke, Rabbi Nechunia also appears to be making reference to the humility and self-sacrifice necessary for acquiring it. Rabbi Mendel of Kotsk teaches that although we know many examples of sages and Torah scholars that had worldly obligations and were even professionals, they did not feel that such obligations were a yoke or source of concern.[83]

This week, the combination of the *sefirot* is *netzach shebetiferet*: victory and persistence within beauty and balance. A tree represents a balance between roots, trunks, branches and leaves—it is only by having such a balance that the tree survives. Without roots, or with too many branches, a tree cannot stand. Without enough branches and leaves, trees cannot create enough energy to fully grow. In *Shevat*, still in the midst of winter, the tree has to persist

---

[83] Marcus, p. 87

and struggle in order to survive. A similar equilibrium is required when balancing the yoke of Torah with the yoke of government and worldly obligations—the balance is required is often different for each individual person, as well as during different periods in their lives.

We learn from the song of the grasshopper that help will always come from G-d, as long as we are willing to lift our eyes above our limited perspective, and look up, to the mountains. The *Midrash* teaches us that the mountains are also a reference to our patriarchs, and that it is largely in merit of their deeds that G-d saves us. It is important to try to perceive more than just our current situation. Let us focus instead on the whole of our existence: who we are and where we came from: our parents.

WEEK 19: TO FEEL THAT G-D IS CLOSE EVEN WHEN HE SEEMS FAR AWAY

The locust is saying, "O G-d, You are my Lord; I will exalt You, I will praise Your Name; for You have done wondrous things; Your counsels of old are faithfulness and truth." (Isaiah 25:1)

Rabbi Chalafta the son of Dosa of the village of Chanania would say: Ten who sit together and occupy themselves with Torah, the Divine Presence rests amongst them, as is stated: "The Almighty stands in the congregation of G-d" (Psalms 82:1). And from where do we know that such is also the case with five? From the verse, "He established his band on earth" (Amos 9:6). And three? From the verse, "He renders judgment in the midst of the tribunal" (Psalms 82:1). And two? From the verse, "Then the G-d-fearing conversed with one another, and G-d listened and heard" (Malachi 3:16). And from where do we know that such is the case even with a single individual? From the verse, "Every place where I have My name mentioned, I shall come to you and bless you" (Exodus 20:21).

Hod shebeTiferet (glory and gratefulness within the context of beauty and balance)

In the nineteenth week, when we celebrate the Chassidic holiday of *Yud Shevat*, in *Perek Shirah*, the locust blesses and praises G-d, recognizing His wonders as well as His true and loyal advice given from afar. (Isaiah 25:1) *Yud Shevat* is the *yahrzeit* of the Sixth Rebbe of Lubavitch, and also the date in which his successor, Rebbe Menachem Mendel Schneerson, became rebbe exactly one year later.

As explained above, *Shevat* represents the transmission and the development of the Oral Torah. The first to pass on this tradition was Moses, who transmitted it to Joshua. *Yud Shevat* represents the transition, as well as the transmission of the Torah of *Chassidut* from the Sixth Lubavitcher Rebbe to the Seventh.

This week, which immediately precedes *Tu B'Shvat*, the song of the locust includes the words *etzot* as well as *emunah*. *Etza* means "advice," but *etz* means tree. *Emunah* means faith. As already explained, the month of *Shevat* is related both to trees and to faith. In the middle of winter, the Jewish people celebrate *Tu B'Shvat*, trusting that the trees, which are now cold and leafless, will soon be able to blossom and yield fruit.

Interestingly, the song of the locust includes several different terms used in order to make reference to G-d:

- The first name used, *Hashem*, is the name of G-d that represents how He is above nature and time. It is connected to *rachamim*, mercy.

- *Elohai* (my *Elohim*), refers to G-d as He is expressed in nature. This name is connected to *gevurah*, strength or discipline.

- *Atah*, you, is a way of calling out to G-d that shows closeness. In addition, *Atah* refers to G-d's

essence as manifested even higher and far above
any given name.

The song of the locust, and *Shevat* as a whole, represents
this duality of connecting to G-d in a way that is above
nature yet still within it. Furthermore, the song of the
locust reflects the feeling we have in *Shevat* of feeling
distant from G-d, while still close to Him at the same
time. Faith itself is a concept closely linked to this duality.
Sometimes we might feel very far from G-d, but we need
to understand that in actuality He is always very close.

Rav Moshe Wolfsohn explains the story of the sacrifice
of Isaac, the *Akeidah*, along the same lines, based on the
Zohar. *Ness* means a test, but also to raise. Rav Wolfsohn
teaches that the main test of the *Akeidah*, the tenth and
final test, was not the willing to sacrifice his son (think
about his first test, throwing himself into a furnace
before G-d had even revealed Himself to him), but the
fact that *Hashem* seemed to be so far away, as the verse
states, *"Vaya'ar Et HaMakom Merachok,"* Abraham "saw
the place [he was to sacrifice his son] from a distance."
Hamakom, which is usually translated as "the place,"
is also one of *Hashem*'s names. After years of closeness,
Hashem stripped Abraham of all his levels of greatness,
and Abraham now needed to serve G-d like the simplest of
Jews, with simple *emunah*, like the Jews of our generation,
of *Ikvessa d'Meshicha*, the times of the "heels of *Mashiach*."
Abraham succeeded in this test and was rewarded, *"Ekev
Asher Shamatah beKoli,"* because you hearkened to My
voice. *Ekev*, however, also means heel. The words can
therefore mean that Abraham was rewarded because he
made himself like an *ekev*, a heel. Abraham's test is the

test of *emunah* of our generation. Our sages state that, "Everything which occurred to the Patriarchs is a sign to their descendants, "*Ma'aseh Avot Siman LeBanim.*[84]" Interestingly, the *Perek Shirah* verse for this week ends with the words, "*Merachok Emunah Amen.*" (one of the verse's first words is *Aromimchah*, which means, "I will raise You," like the word *Ness*) Rav Wolfsohn concludes stating that our generation, in which we do not have with us *tzadikim* for whom miracles were a regular occurrence, has a particularly difficult test in *emunah*. Certainly, *Yud Shevat*, which marks the passing of the Previous Rebbe, Rabbi Yosef Yitzchak Schneersohn, was an example of such a test.

The connection of the song of the locust to *Yud Shevat* is also very strong. *Bati LeGani*, the last *ma'amar* (Chassidic discourse) of the Previous Rebbe, as well as the first *ma'amar* of his successor, the Rebbe, Rabbi Menachem Mendel Schneerson. For over forty years, the Rebbe delved deeper and deeper into the teachings of this *ma'amar*, and its contents are still studied every year on this date by Chabad *chassidim*. The discourse is about how at first in the beginning of creation, the *Shechinah* resided and was revealed in the world, but then became distanced and hidden due to certain sins, beginning with the eating of the Tree of Knowledge by Adam and Eve. However, through the righteous acts of certain *tzadikim*, the *Shechinah* gradually returned to its closeness to us, culminating with the giving of the Torah at Mount Sinai. The discourse then draws a parallel to the final redemption.

---

[84] *Ramban* on Genesis 12:6

The number nineteen is also related to the idea of increments: the prayer of *Shmoneh Esreh* was increased from 18 to 19, and represents a ladder to G-d, just as the ladder in Jacob's dream. In that dream, the angels ascended and descended a ladder. With every blessing of the *Shmoneh Esreh*, we ascend this ladder, getting closer and closer to G-d.

Nineteen also equals the *gematria* of Eve (*Chavah*); some Biblical commentaries state that Eve, who was created after Adam, is a loftier version of him. It is well known that women generally have stronger and purer faith than men. It was in the merit of the Jewish women that we were redeemed from Egypt, and it will be in the merit of the Jewish women that we will be redeemed from this last exile through *Mashiach*.

The teaching of *Pirkei Avot* for this week is that of Rabbi Chalafta the son of Dosa of the village of Chanania. He asserts that ten men gathered and involved in the study of Torah have the *Shechinah* with them, as it is said, "G-d resides in the assembly of G-d "(Psalm 82:1). The same is true with five: "He established His band on earth" (Amos 9:6). The same happens with three, as we read: "G-d renders judgment in the midst of the tribunal." The same happens with two: "Then the G-d-fearing conversed with another, and G-d listened and heard." (Malachi 3:16) And finally, G-d is present even if there is only one: "In every place where I have My name mentioned, I will come to you and bless you" (Exodus 20:24; *Pirkei Avot* III:6).

Just as with the song of the locust, Rabbi Chalafta teaches about the different levels of G-d's closeness and revelation.

Rabbi Chalafta also teaches about the greatness of the Torah and of its ability to bring down G-d's presence into the material world. The Rebbe specifically comments about how the actions of the ten men show different levels of G-d's Presence. First the men are gathered—that's one level; then they become involved—that's a second level; then they become specifically involved in the study of Torah, that's a third level and an even higher revelation of the Shechinah.[85]

The combination of *sefirot* for this week is *hod shebetiferet*: grateful service within beauty and balance. During the month of *Shevat*, as we celebrate trees and nature as a whole, we have the ability to behold the wonderful and beautiful works of G-d, and to be uplifted and dazzled by it.

A similar lesson can be taken from the words of the locust: with the right amount of gratitude, appreciation, and humility, it becomes much easier to have faith and hope in our Creator. After all, are we not here witnessing His works at every moment? Conversely, we must try to fully internalize the truth that He too, is with us at every moment, even when He may seem to be very distant. In fact, those "distant" and difficult moments are when He is with us the most. In order to feel Him around us and within us, all we need to do is let Him in. As a child, the Kotzker Rebbe was once asked, "Where is G-d?" The expected answer was for a child to say what is normally taught in school, "everywhere." Instead, the Kotsker responded: "G-d is wherever you let Him in."

---

[85]   Marcus, p. 88

WEEK 20: TO BE SOLID AND GIVING IN OUR RELATIONSHIPS

> **The spider is saying,** "Praise Him with sounding cymbals! Praise Him with loud clashing cymbals!" (Psalms 150:5)
>
> **Rabbi Elazar of Bartota would say:** Give Him what is His, for you, and whatever is yours, are His. As David says: "For everything comes from You, and from Your own hand we give to You" (I Chronicles 29:14).
>
> *Yesod shebeTiferet* (foundation and firmness within the context of beauty and balance)

The spider is the twentieth animal in *Perek Shirah*. It cries out to the Jewish people to praise G-d with clanging cymbals and sounding trumpets (Psalm 150:5). This is the week of *Tu B'Shvat*, the New Year of the Trees.

For King David, to whom *Perek Shirah* is attributed, the spider had a very special significance. A *Midrash* teaches that once King David pondered on the purpose of why G-d had created the spider—he could not find a purpose for it. Later, when King David was fleeing from Saul, he entered a cave. A spider then spun an entire web at its entrance. When Saul's men saw the spider's web they figured no one could have been inside the cave for long, so they went away, not bothering to check the cave. The spider's web not only saved his life, but also made him realize that everything that G-d creates has a glorious purpose. That is perhaps why King David reserved the spider for *Tu B'Shvat* itself, the New Year of the Trees, and the highpoint of Judaism's celebration of nature, and why the verse of the spider comes from the very last Psalm, which also serves as a culmination of G-d's praise.

There is also a remarkable parallel between spider webs and trees. A tree takes a long time to grow, but eventually it bears fruit. Similarly, the spider takes a long time to make its web, and its "fruits" are the insects caught in it. The spider web is an example of balance and resistance, just like a tree. Both the tree and the spider web are somewhat delicate, yet can withstand very strong winds, due to their ability absorb impact flexibility, without breaking or falling. Both are testimonies to G-d's greatness and to the complexity of His creation.

The number twenty represents two complete units. It represents an intensification of the concepts of duality and relationship represented by the number two. In addition, twenty is the age of full maturity, when a man may be enlisted for war, and is expected to fully provide for his own sustenance. Beginning at the age of twenty, we are held accountable for our actions in the Heavenly court.

The *Pirkei Avot* teaching of this week comes from Rabbi Elazar of Bartota, who states: give to Him what is His, for you and all that is yours is His, as said King David: everything comes from You, and from Your hand we give to You (*Pirkei Avot* 3:7, Chronicles I 29:14). It is very appropriate that King David be quoted since the *Perek Shirah* section of this week is so intrinsically related to him.

Tzedakah, in a general sense, is the commandment to give charity, and comes from the word justice. The Tanya explains that is arguably the highest of all *mitzvoth* because when we give *tzedakah,* a part of our livelihood and sustenance, it is as if we are giving away part of our very lives. We usually have to fight very hard to obtain this money, and to give it away is the ultimate realization that everything we have is really a gift from *Hashem*. Even after *Hashem* gives, it still remains His, because ultimately He is the Supreme Owner and Ruler over everything.

Rabbi Elazar's statement is also related to *Tu B'Shvat*, because the first fruits one would reap would be brought as an offering to the Temple, and all fruits require *ma'aser* (tithing). In fact, on *Tu B'Shvat* is when one would first be obligated to bring the tithe of the fruits, and that is why it is called the *Rosh Hashanah* of the Trees. *Hashem* is the One who grants us various kinds of fruits and produce. It is therefore appropriate that we give (at least) ten percent of these to Him in return, just as we are supposed to set aside at least ten percent of our income towards *tzedakah*.

A similar principal holds true when it comes to transmitting the Oral Torah. One has to be extremely conscious that one is transmitting that which comes from and belongs to G-d, the Ultimate Teacher. Both regarding what one receives directly from a teacher as well as new Torah insights that appear to have been independently conceived, everything comes from G-d. He grants us knowledge for safekeeping, and for us to put to the best use possible. There is also a concept of "tithing" one's time to teach Torah.

In this week, the resulting *sefirah* combination is *yesod shebetiferet*. On *Tu B'Shvat*, we see that a tree represents this very concept: a foundation that has both beauty and balance.

We learn from the spider that with total confidence, and with a loud and firm voice (like the smashing of cymbals), we can be good examples and good influences on others. We can help others understand that we are never alone—we all have the inner strength that comes from having G-d always on our side.

WEEK 21: To Keep Things in Perspective

The fly says, when Israel is not busying itself with Torah, is saying: "The voice said, 'Call out'. And he said, 'What shall I call out? All flesh is grass, and all its grace is as the flower of the field.' ' . . . The grass withers, the flower fades, but the word of our Lord shall endure forever.'" "I will create a new expression of the lips: Peace, peace for him who is far off and for him who is near, says G-d, and I will heal him." (Isaiah 40:6,8; 57:19)

Rabbi Yaakov would say: One who walks along a road and studies, and interrupts his studying to say, "How beautiful is this tree!", "How beautiful is this ploughed field!"—the Torah considers it as if he had forfeited his life.

Malchut shebeTiferet (kingship within the context of beauty and balance)

On the twenty-first week, coming to the end of the month of *Shvat*, in *Perek Shirah* the fly calls out to the Jewish people when they are not engaging in the study of Torah. The song of the fly appears to be a kind of dialogue. One voice exclaims, "Call out!" and then a second voice responds, "What shall I say? All life is like the grass and the flower of the field . . . the grass withers and the flower fades . . . but the word of the Lord our G-d shall stand forever. The Creator of speech of the lips is saying, Peace, peace to the distant and to the near, says the Lord, and I shall heal." (Isaiah 40:6-8 and 57:19). This week marks the *yahrzeit* of Rebbetzin Chaya Mushka, the Rebbe's wife, on the 22nd of *Shevat*.

Soon after *Tu B'Shvat*, when we emphasize the importance of trees and nature, the fly comes to remind us that nature and life itself, although beautiful, pleasurable, and meaningful, are ultimately fleeting. Even though they are a reflection of the Creator, but it is ultimately only the Creator Himself, and those indelibly attached to Him, that are eternal. Interestingly, flies do not disturb the *tzadikim*. Perhaps this explains why we only know the song that the fly sings when the Jews are not studying Torah. When we are truly engaged in the study of Torah, we are all *tzadikim*. Flies do not approach us, and therefore we cannot know what they are singing.

The fly reminds us of one of the most beautiful and happy stories of our people linked to a woman: the story of *Ishah Shunamit*, the Shunammite woman. This woman performed the great mitzvah of *hachnasat orchim*, hospitality, based on a tradition inherited from our father Abraham. She prepared a special room for the prophet Elisha to always be able to stay with her and her husband. The Talmud and the Zohar explain that she understood the greatness of the prophet Elisha, because she never saw a fly land on his table.[86] This story is about the sanctification of pleasure—Elisha's table was like the Temple's altar, where there were never any flies, despite the constant meat and blood.

Even though she was childless, the *Ishah Shunamit* was always very satisfied with what she had. When asked by the prophet if she needed anything, she replied by stating, "I dwell within my people." Her behavior towards Elisha the

---

[86]   *Brachot* 10b

prophet, the disciple of Elijah, is one of the prime biblical examples of humility, modesty, kindness and hospitality.

These characteristics also find expression in the life of Rebbetzin Chaya Mushka. The Rebbetzin also had no children of her own, yet considered all her "people," the Chassidim, to be her children. She was the Rebbe's best friend and most devout partner throughout his life. The Rebbetzin was also known for her great kindness, hospitality, and modesty, which she learned from the home of her father, Rabbi Yosef Yitzchak Schneersohn, the Sixth Lubavitcher Rebbe. (*See* Week 19)

The number twenty-one is the sum of the first three letters of *Hashem*'s name. Interestingly, 21 is also the square root of 441, the *gematria* (numeric value) of the Hebrew word *Emet*, truth, which, as explained in Week 4, is G-d's "seal." This continues building on the above themes of maintaining the proper focus on *Hashem* and his eternal truth.

The lesson in *Pirkei Avot* for the week after *Tu B'Shvat*, taught by Rabbi Yaakov, continues on this same theme: "When one is on a path studying Torah, if one interrupts his study and exclaims: 'How beautiful is this tree! How beautiful is this plowed field,' it is considered by Scripture as if he were endangering his life. (III:7) Rabbi Yaakov's words parallel the song of the fly. We must maintain our focus on what is truly important and everlasting, and continue in our main path, which is to advance in our study and transmission of Torah knowledge. The study of the eternal words of the Creator should not be interrupted in order to enjoy fleeting occurrences or even to exalt His own Creation.[87]

During this week, we complete the third cycle of seven weeks, and the *sefirah* combination results in *Malchut shebeTiferet*: kingship within beauty. *Malchut* is a female *sefirah*. The truest and everlasting feminine beauty is inner beauty, as the verse in Psalms states, "*Kol Kvudah Bat Melech Pnimah*, all the glory [and beauty] of the princess is within." Similarly, one of the last verses of *Eshet Chayil* sung before *Kiddush* on *Shabbat* night, "charm is deceitful and beauty is vanity; a woman that is G-d-fearing, she is the one to be praised." These verses are also one of the last verses in Solomon's Book of Proverbs. King Solomon, who also wrote Ecclesiastes, knew very well which things were of permanent value, and which were simply "vanity of vanities."

Similarly, we can learn from the fly the invaluable lesson that while most things are temporary, *Hashem* and His Torah are eternal and permanent. Therefore, we should also try to strengthen even more our connection with G-d, speaking directly to Him—there is no need of intermediaries. Healing always comes through Him, and only the ways of the Torah can bring true peace and satisfaction.

---

[87] The *Maggid* of Mezritch explains that this teaching is referring to someone who stops learning in order to reflect on how much he has learned. (Marcus, p. 91) The 22nd of *Shevat* is also the *yahrzeit* of Rabbi Menachem Mendel of Kotsk, known for cutting through people's "flowery" egocentric behavior and focusing completely on the truth.

WEEK 22: TO COMPLEMENT ONE ANOTHER IN HAPPINESS

> **The sea monsters[87] say**: "Praise G-d from the land, the sea monsters and all the depths." (Psalms 148:7)
>
> **Rabbi Dusta'i the son of Rabbi Yannai would say in the name of Rabbi Meir:** Anyone who forgets even a single word of this learning, the Torah considers it as if he had forfeited his life. As is stated, "Just be careful, and verily guard your soul, lest you forget the things that your eyes have seen" (Deuteronomy 4:9). One might think that this applies also to one who [has forgotten because] his studies proved too difficult for him; but the verse goes on to tell us "and lest they be removed from your heart, throughout the days of your life." Hence, one does not forfeit his life unless he deliberately removes them from his heart.
>
> ***Chesed shebeNetzach*** (kindness within the context of victory and endurance)

In the twenty-second week, in *Perek Shirah*, the sea monsters sing that the Lord is to be praised on earth as well as in the depths. (Psalm 148:7)   This is the week of *Rosh Chodesh Adar*. The month of *Adar* corresponds to the zodiac sign of Pisces. Therefore, it is very much appropriate that the water creatures in *Perek Shirah* be the ones to sing during the four weeks of this month.

---

88   Rabbi Lazer Brody translates these animals as "giant sea creatures."

Adar is the month of Purim, and when it begins, we "increase in joy." The depths mentioned in the song of the sea monsters refer to the deep and hidden miracles that *Hashem* performed for us during this month, especially on Purim.

The month of *Adar* is represented by the tribe of Naftali. Naftali, and *Adar* as a whole, is also connected to the quality of being an emissary, a *sheliach*. Jacob's blessing of Naftali describes him as an *ayalah shlucha* (a gazelle that is sent-off). Naftali was sent as a messenger on various occasions. In Moses' blessing at the end of the Torah, Naftali is described as *seva ratzon*, satisfied will. The attribute of *ratzon*, will, is part of the *sefirah* of *keter*, the highest of the *sefirot*, which literally means crown. Interestingly, Naftali is the only tribe described as a feminine animal, and its link to *keter* appears to be connected to the fact that the hero of this month is a woman who was sent on a mission to obtain the crown, Queen Esther.

Like Queen Esther, the tribe of Naftali is also a symbol of self-sacrifice and humility. Even though the tribe was known for its speed and alacrity,[89] its prince accepted to be

---

[89]   *Rashi* explains that the gazelle runs quickly, and that this is the meaning behind Jacob's blessing to Naftali. (Genesis 49:21, *Rashi*; See also the Rebbe's *sicha*, Chassidic discourse, for the 12th Day of *Nissan*, 5747, *available at: http://www. sichosinenglish.org/books/sichos-in-english/35/06.htm*). *Rashi* also explains there that the men of Naftali dispatched towards the enemy with alacrity, *zrizut*. *Zrizut* is also the main characteristic of the *Kohanim*, of the tribe of Levi, which is

the last ones to bring an offering during the inauguration of the Tabernacle.[90] Being a *sheliach* requires enormous nullification and submission to the one that sends him or her, as well as tremendous will power, *ratzon*, to see to it that the mission gets accomplished.

The *sheliach* qualities and self-nullification of *Naftali* also appears to be related to the phrase, "*Ve'anochi Tola'at ve lo Ish*," which means, "I am a worm and not a man." *Velo Ish*, not a man, has the same numerical value as *Sheliach*. This phrase is taken from Psalm 22 (the same number as this week), which has in its open verse, the term "*ayelet hashachar*," the gazelle of the morning. As mentioned above, the gazelle is connected to Naftali. Our sages teach us that "*ayelet hashachar*" is also a reference to the planet Venus, the last "star" to appear in the sky before morning, and a reference to Queen Ester, the last prophet to appear before redemption.

Similarly, *Adar* is the last month of the Jewish calendar counting from *Nissan*. As mentioned above, the prince of Naftali was the last tribe to bring an offering at the inauguration of the Tabernacle, wrapping up the work done by the previous tribe, Asher, and that of the other tribes. That is the work of the *sheliach* and ours as well, to wrap up the work done by those before us, and bring *Mashiach*.

---

also represented by the month of *Adar*, as further explained below.

[90]   Ryzman, p. 109

Adar is the only month in the Jewish calendar that is often counted twice. Seven times every nineteen years, the Jewish calendar contains two *Adar* months: *Adar I and Adar II. Adar II* is represented by the tribe of Levi. As would be expected, there are strong parallels between Levi and Naftali. Like Naftali, which was known for its speed and alacrity, the Levites, especially the *kohanim*, were known for their alacrity and care in the performance of *mitzvot*. Furthermore, the Levites (and again, the *kohanim* in particular) served as emissaries for the entire Jewish people when performing their service in the Temple. As further explained in the weeks ahead, the Levites service was characterized by tremendous self-sacrifice. There is also another interesting link between the tribe of Levi and the sea animals we read about during this month. The animals in the sea did not perish during the Flood. Similarly, the tribe of Levi was never enslaved by the Egyptians.

As demonstrated by the above paragraph, *Adar* contains a very strong theme of duality. The zodiac sign of Pisces is also related to duality: its symbol is two fish facing opposite directions. Unlike other redemptions, the Purim story has not one, but two main heroes: Esther and Mordechai. It is also in the month of *Adar* that we fulfill the *mitzvah* of giving the half-shekel. The half-shekel was a contribution made to the Temple in order that sacrifices could be brought on behalf of the entire public. The *mitzvah* is still done during the month of *Adar*, although for now it plays more of a symbolic role. Each person's giving a half-shekel, as opposed to a whole one, symbolizes the idea that no Jew is complete by him or herself. Each of us complements the other.

The number twenty-two represents the total number of letters in the Hebrew alphabet. *Hashem* used these letters to create the Torah and the world by combining them to each other. In this sense, each of the letters complements the other. Similarly, the Torah begins with the letter *beit*, representing the idea of duality and relationship, the relationship between *Hashem* and His creation.

Duality and relationship are also found in the song of the sea monsters. At first glance it appears strange that the sea monsters should be singing about praising *Hashem* on land as well as in the depths of the sea. However, the sea monsters understand that their song is not enough by itself. It must be complemented by the songs in the land as well.

The duality of the month of *Adar* is also one the contrast between "the hidden" and "the revealed." The miracle of Purim was performed through "hidden" means, and despite the hand of G-d being more than apparent in the events that led to the Jewish redemption of this month, the actual name of G-d does not appear in the Purim story found in the *Megillah*. The name of the scroll we read, *Megillat Esther*, is further evidence of this duality. *Megillah* comes from the verb *nigleh* (revealed) and *nistar* (hidden). In the song of the sea monsters, the sea depths represent that which is hidden, while the land represents that which is revealed.

The song of the sea monsters is also reminiscent of the blessing Jacob gave to his two grandchildren, Ephraim and Menashe (here again, the number two appears): "You will multiply like fish in the face of the *land* [not the water]."

Rabbi Yitzchak Ginsburgh explains that the *gematria* of Naftali, which represents *Adar*, is equal to the *gematria* of Ephraim and Menashe.

This week, the lesson in *Pirkei Avot* comes from Rabbi Dusta'i the son of Yannai, who states that forgetting one's study is comparable to committing a mortal sin. One of the main *mitzvot* of the month of *Adar* is remembering the evil done by Amalek and the Divine commandment to destroy it. If we do not remember to destroy evil, we put our own lives in danger.

The combination of *sefirot* for this week is *chesed shebenetzach*, kindness within victory. In the month of *Adar*, we increase in joy. This week marks the beginning of two months of victory and redemption—*netzach*—associated with Purim and Passover. We celebrate the kindness G-d showed us by being more joyful than usual. (This week would also represent the "eighth week," of *Shavuot* and "*Shivah Yemei Miluim*" of the cycle of *Tiferet*)

The lesson in self-improvement we learn from the sea monsters is that it is not sufficient to praise G-d just by ourselves. We must also think of those who are distant, just as the sea monsters think of those on land.

WEEK 23: TO BE HAPPY EVEN WITHOUT KNOWING WHY THINGS ARE HOW THEY ARE

The Leviathan is saying, "Give thanks to G-d for He is good, His kindness endures forever." (Psalms 136:1)

Rabbi Chanina the son of Dosa would say: One whose fear of sin takes precedence to his wisdom, his wisdom endures. But one whose wisdom takes precedence to his fear of sin, his wisdom does not endure.

He would also say: One whose deeds exceed his wisdom, his wisdom endures. But one whose wisdom exceeds his deeds, his wisdom does not endure.

He would also say: One who is pleasing to his fellow men, is pleasing to G-d. But one who is not pleasing to his fellow men, is not pleasing to G-d.

Gevurah shebeNetzach (discipline and judgment within the context of victory and endurance)

We now arrive at the twenty-third week, when the Leviathan in *Perek Shirah* gives thanks to the Lord, for He is good and His mercy is eternal. This week marks the seventh day of *Adar*, the birthday as well as the *yahrzeit* of Moses, *Moshe Rabbeinu*. Moses is from the tribe of Levi. It is also no coincidence that the first three Hebrew letters of the name "Leviathan" spell the word "Levi," one of the tribes of this month.

The Leviathan is clearly a reference to Moses himself. In general, fish represent *tzadikim*, and just as the Leviathan is the biggest of all fish, Moses is the greatest of all *tzadikim*.[91] (*See* Week 4, regarding the eagle) A hidden reference to Moses being like a fish can also be found in the name of his main disciple, *Yehoshua Bin Nun*. *Nun* means fish in Aramaic. The Torah teaches us that a student is considered like a son.[92] The *gematria* of the letter *Nun* is fifty, and when Moses passed away he reached the fiftieth level of holiness. This is implied in the name of the place of his burial, Mount Nevoh, which can also be read as "*Nun Boh*" ("the *Nun* is in it").

The last letter of the Hebrew word for Leviathan (*Leviatan*) is *Nun*. If one exchanges the *Lamed* (which equals 30) and the *Yud* (which equals 10) for a *Mem* (40), the word *Leviatan* is transformed into *Mavet* (death) *Nun*. As mentioned above, *Moshe Rabbeinu* reached the fiftieth level of holiness upon his death, even though we say that *Moshe Rabbeinu* never truly died.

The song of the Leviathan is well known, and repeated many times in Psalm 118. In Hebrew, it reads, "*Hodu l'Hashem Ki Tov Ki l'Olam Chasdoh.*" *Ki Tov*, which means "for [He] is good," is exactly the Torah's description for what Yocheved saw in her newborn son, Moses. She saw *Ki Tov*, that he was good. That is why one of Moses' names is also *Tuviah*, from the word *Tov*. *Rashi* explains that at the time of Moses' birth, his mother saw that the house

---

[91] *Shnei Luchot HaBrit*
[92] Rabbi Tzvi Aryeh Rosenfeld

became filled with light.[93] Our sages explain that this is also a reference to the light that will only be revealed in the end of creation.

The number twenty-three has the *gematria* of *ziv*, which means light, radiance. Rabbi Yitzchak Ginsburgh explains that *ziv*, as opposed to *or*, refers to a light that shines far away from its source. The Leviathan is an animal that is mysterious and unknown. Its existence will only be fully revealed in the messianic era. Our current understanding of the Leviathan is negligible, equivalent to the brightness of a light coming from far away, like the *ziv*. We know through Psalm 104:26 and *Midrashim*, that G-d created the leviathan to "play" with it, but we certainly do not know exactly what that means. We also know that the Leviathan will be the food served to us in the final redemption, the end of creation.

Ziv is also a biblical name given to the month of *Iyar*. The Torah states that it was "in the month *Ziv*" that Solomon began to build the Temple.[94] The construction of the Second Temple also began in the month of *Iyar*. Furthermore, we know that it is during *Iyar* that we count the *omer*, and that the word *Sefirat Ha'Omer* comes from the word *sapir*, saphire. During *Iyar* we work on ourselves to become radiant like saphire. We make ourselves into proper vessels so that G-d can dwell within us.

As we enter the month of *Adar* and experience Moses' birthday and passing, we also begin to work on our inner

---

[93]   Exodus 2:2
[94]   Kings I, 6:1

Temple. The Torah reading for this week is usually related to the construction of the Tabernacle, and we continue to collect the half-shekel, which historically was given towards the Temple's upkeep.

In order to achieve balance in the world, *Hashem* had to allow the female to die. Despite this tragedy, the Leviathan still sings about G-d's kindness. The Leviathan knows perfectly well that all that *Hashem* does is for the good.

The Leviathan praises *Hashem* for His eternal kindness, and Moses also showed great kindness to the Jewish people, leading them out of Egypt in order to receive the Torah at Mount Sinai. Furthermore, as the largest of all fish and the one that has the closest relationship with G-d, the Leviathan is not content with praising *Hashem* by itself. It commands that others to do their part to praise G d as well.

The last *ma'amar* reviewed and edited by the Rebbe, *Ve'Atah Tetzaveh*, was delivered during *Adar*, and it is about the relationship between Moses and the rest of the Jewish people. *Tetzaveh* means "to command," but also to tie, unite—the same root as the word *mitzvah*. *Tetzaveh* is the one weekly portion of the Torah since the introduction of Moses, in which his name is not mentioned. This is said to be a hidden reference to Moses' passing, on the 7th of *Adar*, since *Tetzaveh* is usually read around this time. The connection between *Tetzaveh* and Moses' death is so strong that when there are two *Adars*, Moses' *yahrzeit* is commemorated on the first *Adar*, because it will be then that *Tetzaveh* will be read. Usually, when there are two *Adars*, the "main" date is usually the one in the second

Adar. It is worth noting that the Rebbe's stroke was on *Adar* I, on the 27th day of that month. Two years later, on this exact day, 27th of *Adar* I, 5754, the Rebbe suffered another stroke, which ultimately led to his passing a few months later.

Less than two months prior to the Rebbe's stroke, he gave an enigmatic talk in which he described how his late father-in-law, the Previous Rebbe, was not able to speak clearly in the last years of his life. At that time, even though it was now more than forty years after the Previous Rebbe's passing, the Rebbe exclaimed that we all had to do our part, and take upon ourselves as a personal challenge to increase Torah study and Chassidic gatherings in order to compensate for the Previous Rebbe's difficulty in communication, and to do so with happiness.[95] How unbelievable was it then that two months later the Rebbe would find himself in the same condition.

The *Pirkei Avot* teaching for this week comes from Rabbi Chanina the son of Dosa, who says that anyone whose fear of sin precedes his wisdom, his wisdom will endure, but all those whose wisdom precedes their fear of sin, their wisdom will not endure. This teaching is perfectly related to Moses, who showed fear of *Hashem* since his first interaction with Him at the burning bush.

Moreover, Rabbi Chanina also teaches that whoever is pleasing to mankind is pleasing to G-d, and whoever

---

[95] From the Rebbe's *Sichos*, 3rd of *Shvat* after *Mincha* prayers, *available at:* http://www.sichosinenglish.org/books/ sichos-in-english/51/17.htm

is not pleasing to mankind is not pleasing to G-d. This lesson also applies to Moses, whose acts were pleasing to the Jewish people and to *Hashem*.

Rabbi Chanina, similar to Moses himself, exemplifies a *tzadik* who is the foundation of the world. The Talmud teaches that every day a heavenly voice exclaims that, "the entire world is sustained in merit of Chanina my son, yet for Chanina my son, one measure of carobs is enough from Friday to Friday."[96]

In this twenty-third week, the combination of *sefirot* results in *gevurah shebenetzach*: discipline and strength within determination and victory. As explained earlier, Moses represents the *sefirah* of *netzach*, and his death is connected with the attribute of *gevurah*. From the above teaching, we see that Rabbi Chanina himself also is very much connected to the *gevurah shebenetzach*.

The lesson in self-improvement we can extract from the Leviathan is that everything that G-d does is for good, and therefore we should fully trust in Him.

---

[96] *Brachot* 17b

WEEK 24: TO LIVE ABOVE OUR WORLDLY CONCERNS

> **The fish are saying:** "The voice of G-d is upon the waters, the G-d of glory thunders; G-d is upon many waters." (Psalms 29:3)
>
> **Rabbi Dosa the son of Hurkinas would say:** Morning sleep, noontime wine, children's talk and sitting at the meeting places of the ignorant, drive a person from the world.
>
> *Tiferet shebeNetzach* (beauty and balance within the context of victory and endurance)

In the twenty-fourth week, the fish in *Perek Shirah* sing that the voice of *Hashem* hovers above the waters—the G-d of glory thunders—*Hashem* is above many waters. (Psalm 29:3) This is the week of Purim, when we remember that *Hashem* is with us during all our trials and tribulations, even if sometimes in a hidden way.

In Purim, we celebrate the great salvation experienced in the times of the Persian exile, when the evil Haman, with the initial support of the King, Achashverosh, sought to exterminate the entire Jewish people. Through the efforts of Mordechai and Esther, the decree against the Jewish people is miraculously annulled, and instead Haman, his sons, and the enemies of the Jews are the ones killed.

The Zohar states that *Yom Kippur* (also called *Yom haKippurim*) is a day that is "*KePurim*," like Purim, meaning that Purim is even higher than *Yom Kippur*. If on *Yom Kippur* we are on the level of angels, then on Purim we must be at a level that is even higher than angels, on the level of *tzadikim*. As mentioned in the previous week, fish symbolize *tzadikim*.

Furthermore, on Purim, in an attempt to become closer to G-d, we drink "many waters." We try to reach a level of *ad deloyadah*, of not knowing the difference between "blessed be Mordechai" and "cursed be Haman." We have an experience that in many ways is similar to that of the four rabbis that entered the *Pardes*. When describing this experience, Rabbi Akiva stated, "When you reach the stones of pure marble, do not say: 'Water, water.'" On Purim, we realize that there are no divisions or separations on-high, all is One, and there is no difference between the effects of what we perceive as good and what we perceive as evil. When a person reaches these levels, the desire to cleave to *Hashem* is so strong that it is like great waves pulling us out of this world. The voice of *Hashem* thunders, like at Mount Sinai, and we want to nullify ourselves completely (*ratzo*). In order to survive this experience, we must do like Rabbi Akiva, who "entered in peace and returned in peace." We must understand that ultimately *Hashem*'s desire is that we return and make a dwelling place for him *within* this world (*shov*).[97]

The song of the fish states that the voice of *Hashem*, and *Hashem* Himself, are above the waters. However, the fish are not above the waters, but actually inside them. In order

[97] <u>Attaining Sagacity</u>, Eliyahu Touger, *available at* http://www.sichosinenglish.org/books/attaining-sagacity/10.htm

to perceive G-d fully, the fish also need emissaries. The role of *shlichut* (being an emissary) is very prominent in the Purim story. Not only is Esther an emissary of Mordechai and vice-versa, but also the communications between Mordechai and Esther were often done through *shluchim*. It is therefore no coincidence that on Purim we give each other *mishloach manot* (from the word *sheliach*), preferably through a third person.

The term "many waters" is also in the Song of Songs, when King Solomon writes that many waters cannot extinguish the love [for G-d].[98] The "many waters" are a reference to the difficulties and turbulences involved in making a living, which however great, cannot extinguish the love of a Jew for G-d.[99]

The Hebrew word for fish is *dag*. Rabbi Yitzchak Ginsburgh explains that fish represent the *tikkun* (rectification) of worry (*da'agah*), especially in relation to earning a livelihood. The Torah relates that at the time of Nehemiah, certain Jews desecrated the Sabbath by selling fish in the market of Jerusalem. These men did not trust in G-d in earning a living. The fish (*dag*) then became a source of excessive concern (*da'ag*).

Fish are constantly aware of their dependence on water, given that water is more tangible than air. Similarly, they are constantly aware of the Source of their existence, *Hashem*.

---

98 Chapter 8:7
99 *Ma'amar "Mayim Rabbim"* of the Alter Rebbe

The number twenty-four is related to the twenty-four presents of the *kohanim*, of the tribe of Levi. In addition, the priesthood was later divided into twenty-four watches. The letters *caf* and *dalet* spell *kad*, which means jar, or pitcher. There is the famous *kad* found during *Chanukah*, which contained pure oil with the seal of the high priest, the *Kohen Gadol*. This oil lasted eight days instead of one. Even the great impurity and turbulences that took place during the Hellenistic period did not extinguish the love of the Jewish people for *Hashem*. The Jews emerged from the struggle with the Greeks even purer than before and with redoubled faith.

In addition to *Chanukah*, the connection between Purim and the role of *kohanim* is also quite strong. Esther has to fast and enter the King's chamber in order to ask for the life of her people, very much the *Kohen Gadol* on *Yom Kippur*. The *Mishnah* states that the *Kohen Gadol* was called a *sheliach Hashem*, an emissary of G-d, although he also served like an emissary of the Jewish people. Esther also played this role, of being at the same time an emissary of the Jewish people, but also G-d's emissary in order to save His people. The *kohen* is also referred to as *malach Hashem*, a messenger, literally an "angel" of G-d.

Purim gives emphasis to two different types of relationship and duality. Mordechai, of the tribe of Benjamin, of King Shaul, and Haman, a descendant of Amalek, are polar opposites. Esther and Mordechai complement each other for the good, while Haman and King Achashverosh complemented each other for evil.

In the *Pirkei Avot* saying for this week, Rabbi Dosa the son of Harkinas teaches that late sleep in the morning, wine at midday, the chatter of children, and sitting in the meeting places of the ignorant, all take a person out of this world. Interestingly, these acts are all encouraged on Purim! On Purim, there are two ways to reach a level of *ad deloyada*: sleeping or drinking during the day. Moreover, the Purim story highlights the importance of the words spoken by children studying Torah, the very source for the redemption. Additionally, on Purim we emphasize our unity and do not distinguish between rich and poor, be it material wealth or Torah knowledge. We distribute *mishloach manot*, give gifts to the poor, and all sit together to partake in the Purim feast. All these actions take us out of this world of illusion (*olam*, world, comes from the word *he'elem*, hidden) and bring us to higher levels of reality and connection to G-d.

This week, the combination of *sefirot* is *tiferet shebenetzach*, beauty and balance within redemption, persistence and determination. These qualities are very much linked to Esther and Mordechai and to Purim in general. The lesson we draw from the fish is that material concerns must not take away from our trust and faith in *Hashem*. Nothing should be a hindrance to our direct relationship with Him.

WEEK 25: TO HAVE SELF-SACRIFICE IN ORDER TO FULFILL OUR MISSION IN LIFE

The frog is saying, "Blessed is the Name of the honor of His Kingdom for all eternity." (Talmud, *Pesachim* 56a)

Rabbi Elazar of Modi'in would say: One who profanes the *kodoshim* ("holy things" consecrated for the service of G-d in the Holy Temple), degrades the Festivals, humiliates his friend in public, abrogates the covenant of our father Abraham (i.e., circumcision), or who interprets the Torah contrary to its true intent—although he may possess Torah knowledge and good deeds, he has no share in the World to Come.

Netzach shebeNetzach (victory and endurance within the context of victory and endurance)

And we come to the twenty-fifth week, still in the month of *Adar*, when the frog in *Perek Shirah* blesses His name and His reign for all eternity, *Baruch Shem Kevod Malchuto L'Olam Va'ed* (Talmud, *Pesachim* 56A). The frog also appears in the introduction to *Perek Shirah*, in a story of great personal self-sacrifice. The frog's song is said every day, at least twice a day, since it is an essential part of the prayer of the *Shemah*. The *Shemah* expresses our complete acceptance of the kingship of G-d, and of His commandments, with great self-sacrifice.

It also worth noting that this week marks the *yahrzeit* of Rebbe Elimelech of Lizhensk. Rebbe Elimelech completely exemplified self-sacrifice. One of his main meditative techniques was to imagine throwing himself into a great pillar of fire in order to sanctify G-d's name. The technique would ensure that any other task he would perform during the day would be on this same level of self-sacrifice.

The story of the frog in *Perek Shirah*'s introduction is a great example of how to be an emissary with true self-sacrifice. G-d's second plague upon Egypt was that of frogs. The frogs would jump inside the ovens of the Egyptians, giving up their lives without hesitation. Their self-sacrifice was later a source of inspiration for Chananya, Misha'el and Azariah, who sanctified G-d's name by refusing to bow down to an idol, knowing full well they would be thrown into a burning furnace. Miraculously, they emerged from the furnace unscathed.[100]

The second plague was in response to the fact that the Egyptian taskmasters worked the Jewish people so hard in the open sun that they had no time to eat or drink and felt completely dehydrated. Frogs are water creatures and their bodies absorb moisture in order to survive. The *Midrash* teaches that during the plague, a large number of frogs would search out and absorb all the moisture in Egypt, making the Egyptians feel dehydrated as well. It is well known that water is a metaphor for Torah. It is the job of the *sheliach* is to find Torah and the holy sparks of the Diaspora in order to absorb them and elevate them,

---

[100] "Chananya, Mishael, and Azarya," Nissan Mindel, Kehot Publication Society, *available at*: http://www.chabad.org/library/article_cdo/aid/112288/jewish/Chananya-Mishael-and-Azarya.htm

searching even in the driest of places. The reality is that we are all emissaries.[101]

Perek Shirah explains that the frog, as an amphibian, does what no other animal can. It voluntarily serves as food for a land animal which feed itself only from water animals. Again, using water as a metaphor for Torah, the frog is willing to sacrifice its own life in order to bring Torah to those animals on dry land. The frog tells King David that because of this self-sacrifice, *Hashem* will make it whole, will complement it. Here again we see the idea that each Jew complements the other, like the half-shekel giving during this month.

Interestingly, in *Perek Shirah* itself, the frog again plays the role of bringing together land and sea. The frog comes after the fish and before the sheep and goat, literally making the link between the water animals of the month of *Adar* and the land animals of the month of *Nissan* and beyond.

The week of the frog always falls after the week of Purim and close to the special Torah reading of *Parah* (the animal of the second week of *Nissan*), which is primarily about how to purify a person from the greatest source of impurity (contact with the dead). Interestingly, the *kohen*

---

[101] "There is not the vaguest shadow of doubt that, wherever our feet tread, it is all in order to cleanse and purify the world with words of Torah and *tefilla* (prayer). We, all of Israel, are emissaries of G-d, each of us as Divine Providence has decreed for us. None of us is free from this sacred task placed on our shoulders." *Hayom Yom*, 5th of *Adar I*.

that performs the purification also sacrifices himself by becoming impure in the process, although only temporarily. A similar self-sacrifice is performed by Queen Esther, who makes herself impure by marrying King Achashverosh in order to save the entire Jewish people. It is also no coincidence that Purim and *Parah* have such similar roots.

This dual role, superficially negative, yet extremely positive, is found in the verse *Baruch Shem Kevod* itself. The Talmud in *Pessachim* suggests that this verse is somehow embarrassing to be said out loud, and that is why we say it quietly. Some authorities state that this verse represents a lower form of declaring G-d's unity. However, many other famous commentaries teach us that this saying was actually much higher, and said by the angels themselves. We say it quietly only because it is too lofty for this world. The only day that we say it openly is on *Yom Kippur*, when we are all on the level of angels.[102] As mentioned previously, angels are emissaries of G-d.

There are many other sources that connect the frog to the idea of being a *sheliach* with total self-sacrifice. There's also a famous *Midrash* that teaches that in fact the plague of frogs started out as only a single giant frog. When the Egyptians would try to strike this single frog it would multiply into many more mini-frogs, who in turn would also split into more, like emissaries of the giant frog.

---

102 Rav Mordecai Kornfeld, *available at* http://www. shemayisrael.co.il/dafyomi2/pessachim/insites/ps-dt-056.htm

Rebbe Elimelech of Lizhensk is known as a "Rebbe of Rebbes," because the most prominent Polish Rebbes were all his disciples, or disciples of his disciples. They were all like emissaries, continuing his legacy. Among these giants are the Chozeh of Lublin (who would thank G-d an hour a day for bringing down the soul of his Rebbe), the Ohev Yisrael (the Apter Rov), the Rimanover, the Maggid of Kozhnitz, and many others. Rebbe Tzvi Elimelech of Dinov, the Bnei Issachar, was his nephew.

This concept of *shlichut* is found again in the words that the frog says to King David in the introduction of *Perek Shirah*: "Every song I say contains three thousand parables." A parable represents the concept of taking an idea and bringing down, so that it is more accessible to others. The frog has three thousand other "emissaries" linked to its song. It is worth noting that at the time of his passing, the Lubavitcher Rebbe had roughly three thousand emissaries, and that today there are roughly three thousand Chabad centers worldwide.

The three thousand parables are also comparable to the three thousand men that "fell" by the hand of the Levites, who served as Moses' emissaries after the incident of the golden calf:

> 26. So Moses stood in the gate of the camp and said: "Whoever is for the Lord, [let him come] to me!" And all the sons of Levi gathered around him.

> 27. He said to them: "So said the Lord, the G-d of Israel: 'Let every man place his sword

> upon his thigh and pass back and forth
> from one gate to the other in the camp, and
> let every man kill his brother, every man his
> friend, every man his kinsman.'

> 28. The sons of Levi did according to Moses'
> word; on that day <u>some three thousand men</u>
> fell from among the people.

Perhaps the phrased "roughly three thousand men" is a reference to the men of Levi, who followed the word of Moses, falling upon those that needed to be punished.

In fulfilling Moses' word, the Levites acted with extreme self-sacrifice and did not consider brother and friend. This was an extremely positive behavior at the time, but perhaps still required a sort of *tikkun*, correction. In contrast, the Chabad *shluchim* consider *everyone* to be their brother and friend, and treat them as such. Chabad *shluchim* also "fall" from their pure and holy lifestyle in order to reach out to those that need guidance.

Similarly, three thousand *halachot* were forgotten at the time of the mourning for Moses. Perhaps the three thousand *shluchim*, who methodically study the Rebbe's words, are a *tikkun* for this as well.

The term "roughly three thousand men" also appears in the story of Samson, which he also showed extreme self-sacrifice, to the point of giving up his life.

> 27. Now the house was full of men and
> women, and all the lords of the Philistines

were there. And upon the roof (there were) *about three thousand men and women*, the spectators of Samson's sport.

(. . .)

30. And Samson said, "Let my soul die with the Philistines," and he bent with (his) might, and the house fell upon the lords, and upon all the people that were therein. And the dead that he killed at his death were more than he had killed in his lifetime.[103]

Like the *kohen* that performs the purification through the red heifer, and Queen Esther in the Purim story, Samson was willing to sacrifice himself, both spiritually and physically, in order to bring redemption to the Jewish people. The verses above also appear to make a slight reference to Purim. Verse 27 states that there were about three thousand men and women "upon the roof." In the original Hebrew, this part is written, "*Al haGag*." In Aramaic, it would be "*Agag*." Haman was a descendant of Agag, the king of the Amalekites. At the end of the Purim story, not only are Haman and his sons killed, but also 75,000 (25 x 3,000) Amalekites.[104]

The number twenty-five is connected to the Jewish festival of *Chanukah*, since this festival, as well as the dedication of the Temple that is celebrated on this day took place on the twenty-fifth day of *Kislev*. The word "*Chanukah*"

---

[103] Judges 16: 27-30
[104] Esther 9:16

itself means "*Chanu*" (they rested)—"*Kah*" (twenty-five), a reference to the twenty-fifth of *Kislev*. The twenty-fifth letter in the Torah is "*or*," a reference to the light of *Chanukah*.

The *Chashmonaim* played a dual role of both the *kohanim* and the kings. Rebbe Elimelech (whose name means "G-d is my King") also had a strong complementary relationship with his saintly brother, the Tzadik Reb Zusya of Anipoli.

This week in *Pirkei Avot*, Rabbi Elazar of Modi'in teaches that he who profanes holy objects/animals, degrades the festivals, publicly humiliates his neighbor, repeals the covenant of our father Abraham (circumcision) and interprets the Torah in a way that is opposed to its true meaning—even if they have Torah and good deeds, they have no part in the World to Come.

During this week, just after Purim, we begin preparing for Passover. The *Shulchan Aruch*, the Code of Jewish Law, explains that one should prepare for Passover thirty days before the festival. During these days it is customary to give money to the poor (*Maot Chitim*) so that they too can properly celebrate Passover. And see the tremendous connection with *Pirkei Avot*, namely:

1) "Profaning the holy" appears to be a reference to the times of the Temple, when everyone had to bring the Passover sacrifice. The animal and subsequently the meat of the sacrifice were sacred and had to be treated properly.

2) "Degrading the festivals" is a more direct reference to the importance to the festival of Passover, both in its

physical preparations (destroying the physical *chametz*, yeast and other leavened breads) and spiritual preparations (eliminating the inner spiritual *chametz*, our egotism and inflated self-importance).

3) "Publicly humiliating his neighbor" relates to the charity given in advance of the holiday, so no one should feel ashamed of having to beg for money in order to celebrate Passover.

4) "Revoking the covenant of Abraham our father" is related to circumcision. Passover is linked to Abraham, because it was on Passover that angels came to visit him and Sarah, and Abraham gave them *matzot* to eat. Also, just before the first Passover in Egypt, all the men of the people underwent circumcision. Again, 40 years later, before entering Israel, Joshua made all men undergo circumcision. During the 40 years in the desert no men were circumcised. In the days of the Temple, those who were not circumcised they could not eat the Passover sacrifice.

5) "Interpreting the Torah in a way that is opposed to its true meaning" relates to the various legal rulings that are made during Passover cleaning. Cleaning the house for Passover and preparing for the *Seder* involves a lot of work. It is therefore easy to find excuses not to have to clean so much: "After all, by Torah law is it not enough simply to verbally nullify the *chametz*?" Hence the importance of this teaching: we have to do everything possible to strictly adhere to the letter and the spirit of the Law, each one at his or her own spiritual level.

The list of wrongdoing mentioned by Rabbi Elazar also relates to problems that occurred during the time period of *Chanukah*. The Greeks defiled the sacred objects of the Temple; they were against celebrating sacred dates, such as *Shabbat* and *Rosh Chodesh*. The Hellenistic Jews had no shame and fought naked in gymnasiums, many even reversed their circumcision. Hellenistic Jews, Saducees, and other cults also sought to corrupt the true interpretations of the Torah, and the Greeks tried to misrepresent the sacred nature of the Torah, and forced it to be translated into Greek.

This week, the *sefirot* combination results in *netzach shebenetzach*, victory within victory. This week represents the midpoint and link between the victory and redemption of *Adar* (Purim), with the victory and redemption of *Nissan* (Passover). Twenty-five is also exactly midway through the Counting of the *Omer*, linking the two different modes of divine service related to the first and second halves of the year. (*See* Appendix I)

The lesson we learn from the frog is that we must serve G-d with great self-sacrifice, remembering how temporary our stay is on this Earth, and how we are infinitely small and limited when compared to G-d.

WEEK 26: TO BE HUMBLE AND LET G-D GUIDE US

> **The sheep [and goat] is saying:**[104] "Who is like You among the might ones, G-d, who is like You, mighty in holiness, awesome in praise, worker of wonders." (Exodus 15:11)
>
> **Rabbi Yishmael would say:** Be yielding to a leader, affable to the black-haired, and receive every man with joy.
>
> **Hod shebeNetzach** (glory and gratefulness within the context of victory and endurance)

In the twenty-sixth week, that of *Rosh Chodesh Nissan*, in *Perek Shirah*, the small pure (kosher) domestic animal proclaims that no one is as strong, awesome and miraculous as *Hashem* (Exodus 15:11). The small pure domestic animal is a reference to the sheep (the month of *Nissan* corresponds to the zodiac sign of Aries), as well as to the goat. *Rosh Chodesh Nissan* marks the inauguration of the *Mishkan*, the Tabernacle, in which sacrifices of pure kosher animals, such as the sheep and goat, were brought.

Nissan is the month of redemption and miracles. The relationship of shepherd and flock is one of the most important metaphors for the relationship between G-d and

---

105 While Rabbi Slifkin translates this animal only as sheep, Rabbi Lazer Brody includes goats as well. The Hebrew term can be translated literally as "small/thin pure animal."

the Jewish people. G-d is far above our comprehension, just as the shepherd is also completely beyond the understanding of his flock. At the same time, like sheep, we have total humility and faith that our Shepherd will lead us in the right path, despite perhaps having to face foxes and lions along the way.

The goat is also used a symbol for the Jewish People in the famous song that is sung by many Jews on Passover night, *Chad Gadya*. The song's name means "One Goat," and also appears to be phonetically similar to the word *Haggadah*, the text that is read during the Passover *Seder*. *Chad Gadya* is similar to *Perek Shirah*, in that it also includes many animals and natural elements. The animals in *Chad Gadya* function primarily as symbols for various exiles we have endured and the different nations that conquered the Land of Israel. The cat that eats the goat is a reference to Assyrians; the dog that eats the cat is a reference to Babylon; the stick is Persia; the fire is Macedonia; the water, Rome; the ox, the Saracens; the slaughterer, the crusaders; the Angel of Death, the Turks. At the end, G-d saves us from all these enemies and returns us to our Land.[106] The two *zuzim*, the coins used to purchase the goat are said to be a reference to the two tablets containing the Ten Commandments given to Moses at Mount Sinai,[107] but also appear to be a reference to the two Temples that were destroyed, and its people exiled. *Zuz* means to move, to change places. The Third Temple, however, will not move, it will be everlasting.

[106] Jewish Encyclopedia, *available at*: http://www.jewishencyclopedia.com/articles/6998-had-gadya

[107] The Book of Passover, Rabbi Benjamin Blech, p. 163

Similarly, each animal in *Perek Shirah* that sings during *Nissan* represents a different exile, as well as a redemption from it. Sheep were gods to the Egyptians, our first exile, and the goat, *Seir* in Hebrew, is a reference to Esau, our last. It was in this month that we were redeemed from Egypt, and it is in this month that we will be redeemed in the future.

The Torah states unequivocally that *Nissan* is the head of all months, *Rosh Chodashim*. It is therefore represented by the Tribe of Judah, who was the leader of his brothers, and from whom King David descends. All legitimate kings of the Jewish people—including *Mashiach*—are descendants of King David and therefore of Judah. The word for Judah in Hebrew, *Yehudah*, comes from the word *hoda'ah*, which means acknowledgement. This is the same root of the word *Modeh*, as in the prayer we make when we first get up in the morning, the *Modeh Ani*, in which we acknowledge G-d as our King and thank Him for returning our soul. The tribe of Judah is characterized by self-sacrifice, acknowledgement, and thankfulness.

Because the Egyptians idolized sheep, it is extremely appropriate that it be the one to proclaim the absolute greatness of *Hashem*. The Sheep is the animal used in the Passover sacrifice, showing the Egyptians that G-d is far greater than any other god. On *Shabat HaGadol* (the "Great Shabbat," which takes place right before Passover), we celebrate the miracle of how the Egyptians did not react negatively toward the Jewish people, when they tied sheep to their bedposts, and told the Egyptians that they were about to sacrifice their gods in the coming days.

Nissan is the month of Passover, and it is therefore appropriate that this week's song be from the Song of the Sea, which was sung after the miracle of the splitting of the Sea of Reeds.[108]

The number twenty-six is the *gematria* of G-d's name, "*Hashem*." Twenty-six also equals two times the number thirteen, the *gematria* of the word *echad*, one, as well as *ahava*h, love.

Rabbi Yishmael in *Pirkei Avot* teaches us this week that we must submit to a superior (literally "the head"), and be courteous to a younger person, greeting every person with joy (III:12). Among the *kohanim*, Rabbi Yishmael was the head, the *Kohen Gadol*. In addition to his close connection with *Hashem*, Rabbi Yishmael, as Aaron before him, had a great love for each member of the Jewish people, independent of his or her status or stature. This verse also has a clear connection with *Nissan*, the head of the months.

The *sefirot* combination for this week results in *hod shebenetzach*. With humility and gratitude, self-sacrifice and acknowledgement, we achieve the miraculous victory and redemption that takes place during this month.

We learn from the sheep and the goat that our work of improving ourselves physically and spiritually must be based on our strong belief that only *Hashem* can truly redeem us.

---

[108] Exodus 13:16

WEEK 27: TO PURIFY OURSELVES IN ORDER TO CHANGE

The cow is saying, "Rejoice to the Lord over our strength, trumpet to the Lord of Jacob!" (Psalms 81:2)

Rabbi Akiva would say: Jesting and frivolity accustom a person to promiscuity. Tradition is a safety fence to Torah, tithing a safety fence to wealth, vows a safety fence for abstinence; a safety fence for wisdom is silence.

He would also say: Beloved is man, for he was created in the image [of G-d]; it is a sign of even greater love that it has been made known to him that he was created in the image, as it is says, "For in the image of G-d, He made man" (Genesis 9:6). Beloved are Israel, for they are called children of G-d; it is a sign of even greater love that it has been made known to them that they are called children of G-d, as it is stated: "You are children of the L-rd your G-d" (Deuteronomy 14:1). Beloved are Israel, for they were given a precious article; it is a sign of even greater love that it has been made known to them that they given a precious article, as it is stated: "I have given you a good purchase; My Torah, do not forsake it" (Proverbs 4:2).

All is foreseen, and freedom of choice is granted. The world is judged with goodness, but in accordance with the amount of man's positive deeds.

He would also say: Everything is placed in pledge, and a net is spread over all the living. The store is open, the storekeeper extends credit, the account-book lies open, the hand writes, and all who wish to borrow may come and borrow. The collection-officers make their rounds every day and exact payment from man, with his knowledge and without his knowledge. Their case is well founded, the judgment is a judgment of truth, and ultimately, all is prepared for the feast.

Yesod shebeNetzach (foundation and firmness within the context of victory and endurance)

As we arrive at week twenty-seven, even closer to Passover, it is the turn of the large pure (kosher) domestic animal to proclaim that we rejoice to the G-d of Jacob, the source of our strength. (Psalm 81:2) The large pure domestic animal is seen as a reference to the cow. The Jewish people are called by the names Israel and Jacob. Jacob is usually the name used when we are in a more fragile, humble state. When we are feeling weak, we must rely even more on *Hashem* as the source of our strength. This is also the week of the *yahrzeit* of the Rebbe Rashab, on the 2nd of *Nissan*. The Rebbe Rashab's leadership took place during a tumultuous time in Jewish history, when the Jewish people were in a particularly fragile state (like the song of the cow), and faced the harsh anti-religious oppression of the Bolsheviks in Russia.

The cow also represents the spiritual exile and impurity of Egypt, embodied by the golden calf. Conversely, the cow also represents the purification through the *Parah Adumah*, the Red Heifer. The Red Heifer had to be completely red, pure and complete/whole (*tamim*).[109] The Red Heifer's ashes were used for purification of the highest form of impurity—contact with the dead. This purification process had to be performed by every Jew that found himself in a state of impurity in order to bring the Passover offering during this month. It is for this reason that we read a special Torah portion about the Red Heifer, known as *Parashat Parah*, in a few weeks before this holiday. The Rebbe Rashab also is a tremendous example of purity. He established *Tomchei Tmimim* yeshiva system—its students were known as *tmimim*, the pure, wholesome ones. The Rebbe Rashab's last *ma'amar* was about the ultimate destruction of Amalek and the husks of impurity (*kelipah*).

The number twenty-seven is formed by the Hebrew letters *kaf* and *zayin*, which form the word *zach*, "pure." In preparation for Passover, we must purify ourselves physically and spiritually, returning to G-d, and eagerly awaiting his redemption.

The *Pirkei Avot* for week twenty-seven is found in the lessons of Rabbi Akiva. Rabbi Akiva is known for his many popular sayings, one of which is directly related to the purification of the people of Israel. Rabbi Akiva states how praiseworthy are the Jewish people, whose purification comes directly from our Father in Heaven.[110] In the *Pirkei Avot* for this week, Rabbi Akiva first describes

---

[109] The word *tamim* is related to the word *tam*, simple/pure, which is also connected to Jacob. In his early years, Jacob is called an "*Ish Tam Yoshev Ohalim*," a pure/simple man who dwells in the tents (of study). (Genesis 25:27)

[110] Mishnah, *Yoma* 8:9

how to maintain one's purity, by not engaging in jest. He also describes how dear is man, since he was created in the image of G-d, and how beloved are the People of Israel, who are called G-d's children and were given the Torah. Rabbi Akiva's section in *Pirkei Avot* includes several other fundamental and profound teachings that serve as the intellectual foundation of the Jewish religion. Similarly, the teachings of the Rebbe Rashab serve as intellectual foundation of Chabad philosophy.

Rabbi Akiva ends his words in *Pirkei Avot* stating that everything is prepared for the feast. In *Nissan*, too, everything is prepared for the feast of Passover. There is no one better than Rabbi Akiva to be sharing his lessons during the month of *Nissan*, given that he is one of the greatest examples of complete humility and self-sacrifice (qualities related to this month and to Passover). This sage began to study Torah at the age of 40, sitting silently and humbly alongside small children . . . and the result? Rabbi Akiva became one of the greatest Torah scholars of all time. Rabbi Akiva's name also has the same root as the name Jacob. Both names come from the word *eikev*, which means heel. This is in contrast to the name Israel, which contains the same letters as *Li Rosh*, "mine is the head." While the head is the highest part of the body, the heel is the lowest.

This week's *sefirot* combination results in *yesod shebenetzach*, that is, foundation within determination, victory and redemption. This is perhaps the most prominent feature of Jewish education during our long exile. *Nissan* is when we were liberated from Egypt, physically and spiritually, and when we will be liberated from the current exile as well.

The lesson learned from the cow is that in the journey to make our *tikkun*—our spiritual correction, the very reason why we came into the world—G-d is the source of our strength. The cow sings about Jacob, who worked hard all his life to overcome the obstacles laid out before him along the way. Only after much perseverance and determination did Jacob manage to overcome these difficulties and become Israel. Each of us also undergoes changes and progress, even if we do not realize it. In this process, G-d is always by our side.

Week 28: To Recognize our Limits in order to Free Ourselves from Them

---

The pig [and rabbit] is saying:[110] "G-d is good to the good, and to the straight-hearted." (Psalms 128:2)

Rabbi Eliezer the son of Azariah would say: If there is no Torah, there is no common decency; if there is no common decency, there is no Torah. If there is no wisdom, there is no fear of G-d; if there is no fear of G-d, there is no wisdom. If there is no applied knowledge, there is no analytical knowledge; if there is no analytical knowledge, there is no applied knowledge. If there is no flour, there is no Torah; if there is no Torah, there is no flour.

He would also say: One whose wisdom is greater than his deeds, what is he comparable to? To a tree with many branches and few roots; comes a storm and uproots it, and turns it on its face. As is stated, "He shall be as a lone tree in a wasteland, and shall not see when good comes; he shall dwell parched in the desert, a salt land, uninhabited" (Jeremiah 17:6). But one whose deeds are greater than his wisdom, to what is he compared? To a tree with many roots and few branches, whom all the storms in the world cannot budge from its place. As is stated:

---

[110] The Artscroll translation, by Rabbi Nosson Scherman, includes a picture of a rabbit, not a pig. The Hebrew term can be translated literally as "small/thin impure animal."

> "He shall be as a tree planted upon water, who spreads his roots by the river; who fears not when comes heat, whose leaf is ever lush; who worries not in a year of drought, and ceases not to yield fruit" (ibid., v. 8).
>
> *Malchut shebeNetzach* (kingship within the context of victory and endurance)

On this twenty-eighth week, which includes the first night of Passover, in *Perek Shirah*, the small impure (non-kosher) domestic animal sings that, "G-d is good to those that are good, and to those that are upright of heart. (Psalm 125:4) Some translations believe this to be a reference to the pig, while others to the rabbit. This week also includes the *yahrzeit* of the Third Lubavitcher Rebbe, Menachem Mendel (the Tzemach Tzedek), and the birthday of the Seventh Rebbe, who carries the same name of the Third, his ancestor through direct patrilineal descent.[112]

The pig is considered by the sages to be a hypocrite, because it proudly displays the external characteristics of being kosher, split hooves, but internally, its intestines, make it a non-kosher animal. The physical makeup of the rabbit and other animals of its kind (such as the hare and the hyrax) is the exact opposite. These animals do not have split hooves, yet their intestines are that of a kosher animal. Internally, they are "upright of heart," but their actions and external characteristics are clearly not so.

---

[112] It is worth noting that their respective wives also carry the same name, Chayah Mushka.

Aside from the pig and the camel (Week 30), the hyrax and the hare are the only other two animals explicitly mentioned in the Torah as not being kosher. The Midrash in *Vaikra Rabbah* 13:5 explains that the hyrax represents the Persian exile, while the hare represents the Greek one. The pig represents the Roman exile, connected to Esau and his descendants. This is the exile we are currently in. The song these animals sing is a reference to the final redemption, when even the pig will be "upright of heart," and all these animals will be kosher.

The Tzemach Tzedek and the Rebbe represent the main thrust of the message of Passover: redemption. The name "Tzemach Tzedek" is actually one of the names of *Mashiach*, as is also the name "Menachem." As we see from the animals above, redemption has two major aspects: internal traits (intellectual, emotional) and external ones (material, physical). In relation to "internal" redemption, both the Tzemach Tzedek and the Rebbe introduced very important new concepts in Chassidic thought and were finally able to publish and disseminate the works of previous Rebbes. At the same time, both were extremely successful externally, in the realm of action. The Tzemach Tzedek established agricultural settlements that saved many Jews from dire poverty, and also rescued thousands upon thousands of children forced to enlist in the Russian army. Similarly, the Rebbe was able to establish Jewish centers all over world, and helped save thousands of Jews trapped in the "iron curtain" of the Soviet Union.

The number twenty-eight represents twice the value of fourteen, *yad,* a reference to the strong and outstretched arm of G-d that took us out of Egypt. (See Week 14) Here, that concept is doubled, representing two outstretched arms. On Passover, we celebrate that *Hashem* saved us then, while fully believing that He will soon save us again, in a way that is even more miraculous than what took place in Egypt.

Twenty eight is formed by the letters *kaf* and *chet*, forming the word *koach*, which means strength. *Koach* also means potential energy, that which is yet to be revealed. The pig seems to have the possibility and potential to be kosher, but ultimately it is not—at least not yet. As mentioned earlier, the pig represents Esau, the brother of Jacob, who had enormous potential; that potential made Isaac believe that Esau would ultimately be worthy of the rights and blessings of the firstborn. Like the pig, Esau would also pretend to be a *tzadik* before his father, so much so that the *Midrash* relates that Esau would ask Isaac how to tithe salt and straw. Salt and straw do not need to be tithed, and therefore Esau's request made him look like he was ready to go beyond the letter of the law. The Rebbe explains that salt is an example of potential energy. Salt by itself is just salt, but when combined with other food it can enhance its flavor, and even preserve it from spoiling.

This week, the lesson from *Pirkei Avot* comes from Rabbi Elazar the son of Azariah. Interestingly, rabbinical discussion in the Passover *Haggadah* begins with this rabbi's remarks. In *Pirkei Avot*, Rabbi Elazar teaches us that without Torah there is no work (also translated as proper social conduct), and without work (or proper social conduct) there is no Torah. Without wisdom there is no fear of G-d, and without fear of G-d, there is no wisdom. Without knowledge, there is no understanding, and without understanding, there is no knowledge. Without flour (sustenance) there is no Torah, and without Torah there is no flour. Rabbi Elazar also states that anyone whose knowledge exceeds his good deeds is like a tree with many branches and few roots, but one whose good deeds exceed his knowledge is like a tree that has few branches but many roots.

In Rabbi Elazar the son of Azariah's words we also see the duality and relationship between required internal and external kosher characteristics. Knowledge requires action, and vice versa. Rabbi Elazar does make clear, however, that action must take priority. This was also something emphasized by the Rebbe, who stressed that the main thing is action, "*HaMa'aseh Hu HaIkar.*"

The flour mentioned here is perhaps also reference to *matzah* and also to the custom of providing flour to the poor (*Maot Chitim*, literally "wheat" money), so that they can also properly celebrate Passover. Furthermore, in order to prepare for Passover, we must rid ourselves of our own *chametz*, both the external leavened (self-inflated) bread, as well as our "internal" *chametz*, our inflated ego.

This week we complete one more cycle of seven weeks. This week's *sefirah* combination is *malchut shebenetzach*. During the Passover Seder, we experience victory, humility, and redemption, all expressed openly in this physical world. Through the song of the pig and rabbit, we learn to aspire to a life of complete integrity and complete redemption.

WEEK 29: AFTER THE INITIAL INSPIRATION, TO GET TO WORK

The beast of burden is saying, "When you eat the fruit of your labors, happy are you and good is your lot." (Psalms 128:2)

Rabbi Eliezer [the son of] Chisma would say: the laws of *kinin* (bird offerings) and the laws of menstrual periods—these, these are the meat of *Halachah* (Torah law). The calculations of solar seasons and *gematria* are the condiments of wisdom.

Chesed shebeHod (kindness within the context of glory and gratefulness)

As we enter the twenty-ninth week, the week of Passover, in *Perek Shirah*, the large impure (non-kosher) domestic animal sings that those that eat from the work of their own hands are praiseworthy and are blessed with good. (Psalm 128:2) This animal has been translated by Rabbi Slifkin simply as the "beast of burden."[113] On Passover, we feel the influx of *Hashem*'s blessings and redemption. At the same time, from the second day of Passover onwards, the Jewish people begin counting the *omer* and begin working towards self-improvement. Thus, by the time *Shavuot* arrives, we will have merited to receive the Torah, at least in part through the work of our own hands.

---

[113] Slifkin, p. 11

This week's animal appears to be a reference to Yishmael and his descendants. This son of Abraham was known for his great capacity for praying and for trusting in G-d's blessings and salvation.[114] In fact, Yishmael did receive great blessings, although part of the blessings showed that there were aspects of his lifestyle that still needed to be improved. The angel tells Hagar, Yishmael's mother, that "his hand would be on everyone."[115] Later in life, Yishmael repents, returns to G-d, and has a good relationship with Isaac.[116] In messianic times, Isaac and Yishmael will coexist in peace.

Our sages interpret the verse of the beast of burden to be a dual blessing, "praiseworthy"—in this world, and "good for you"—in the world to come. There is a custom in Chassidic circles, instituted by the Ba'al Shem Tov, to make a meal on the eighth day of Passover called *Moshiach Seudah*, in honor of *Mashiach* and the world to come.

The number twenty-nine is connected to the cycle of the moon (29.5 days to be exact), on which the Jewish month is based. Muslims, who consider themselves descendants of Yishmael, follow a purely lunar calendar. Twenty-nine is also the number of days in a woman's menstrual cycle. (*See Pirkei Avot* below)

The lesson in *Pirkei Avot* for this week is found in the teaching of Rabbi Elazar the son of Chismah. He explains that the laws relating to bird sacrifices and menstrual

---

[114] Genesis 21:10, 48:22, *Targum*
[115] Ibid.
[116] Genesis 25:9, *Rashi*

cycles are essential, while astronomy and numerological calculations (*gematria*) are the spice of wisdom. (III:18) On Passover, we do not eat *chametz*, leavened bread. Spiritually, this represents the notion that on Passover we set aside everything that makes us feel "inflated" and takes away from our essence, our core identity as reflected in our relationship with G-d and with each other.

Furthermore, on Passover, G-d connects to us on a deeply personal level, primarily as our Redeemer, instead of as the Creator of the Universe. (See Appendix I) This appears to be taught in this week's *Pirkei Avot*: G-d does not want us to lose ourselves in grandiose and esoteric topics, such as astronomy and *gematria*. He would rather see us involved also in the details of properly serving Him in how we conduct ourselves on a daily basis.

The two sets of laws mentioned in *Pirkei Avot* are particularly important to daily conduct. They are fundamental to the relationship between G-d and the Jewish People, and between husband and wife (which is also a metaphor for our relationship with G-d, as expressed in Solomon's Song of Songs). Bird sacrifices are related to our ability to come closer to G-d. The word for sacrifice in Hebrew is *korban*, from the word *karov*, which means close (nowadays, because we cannot bring sacrifices, prayer and study serve as substitutes). Similarly, the laws related to the female menstrual cycle are essential in order to make wives permissible to their husbands.[117]

---

[117] The Torah sets forth laws regarding times during a woman's menses in which husband and wife do not touch, and instead interact primarily on a spiritual plane. These

This week, the combination of *sefirot* results in *chesed shebehod*. This week, we work on ourselves in order to properly receive and appreciate G-d's blessings that we receive during Passover. (This week would also represent the "eighth week" of *Shavuot* and "*Shivah Yemei Miluim*" of the cycle of *Netzach*. This is appropriate, as *Pessach* is the festival of redemption)

We learn from the beast of burden that in our path towards righteousness, *Hashem* helps us and journeys with us along the way. Nevertheless, we should not want or expect our spiritual development to be "spoon-fed." Even if ultimately everything comes from G-d, we must work hard to achieve spiritual elevation ourselves.

---

essential laws help preserve a higher level intimacy and attraction, since the physical side of the relationship is renewed each month.

WEEK 30: TO KNOW THAT THE WORLD NEEDS MORE LOVE AND RESPECT

The camel is saying, "G-d shall roar from upon high and cause His voice to sound forth from His holy place, His shout echoes profoundly over His dwelling place. (Jeremiah 25:30)

Ben Zoma would say: Who is wise? One who learns from every man. As is stated (Psalms 119:99): "From all my teachers I have grown wise, for Your testimonials are my meditation."

Who is strong? One who overpowers his inclinations. As is stated (Proverbs 16:32), "Better one who is slow to anger than one with might, one who rules his spirit than the captor of a city."

Who is rich? One who is satisfied with his lot. As is stated (Psalms 128:2): "If you eat of toil of your hands, fortunate are you, and good is to you"; "fortunate are you" in this world, "and good is to you" in the World to Come.

Who is honorable? One who honors his fellows. As is stated (I Samuel 2:30): "For to those who honor me, I accord honor; those who scorn me shall be demeaned."

Gevurah shebeHod (discipline and judgment within the context of glory and gratefulness)

In the thirtieth week, the last week of *Nissan* and the week of *Yom HaShoah*, Holocaust Remembrance Day, it is the turn of the camel in *Perek Shirah* to proclaim that, "the Lord roars from upon high; His voice is heard from His holy place; His roar echoes loudly over His dwelling place. (Jeremiah 25:30) The verse of the camel describes how *Hashem* strongly laments the destruction of the Temple. Due to its destruction, the Jewish people have had to survive for a very long period of time without its basic source of spiritual sustenance, just like the camel survives for long periods without water. *Nissan* is the month of redemption, both the redemption from Egypt as well as the future redemption. However, even on Passover itself we have an egg on the Seder plate as a sign of mourning to remember the destruction of the Temple and that the final redemption has not yet taken place. This week also marks the *yahrzeit* of *Yehoshua Bin Nun*, on the 26th day of this month.

As is explained in the same *Midrash* cited in week twenty-eight, the camel represents the Babylonian exile, when the First Temple was destroyed. Moreover, like the beast of burden, the camel also appears to be a reference to Yishmael.[118] As we complete the month of *Nissan*, we relive all the exiles and the redemptions that the Jewish people experienced throughout history, while hoping to soon experience the final redemption that will take us out of the current exile.

---

[118] Talmud, *Brachot* 56b (where the description of a dream with a camel follows description of a dream with Yishmael); *Midrash Asseret Melachim*, *Midrash Pitron Torah*

Thirty is an intensification of the qualities of balance represented by the number three. The number thirty also has the numerical value of the name *Yehudah*. As mentioned previously, *Nissan* is represented by the Tribe of Judah. *Pirkei Avot* teaches that thirty is also the age of *koach*, strength and potential. (*See* Week 28) At thirty, one is at the height of his or her physical and intellectual capacity. It was at the age of thirty that the *kohanim* would begin serving in the Temple. Such strength and potential are associated with Judah and his descendant, King David, who unlike Esau, acknowledged and repented from their mistakes, and were able to fully tap into their capacity for good.

In *Pirkei Avot* this week, Ben Zoma teaches: "Who is wise? One who learns from every person; Who is strong? He who conquers his evil inclination . . . Who is rich? He who is satisfied with his portion." This teaching is closely related to the tragic events that took place during the time of the Counting of the *Omer*. The death of Rabbi Akiva's 24,000 disciples was caused by the difficulty they had in respecting, accepting, and learning from each other's interpretations and applications of their master's teachings.

The destruction of the Temple and the exile in which we find ourselves to this day (which includes also the events of the Holocaust) is due to *sinat chinam*, baseless hatred. We will be redeemed from this final exile through *ahavat chinam*, baseless love for each individual.

Ben Zoma's lesson is closely related *Yehoshua Bin Nun*. He was Moses' closest disciple and successor, and yet also could relate to everyone: "on the verse describing Joshua as 'a man in whom there is spirit,' *Sifrei* explains "that he was able to meet the spirit of every man."[119]

Ben Zoma's second question and answer, "Who is strong? He who conquers his evil inclination," also appears related to the *yahrzeit* of Joshua. The Rebbe once said regarding his *yahrzeit* that, "On this day, assistance from heaven is granted to become a conqueror, like *Yehoshua Bin Nun*, 'the most prominent of the conquerors.'"[120] During this week, we prepare for the conquests related to the following month (*Iyar*), and learn to become strong conquerors like Joshua.

In this week, the combination of *sefirot* results in *gevurah shebehod*. The Counting of the *Omer*, especially after the end if Passover and the month of *Nissan*, marks a period of service to G-d that can be potentially difficult, requiring both strength and discipline in order to conquer our evil inclination.

An additional lesson that we can extract from the words of the camel is that we must always remember our mission in the world: to create a dwelling place for G-d in this world, starting by creating a sacred space for Him within ourselves.

---

119   Tanya, Compiler's forward
120   From the Rebbe's Letters, *available at:* http://www.sichosinenglish.org/books/letters-rebbe-2/07.htm

Week 31: To Be Proud of Our Humble Connection with G-d

> **The horse is saying,** "Behold, as the eyes of the servants to the hand of their master, as the eyes of the maidservant to the hand of her mistress, so are our eyes to G-d our Lord until He will favor us." (Psalms 123:2)
>
> **Ben Azzai would say:** Run to pursue a minor mitzvah, and flee from a transgression. For a mitzvah brings another mitzvah, and a transgression brings another transgression. For the reward of a mitzvah is a mitzvah, and the reward of transgression is transgression.
>
> He would also say: Do not scorn any man, and do not discount any thing. For there is no man who has not his hour, and no thing that has not its place.
>
> *Tiferet shebeHod* (beauty and balance within the context of glory and gratefulness)

The thirty-first week of the year is the week of *Rosh Chodesh Iyar*. It also includes the day of remembrance of the fallen soldiers of Israel and victims of terror, as well as the fifth of Iyar, which marks the miraculous victory of Israel in its War of Independence. In this week, the horse in *Perek Shirah* sings about how like servants, our eyes are fixed on the Lord our G-d, until He has compassion over us. (Psalm 123:2) From beginning to end, during this month we are involved in the *mitzvah* of counting the omer. As mentioned previously, this month is also known as a month of healing, and is formed by the Hebrew letters *alef, yud,* and *reish,* which serve as an acronym for the verse "*Ani Hashem Rofecha,*" "I am G-d your Healer," in which each word begins with one of these three letters.

The month of *Iyar* is represented by the Tribe of Issachar. The Torah describes Issachar as, "a strong-boned donkey" (similar to the horse), which takes upon itself the yoke of Torah study. Issachar and Zevulun had a partnership in which Zevulun was involved in commerce and supported Issachar in its total dedication to Torah. This dedication to Torah is symbolized by Rabbi Shimon Bar Yochai, whose *yahrzeit* is in this month, and of whom it is said, "*Toratoh Emunatoh,*" that his Torah study *was* his profession.

There is a clear connection between this week, the fifth of *Iyar* and the War of Independence. The horse, especially in ancient times, symbolizes military might. An example of this is found in the Song of the Sea, which describes how when Pharaoh came with his chariots to attack the Jewish people, G-d threw "horse and rider into the sea." (This is actually the song of the ox, later this month, in Week 34)[121]

Despite being a symbol of power, the horse sings of constantly looking to *Hashem* for mercy. During the War of Independence, the Jewish people truly fought mightily and heroically, like horses, and yet their victory was only possible due to its miraculous nature, a product of *Hashem*'s great mercy.

---

[121] *See also* the last chapters of the Book of Job.

A horse loyally follows the directions of its rider. Like the horse, the Jewish people waited a long time and suffered greatly until *Hashem* showed us favor and made it possible for us to live in our Holy Land again.

The horse's song also reflects the feelings of one who is ill or injured and prays to G-d for healing. This is connected to the day of remembrance, as well as to the fifth of *Iyar* itself. One must not forget that the miracle of Israel's War of Independence occurred shortly after the Holocaust, when the Jewish people as a whole was like a sick person in urgent need.

The number thirty-one contains the same numerals as thirteen, which, as explained above, represent G-d's thirteen attributes of mercy. Furthermore, the number thirty-one is also connected to the conquest of the Land of Israel. At the end of the conquest of the Land in the times of Joshua, the *Tanach* lists all the kings that were defeated at that time, thirty-one in all.[122]

The number thirty-one is formed by the Hebrew letters *lamed* and *alef*, which in turn spell the word *E-l*, one of the names of G-d. The name *E-l* is an expression of infinite power, but also of infinite mercy.[123] The word *el* appears many times in the horse's song.

In the *Pirkei Avot* for this week, Ben Azzai teaches that one must be fast to perform a *mitzvah* and to flee from

---

122   Book of Joshua, Ch. 12

123   Vedibarta Bam, *available at:* http://www.sichosinenglish.
       org/books/vedibarta-bam/144.htm

a transgression; for a *mitzvah* draws another *mitzvah*, while a transgression draws another. The reward for a *mitzvah* is a *mitzvah*, while the reward for a transgression is a transgression. Similarly, just as one *mitzvah* leads to another, physical and spiritual healing also comes slowly, one step at a time, like the Counting of the *Omer*.

Furthermore, Ben Azzai teaches not to scorn anyone and not to reject any thing, because there is no one who does not have his moment and there is no thing that does not have its place. This teaching's connection with *Yom Ha'Atzma'ut* is similar to that of the song of the horse: the Jewish people and the Land of Israel finally had their moment!

This week's *sefirot* combination results in *tiferet shebehod*. With patience and balance, step by step, we serve G-d and climb the ladder to spiritual fulfillment, getting closer and closer to *Hashem*. In order to perform this task, we inspire ourselves in the horse's example, understanding that despite our strength we are nothing more (and nothing less) than servants of G-d. We should be proud of our humble connection with G-d and know that the journey towards Him may at times be slow, but that the arrival at its destination is certain.

WEEK 32: TO RECOGNIZE DEEP IN OUR HEARTS HOW SMALL WE ARE, HOW GREAT G-D IS

> **The mule is saying,** "All the kings of earth shall acknowledge You, G-d, for they have heard the sayings of Your mouth." (Psalms 138:4)
>
> **Rabbi Levitas of Yavneh would say:** Be very, very humble, for the hope of mortal man is worms.
>
> *Netzach shebeHod* (victory and endurance within the context of glory and gratefulness)

In week thirty-two, the second week of the month of *Iyar*, in *Perek Shirah*, the mule declares that all the kings of the earth will acknowledge the words of *Hashem*. (Psalm 138:4) This week is still connected to the miracles of Israel's independence. (*See* Appendix 2) It was during this time that the right of the Jewish People to the Land of Israel was clearly recognized by the leaders of the world and the United Nations. A verse of the Psalms states, "Do not be like the horse or like the mule, without understanding."[124] It took the nations of the world a long time to understand the right of the Jewish People to the Land of Israel, but at least during this brief moment in history, the world recognized this right.

There is an interesting contrast between this week's animal, the mule, closely related to the gentile prophet

---

[124] Psalm 32:9

Bilaam (whose mule spoke to him), and the animal of the following week, the donkey, which is connected to Abraham, as well as to Moses and *Mashiach*. There is a very strong parallel between some of the main events in Abraham's life and those in the life of Bilaam. *Pirkei Avot* teaches that Abraham and Bilaam are polar opposites. While Abraham was humble and the greatest source of blessing, Bilaam was arrogant and the greatest source of curse. *Rashi* also makes a comparison between when Abraham gets up early in the morning to saddle his donkey, in order to perform the sacrifice of Isaac, and later, when Bilaam gets up early in the morning to saddle his mule, in order to meet Balak, perform sacrifices, and attempt to curse the Jewish people. Abraham and his descendants were promised the Land of Israel, while Balak and Bilaam did everything in their power to take away the Land from the Jewish people. In the end, Bilaam was forced not only to recognize the glory of Israel, but to praise it and bless it tremendously. Both Bilaam and Balak were later defeated by the conquering Israelites.

As explained earlier, the month of *Iyar* is connected to the tribe of Issachar, who in the Torah is called a "strong-boned donkey." The mule is the product of the breeding a donkey with a horse. The mule also represents an aspect of physical deficiency and the need for healing connected to this month: the mule is physically incapable of procreating.

The number thirty-two is a reference to the thirty-two paths of wisdom (*chochmah*) mentioned in Kabbalah. There are three opinions regarding Bilaam's connection to Laban. Bilaam was either Laban himself, Laban's son, or his grandson. Laban's name, *Lamed Beit Nun*, represents the 32 paths of wisdom (*lamed beit*) and the fifty gates of understanding (*nun*). (*See* Week 23) Had Laban nullified himself before Yaakov, the *tzadik* of the generation, the evil in him would have been nullified, and all these levels would be revealed in him.[125]

Thirty-two is formed by the letters *lamed* and *beit*, which together form the word *lev*, which means heart. Sometimes we can understand something with our intellect, but it is still hard to make our heart also understand. Despite the stubbornness of our heart, ultimately we will all fully acknowledge *Hashem*, as the song of the mule so clearly states. Perhaps a way to speed this process along is to focus on the famous expression of our sages in the Talmud, which was often quoted by the Lubavitcher Rebbe: "Words that come from the heart [certainly] enter the heart."

The word *lev* does not only describe the physical heart, but is also used metaphorically. When we use the expression "heart of something," we are referring to the essence of it. The Torah, which is the essence of *Hashem*, ends with the letter *lamed* and begins with the letter *beit*, forming the word *lev*. Similarly, the Land of Israel is the heart of our people, and Jerusalem is "the heart of our heart."[126]

In the episode of the spies, the only one other than Joshua that strongly stood for our ability to conquer the Land of

---

[125]   HaRav Eliezer Berland, *available at:* http://www.shuvubonim.org/vayeshev.html

[126]   Elie Wiesel, open letter to the President, *available at:* http://www.israelnationalnews.com/News/News.aspx/137057

Israel was called Kalev. The very name of Ka*lev* shows his strong connection to our heart, the Land of Israel.

In the *Pirkei Avot* for this week, Rabbi Levitas of Yavneh appears to focus on the potentially negative part of our hearts, the *yetzer harah*. He teaches us to be extremely humble in spirit, for man's hope is [to be fed to the] worms. (IV: 4) Rabbi Levitas reminds us that if we focus on our physical side (the word he uses for man is *enosh*, the lowest of all names for a human being), our only hope is to be food for worms. However, if instead we focus on our soul, the divine aspects within us, then we will know how to better to use our hearts, and will be able to truly love our neighbor as ourselves. This is also the lesson found in Chapter 32, the *lev* (heart) of the Tanya. (*See also* next week)

Rabbi Levitas' words closely resemble the phrase for which perhaps Abraham is most famous: "I am like dust and ashes." Dust, because man comes from dust and returns to it; and ashes because Abraham and Sarah were sterile and could not have children, just like the mule. However, G-d is capable of anything . . . giving children to Abraham and Sarah, making a mule speak, making the kings of the nations recognize his words, and even making Bilaam bless Israel!

This week's *sefirah* combination results in *netzach shebehod*. It takes great persistence to get through to our hearts and achieve higher levels in the service of *Hashem*. The mule itself exemplifies this aspect of persistence and stubbornness. This week is also the *yahrzeit* of Eli the High Priest. Besides being the Kohen Gadol, he was also leader of the generation. He therefore perfectly represented the combination of these two sefirot, *netzach* and *hod* (interestingly, Samuel the Prophet, Eli's disciple, also represents both *netzach* and *hod*, as the Book of Psalms equates him to both Moses and Aaron). Eli's death, in which he fell backwards and broke his neck after hearing about the fate of the *Mishkan*, has a close association with the donkey, next week's animal. The Torah commands that if an owner does not intend to redeem a firstborn donkey with a sacrifice, he must break the donkey's neck. In Kabbalah, the neck is the part of the body most associated with the Holy Temple and the *Mishkan*. Another animal that has a commandment related to the breaking of a neck is a female calf. This is in the case of an unexplained murder. The mule is closely associated with donkey and is female like the calf.

A lesson to be drawn from the song of the mule is that even kings, those that are rich and powerful, have to understand that they are ultimately completely subjugated to *Hashem*. *Hashem* controls everything and everyone, without distinction. If anything, a king's behavior is even more subjugated than others, as is stated in Proverbs: "A king's heart is like rivulets of water in the Lord's hand; wherever He wishes, He turns it."[127]

---

127   Ch. 21:1

WEEK 33: TO RECOGNIZE THE SPIRITUAL TREASURES HIDDEN WITHIN EACH ONE OF US

> **The donkey is saying,** "Yours, G-d, is the greatness, and the might, and the splendor, and the victory, and the glory, for everything in the Heavens and earth [is Yours]; Yours, G-d, is the kingship, and the exaltation over all." (Chronicles I, 29:11)
>
> **Rabbi Yochanan the son of Berokah would say:** Whoever desecrates the Divine Name covertly, is punished in public. Regarding the desecration of the Name, the malicious and the merely negligent are one and the same.
>
> *Hod shebeHod* (glory and gratefulness within the context of glory and gratefulness)

We now arrive at week thirty-three of the Jewish calendar, the week of *Pesach Sheini* and *Lag Ba'Omer*. As explained earlier, *Lag Ba'Omer* is a day of great celebration, because it was then that the students of Rabbi Akiva stopped perishing. On *Lag Ba'Omer*, we also celebrate the *yahrzeit* of the great *tzadik*, *Yesod ha'Olam* (foundation of the world), Rabbi Shimon Bar Yochai. It is customary to light a bonfire in his honor, representing the great light that he brought to the world through his teachings of Kabbalah.

This week, in *Perek Shirah*, the donkey proclaims: "Yours, O Lord, are the greatness, and the might, and the glory, and the victory, and the majesty, for all that is in the heavens and on the earth [is Yours]; Yours is the kingdom and [You are He] Who is exalted over everything as the Leader." (1 Chronicles 29:11) King David recited this verse when he was at the height of his glory, reiterating that everything is from *Hashem*: glory and kingship, the Heavens and the earth.

This is the week of *hod* (acknowledgement) in the Counting of the *Omer*, and therefore it is quite appropriate that the song of the donkey so gracefully acknowledge that everything comes from G-d. The song of the donkey contains all seven emotional *sefirot*: *gedulah* is a reference to *chesed*; then comes *gevurah*, *tiferet*, *netzach*, and *hod*; *hakol* is a reference to *yesod*; and *mamlachah*, a reference to *malchut*.

Pesach Sheni is the *yahrzeit* of Rabbi Meir, one of the greatest Torah scholars of all time. This week also includes the *yahrzeit* of the great Rabbi Yehuda Bar Ilai. All three men, Rabbi Shimon, Rabbi Meir and Rabbi Yehudah, were disciples of Rabbi Akiva. The Zohar (the main text of Kabbalah, written by Rabbi Shimon Bar Yochai) tells us that during this week the Gates of Heaven are wide open.

Rabbi Chanan Morrison, based on the teachings of the Rabbi Avraham Yitzchak Kook, helps us better understand the importance of the donkey. Donkeys are considered extremely impure. They have both signs of not being kosher—they do not chew their cud and do not have uncloven hooves. The Zohar teaches that the donkey is so impure that is considered an *avi avot hatumah*, a great source of impurity (as mentioned previously in Week 12, Kabbalah and Chassidism have the power to elevate even the most impure animals).

Despite being extremely impure, the donkey has a *mitzvah* that no other non-kosher animal has: "Every firstborn donkey must be redeemed with a lamb."[128] The Talmud, in the tractate of *Bechorot* (5B), explains that the reason why the donkey has this special *mitzvah* is because it was instrumental in helping the Jews transport the treasures they had received in Egypt. However, there is also a deeper meaning here: the donkey represents the treasure to be found within each one of us.

The word for donkey in Hebrew, *chamor*, comes from the word *chomer*, matter, physicality. In the messianic age, physicality will be merged with spirituality.[129] According

---

128 Exodus 13:13

129 One of the Baal Shem Tov's teachings: "When you see *chamor*, a donkey" (Sh'mot 23:5)-when you carefully examine your *chomer* ("materiality"), your body, you will see . . . . "your enemy"—meaning, that your *chomer* hates your Divine soul that longs for G-dliness and the spiritual, and furthermore, you will see that it is . . . . "lying under its burden" placed upon it—(the body) by G-d, namely, that it should become refined through Torah and mitzvot; but the body is lazy to fulfill them. It may then occur to you that . . . . "you will refrain from helping it"-to enable it to fulfill its mission, and instead you will follow the path of mortification of the flesh to break down the body's crass materiality. However, not in this approach will the light of Torah reside. Rather . . . . "you must aid it"-purify the body, refine it, but do not break it by mortification.

There was indeed a method of subordinating the body through afflicting it with ascetic practices, but the Baal Shem Tov rejected this path. He saw the body not as an

to the prophecy of Zachariah, Moshiach will arrive on a donkey!

According to Rav Kook, the Messiah's donkey represents the period of *Ikveta d'Mashicha*, the time when the "steps" (*ikvot*) of messianic redemption begins to be heard. *Ikvot* also comes from the word *ekev*, which means heel or sole of the foot, the roughest and most insensitive part of the body. The era of *Ikveta d'Mashicha* is one of great spiritual decline, full of *chutzpah*, deceit, immorality and corruption. However, the Zohar writes that despite their external faults, the generation of this time will be good on the inside. This inner good will be reflected in the special souls of the pre-messianic era. Despite the gloom weighing on their behaviors and beliefs, they will be blessed with an innate holiness, as expressed in their great love for the Jewish people and for the Land of Israel.

The *Ikveta d'Mashicha* is to be a difficult period, and not all Torah scholars were eager to go through the experience. However, Rav Yosef showed great spiritual strength in saying: "May the Messiah come, and may I have the merit

---

obstacle to the spirit, something intrinsically evil and unG-dly, but as a potential vehicle for the spiritual, a means for the soul to attain heights otherwise inaccessible. The "enemy" is to be transformed into an ally, an instrument. In great measure the Mitzvot employ gross physical matter to fulfill G-d's will, e.g. leather for *tefillin* thongs, wool for *tzitzit*, etc.

http://www.chabad.org/dailystudy/HayomYom.asp?tDate=2/21/2012

to sit in the shadow of his donkey's dung."[130] Rav Yosef was accustomed to look at the inner essence of things. He recognized the holiness hidden in this special generation, symbolized by the Messiah's donkey.

Perhaps the above is also the deeper meaning for the statement: "If the earlier generations were like angels, we are like humans. But if they were like humans, we are like donkeys."[131]

Rabbi Moshe Wolfsohn explains that recognizing inner holiness was also the power of Rabbi Shimon Bar Yochai himself. It is no coincidence that hundreds of thousands of Jews of all backgrounds and levels of religiosity flock to his grave on *Lag Ba'Omer*. Rabbi Shimon was not only able to understand the deep meaning of the mystical side of the Torah, but he also knew of the enormous value hidden inside every Jew. Just as each of the 600,000 letters of the Torah are special, and essential to a scroll's validity, so too is each of the 600,000 souls of the Jewish people holy and an essential part of the Jewish people as a whole. If only one letter in a Torah is missing, even if it seems to be the most insignificant one, that Torah is considered invalid and cannot be read in the synagogue. The same goes for the Jewish people and every soul that is part of it. Without even a single soul, even the lowest of the low, we are not complete.

At this level of thinking, one can understand that no one is above anyone else. This understanding is exactly what was

---

130 *Sanhedrin* 98b
131 Talmud, *Shabbat* 112b

lacking to the 24,000 (12,000 pairs) of students of Rabbi Akiva who died during the Counting of the *Omer*. In a pair, one of the partners might think he is superior to the other in understanding, and come to think that he need not show respect to the other. On the contrary, his partner should show *him* respect. Rabbi Shimon Bar Yochai came into the world to fix this way of thinking.

When one looks at others while focusing on their inner essence, their soul, whose source is the same for all—G-d—there is no room for difference. On this level, we all truly equal, all siblings, children of one Father. This is the primary lesson taught by the Alter Rebbe in chapter 32 (*lev*, heart) of the Tanya; the Alter Rebbe explains that that this is the secret of how to love your neighbor as yourself. It was Rabbi Akiva who stated that to love your neighbor as yourself is the great general principle of the Torah.

It is also worth noting that while Rabbi Akiva's deep love for his fellow might have always existed in potential, in the beginning of his life however, he expressed the exact opposite emotion. The Talmud quotes Rabbi Akiva, who states that before became learned, he hated the sages so much that he wanted to bite them like a donkey. His students ask why he did not want to bite them like a dog. Unlike a dog, Rabbi Akiva says, a donkey's bite can break the bone. The Hebrew word for bone is *etzem*, which also means essence. Perhaps herein lies the secret to Rabbi Akiva's teachings, which is connected to Rabbi Shimon Bar Yochai's path mentioned above: Rabbi Akiva was able to transform tremendous hatred into the greatest love by focusing on people's essence.[132]

The number thirty-three is the number associated with *Lag Ba'Omer* and Rabbi Shimon Bar Yochai. The combination of the Hebrew letters *lamed* and *gimmel* spell *Lag*, but also form the word *gal*, which means to reveal. One of the Rebbe's best known *ma'amarim* on *Lag Ba'Omer* is entitled "*Gal Einai v'Abita Niflaot mi Toratecha*," a verse in Psalm 119.

The lesson of this week's *Pirkei Avot* is the teaching of Rabbi Yochanan the son of Berokah, who states: one who profanes the Name of Heaven in secret, will be punished in public. Either inadvertently or intentionally, it is all the same when it comes to the desecration of the Name (IV:4). This teaching appears related to Rabbi Shimon Bar Yochai, who sanctified the name of *Hashem* in secret and then publicly revealed his greatness. Rabbi Shimon Bar Yochai spent twelve years in a cave studying Torah with his son. After this long period, he left the cave and spread his teachings to the rest of the Jewish world. (Rabbi Shimon's additional teaching in Week 43 found along with that of Rabbi Yehudah Bar Ilai, in which Rabbi Shimon praises the importance of the "crown of a good name:" Having a "good name" means being a good example and thereby publicly sanctifying the name of G-d.)

This week's *sefirot* combination is *hod shebehod*, just as *Lag Ba'Omer* itself. It is a week of tremendous revelation of divine glory. In the yearly count, *Lag Ba'Omer* is *hod shebehod shebehod*.

---

[132] Talmud, *Pesachim* 49b

A lesson in self-improvement that we can learn from the song of the donkey is that everything comes from G-d, both what we perceive as bad and also what we perceive as good. Thus, as explained in the previous week, we must not only direct ourselves to Him when we are in trouble, but also thank Him in moments of glory.

WEEK 34: TO WORK IN A FOCUSED MANNER AND WITHOUT EGO

> **The ox is saying,** "Then Moses and the Children of Israel sang this song to G-d, and they said, I shall sing to G-d, for He has triumphed; He has thrown the horse and its rider into the sea." (Exodus 15:1)
>
> **Rabbi Yishmael the son of Rabbi Yossi would say:** One who learns Torah in order to teach, is given the opportunity to learn and teach. One who learns in order to do, is given the opportunity to learn, teach, observe and do.
>
> *Yesod shebeHod* (foundation and firmness within the context of glory and gratefulness)

In week thirty-four, as we approach the end of the month of *Iyar*, in *Perek Shirah*, the ox declares that Moses and the Children of Israel will sing this song to the Lord, and say: I will sing to the Lord, Who exalts Himself gloriously, horse and rider He has thrown into the sea (Exodus 15:1). It is worth noting that the month of *Iyar* is linked to the zodiac sign of Taurus.

The ox is the last of the farm animals to sing in *Perek Shirah*, and its verse is from the introduction to the Song of the Sea. The sheep and the goat, the first farm animals in *Perek Shirah*, also sing a verse from the Song of the Sea, on *Rosh Chodesh Nissan*. The cow, the second farm animal mentioned after the sheep and the goat, sings a verse that refers to the Jewish people as Jacob, which reflects a more fragile and humble side of our people. The ox, on the other hand, uses the name Israel, which represents a stronger side. The ox sings as we near the end of the Counting of the *Omer*. During this journey of liberation, from the beginning of *Nissan* until now, we make a full transformation Jacob to Israel.

There is a similar journey within the month of *Iyar* itself. The first animal this month to sing was the horse, and now at the end of the month, the ox sings about how G-d threw the horse and its rider into the sea. Both the horse and the ox represent strength. However, while the horse's power reflects somewhat unrestrained military might,[133] the ox is characterized by its humble acceptance of its yoke. The ox's meat is kosher, while the horse's meat is not. The ox's firm acceptance of the yoke of Heaven is what is most precious in the eyes of *Hashem*.

The ox is also connected to the conquest of the Land of Israel, a general theme of this month of *Iyar*: "Moab became terrified of the people, for they were numerous, and Moab became disgusted because of the children of Israel. Moab said to the elders of Midian, 'Now this assembly will eat up everything around us, as the ox eats up the greens of the field.'"[134] As further discussed below, Joseph is called an ox, and Joshua was a direct descendant of Joseph.

The number thirty-four is twice the value of 17, the *gematria* of *tov*, good. It is the combination of the first

---

133 Psalms 20:8, 32:9, and 147:10
134 Bamidbar 22:3-4

17 years that Jacob lived with Joseph in Israel, and an additional 17 that he lived with Josef in Egypt, the best years of his life. 34 is also the *gematria* of *Vayechi*, the Torah portion that describes Jacob/Israel's passing. The number 34 therefore also represents this journey from *Yaakov* to *Yisrael*, as well as the healing that Jacob experienced after being reunited with Joseph and living the best years of his life in Egypt. Thirty-four is also the *gematria* of *ga'al*, "redeemed" in Hebrew.

The *Pirkei Avot* lesson this week is from Rabbi Yishmael, who teaches that one who studies the Torah in order to teach, is given the opportunity to study and teach; those that study in order to practice, are given the opportunity to study, teach, observe and practice. (IV:5) The words of Rabbi Yishmael are related to the passing of Rabbi Akiva's students during the days of the *omer*. Rabbi Akiva's students died because they did not respect one another sufficiently. Those that thought they knew more than others believed that they should be the one receiving respect instead of giving. The most important aspect of learning is to do so in order to teach and practice, not in order to feed one's own ego. The latter leads a person to think that his or her Torah knowledge makes them superior to others, defeating the whole purpose of learning in the first place.

On this week, the combination of *sefirot* results in *yesod shebehod*. Joseph, who represents the *sefirah* of *yesod*, is called an "ox" by Jacob in his blessing to Joseph on his deathbed, which can be found in the weekly Torah portion of *Vayechi*.

A lesson we may learn from the ox is that we must work on ourselves in a very concentrated and humble way, remembering G-d's omnipotence. We must always keep in mind that *Hashem* saved us from our enemies in the past, and does so again in every generation. Therefore, we have nothing to fear.

WEEK 35: TO THANK G-D IN UNISON

The wild animals say: "Blessed is the One Who is good and bestows good." (Talmud, *Brachot* 48b)

Rabbi Tzadok would say: Do not separate yourself from the community. Do not act as a counselor-at-law (when serving as a judge). Do not make the Torah a crown to magnify yourself with, or a spade with which to dig. So would Hillel say: one who make personal use of the crown of Torah shall perish. Hence, one who benefits himself from the words of Torah, removes his life from the world.

Malchut shebeHod (kingship within the context of glory and gratefulness)

On the thirty-fifth week, in *Perek Shirah*, the wild animals sing "Blessed is G-d, who is good and bestows good." (Talmud, *Brachot* 48b) This week includes both *Yom Yerushalayim* as well as *Rosh Chodesh Sivan*. The song of the wild animals is the blessing that is made to G-d according to Jewish law when something substantially good happens. This blessing is called *HaTov veHaMetiv*, and is used when the level of perceived good is even greater than that of the more familiar blessing of *She'ychianu*, because it is made when the good affects not only the individual but also others.

The fact that all wild animals, despite their strong and ferocious instincts, are able to sing in unison a song that shows concerns for others, is directly linked to a special quality we find in *Rosh Chodesh Sivan*. *Sivan* is marked by the giving of the Torah, which was made possible by the unity within the Jewish people at that time. The Torah relates that it was on *Rosh Chodesh Sivan* that all people camped at Mount Sinai "as one man with one heart."[135]

The month of *Sivan* is connected to the tribe of Zevulun, which was known for its merchant skills and its ability to survive in the outside "wild jungle" that is the capitalist world. Zevulun's commercial prowess also benefited his brother, the tribe of Issachar, which had a more insular lifestyle, dedicating itself completely to the study of Torah. Zevulun fully supported Issachar financially.

The Torah also explicitly compares the Jewish women in Egypt to wild animals, and *Rashi* further explains that the entire Jewish people are referred to as wild animals, since Benjamin is called a wolf, Judah a lion, Dan a lion cub, etc.[136] Despite our strong personalities and diverse ways of thinking (two Jews, three ideas, as the traditional saying goes), we nevertheless all manage to get along. This closeness and unity, both among Jews and between us and G-d, is also symbolized by the zodiac sign of this month: Gemini (twins).

On *Yom Yerushalayim*, we celebrate Israel's miraculous victory during the Six-Day War, when Jerusalem was reunited. There is also a deep connection here with the song of the wild animals, as this day marks the time when something substantially good happened to all of the Jewish

---

[135] *Rashi*

[136] Exodus 1:19; *Rashi*

people. As mentioned earlier. Nowadays, we only say the blessing of *HaTov veHaMetiv* when something very good happens. When something substantially bad happens (or at least perceived to be bad in our eyes) we make the blessing *Baruch Dayan Emet* (Blessed be the True Judge). The Talmud teaches that in Messianic times we will say the blessing of *HaTov veHaMetiv* (Blessed is G-d, Who is good and bestows good) in all circumstances, because we will understand that even what we once perceived to be bad is ultimately for the good. The same holds true for *Yom Yerushalayim*. The term *Yom Yerushalayim* is mentioned in the Psalms as a reference to the destruction of the Temple and of Jerusalem, an event perceived as being very bad, perhaps the worst in our history. After 1967, the term *Yom Yerushalayim* now refers to the day Jerusalem became liberated, a very good and happy day indeed, in the spirit of the blessing *HaTov vehaMetiv*. While it is still difficult to understand the meaning behind the great tragedy of the destruction of Jerusalem and the Temple, at least we now know that the new use of the term *Yom Yerushalayim* could not have come into being were it not for the first.

Finally, it is worth noting that the song of the wild animals has a double *tov*, good (*HaTov veHaMetiv*). As explained in the previous week, the *gematria* of *tov* is 17, and twice that amount is 34. This week appears to further build upon this concept.

The number thirty-five is the *gematria* of the term *yehudi*, which refers to all Jews, even though the root of the word comes only from the tribe of Judah. The name *yehudi* appears related to the ability of all the Tribes of Israel to be able to unite behind a single tribe. The first time *yehudi* appears in *Tanach* is in *Megillat Esther*, as a reference to Mordechai, who himself was from the tribe of Benjamin. The entire Jewish people are referred to in the *Megillah* as "*Am Mordechai*," a "Mordechai Nation."

Thirty-five is formed by the Hebrew letters *lamed* and *heh*, the only two letters in the word *Hallel*, a song of praise sung on *Rosh Chodesh Sivan*, and also sung by many on *Yom Yerushalayim*.

The *Pirkei Avot* lesson for this week comes from Rabbi Tzadok, who states that we must neither separate ourselves from the community, nor act as an advocate (when sitting as a judge); one should neither make the Torah a crown to glorify oneself, nor a spade with which to dig. (IV: 5) The words of Rabbi Tzadok are directly linked the concept of Jewish unity emphasized on *Rosh Chodesh Sivan*.

It is worth noting that Rabbi Tzadok fasted for forty years to prevent the destruction of the Temple in Jerusalem. Rabbi Yochanan ben Zakkai commented regarding Rabbi Tzadok that if there were one more tzadik like him Jerusalem would not have been destroyed. How appropriate therefore is it for Rabbi Tzadok's words to fall on the week of *Yom Yerushalayim*!

This week we also complete one more cycle of seven weeks. The *sefirot* combination results in *malchut shebehod*. *Malchut* represents the concept of taking abstract ideas and applying them in the real world. This week, we bring our service of G-d and our pursuit of peace into complete fruition.

A lesson in self-improvement that can be drawn from the song of the wild animals is that everything that G-d does is for the good. Events that appear to be bad for us will ultimately prove to be for our own good.

WEEK 36: TO HAVE EMUNAH

The gazelle is saying, "And I shall sing of Your strength, I shall rejoice of Your kindness in the morning, for You were a refuge to me, and a hiding place on the day of my oppression." (Psalms 59:17)

Rabbi Yossi would say: Whoever honors the Torah, is himself honored by the people; whoever degrades the Torah, is himself degraded by the people.

Chesed shebeYesod (kindness within the context of foundation and firmness)

Week thirty-six in the Jewish calendar marks the holiday of *Shavuot*. The entire week is also known as "*Shivah Yemei Miluim*," in which *Shavuot* sacrifices could still be brought to the Temple. On this week in *Perek Shirah*, the gazelle praises *Hashem*'s kindness in the morning, a shelter and refuge in times of trouble. (Psalm 59: 17)

The Hebrew word for gazelle is *Tzvi*, which has the same *gematria* as the word *emunah*, complete faith in *Hashem*. The word *tzvi* is composed of three letters, *tzadi, beit, yud*, and is an acronym for the phrase "*tzadik b'emunatoh yichieh*," "a *tzadik* lives through his faith," a verse from the prophet Habakkuk. The Talmud explains that this verse is actually a summary of the entire Torah that was given to Moses on Mount Sinai on *Shavuot*.[137]

---

[137] *Makkot*, 24A

The song of the gazelle expresses its faith in *Hashem*, both in the morning and in times of trouble ("night"). A similar concept is found in the beginning of Psalm 92, which states, "It is good to give thanks to the Lord, and to sing to Your name, O Most High; To declare in the morning Your kindness and Your faith at night."[138] After the troubles we encountered during the Counting of the *Omer*, which is associated with the night, on *Shavuot*, we witness the revelation of *Hashem*, clear as day.[139]

The horns of the gazelle are like a double crown, and we know that the Jewish people also received a double crown on *Shavuot*, as a reward for their faith in G-d. The *Midrash* teaches that while other nations refused to accept the Torah, the Jews did not even first ask what was in it. They simply stated, "*Na'aseh veNishmah*," "We will do and we will listen." The Jewish people willingly accepted to fulfill the commandments of the Torah even before knowing and understanding what they entailed. *Hashem* therefore gave each Jew two crowns, one for "*Na'aseh*" (we will do) and another for "*Nishmah*" (we will hear/understand). Unfortunately, these crowns were later removed after the sin of the golden calf.

The number thirty-six represents the thirty-six secret *tzadikim* that sustain the world. The number thirty-six is also the total number of *Chanukah* candles that are lit during the eight days of the holiday. These two concepts seem connected to the light revealed to us on *Shavuot*, when, due to our efforts during the Counting of the

---

138   Psalm 92: 2,3
139   *Shem M'Shmuel, Lag Ba'omer*

Omer, we are all closer to being on the level of *tzadikim*. These thirty-six *tzadikim* are literally the foundation of the world.

This week's lesson in *Pirkei Avot* comes from Rabbi Yossi, who teaches that one who honors the Torah will be honored by others, while one who dishonors the Torah, will be dishonored by others. (IV: 8) This lesson is strongly related to the giving of the Torah, as well as to the unfortunate events that took place shortly thereafter. When we accepted the Torah, we were shown great honor, but when we dishonored the Torah with the sin of the golden calf, that honor was taken away.

On this week, the combination of *sefirot* is *chesed shebeyesod*, kindness within foundation. On *Shavuot*, the Jewish people had to stand firm (by not getting too close to the mountain and not letting their souls expire completely from the tremendous Divine revelation), in order receive from G-d the great good that is the Torah. (As the week of *Shavuot* and the *Shivah Yemei Miluim*, this week also represents the "eighth week" of the cycle of *Hod*)

A lesson in self-improvement we may learn from the gazelle is that we must have faith in *Hashem* at night (during difficult times), knowing full well that the night will eventually pass and we will be able to thank *Hashem* in the openly revealed light of day.

WEEK 37: TO MAINTAIN OUR HUMILITY AND NOT FORGET THE GREATNESS WE EXPERIENCED

The elephant is saying, "How great are your works, G-d; Your thoughts are tremendously deep." (Psalms 92:6)

His son, Rabbi Yishmael would say: One who refrains from serving as a judge avoids hatred, thievery and false oaths. One who frivolously hands down rulings is a fool, wicked and arrogant.

He would also say: Do not judge on your own, for there is none qualified to judge alone, only the One. And do not say, "You must accept my view," for this is their [the majority's] right, not yours.

Gevurah shebeYesod (discipline and judgment within the context of foundation and firmness)

As we arrive at week thirty-seven, the week after *Shavuot*, the elephant in *Perek Shirah* proclaims, "How great are your works, G-d; Your thoughts are tremendously deep." (Psalms 92:6) The Hebrew word for great used by the elephant is *gadlu*, from the word *gadol*, big, and the elephant itself is the largest of all the land animals. The verse of the elephant is also from Psalm 92, mentioned in the previous week.

On *Shavuot*, we were all deeply impressed with the greatness of *Hashem* and His Torah. After this day of great Divine revelation, we all become higher and greater spiritually. The elephant comes to emphasize to us the greatness of that experience, and that it is important not to let ourselves forget it. Elephants, after all, are renowned for their memory. Physical greatness is also associated with the week after *Shavuot* because that is when we read the Torah portion of *Nasso*, the largest one in all of the Five Books of Moses.[140]

The number thirty-seven has the *gematria* of the root of the word *gadol* (big). Thirty-seven is also the numerical difference between the name of Moses (345) and Korach (308).[141] The "deep thoughts" mentioned by the elephant may actually be a reference to the rebellion of Korach against Moses and Aaron. Korach wanted the leadership position to himself and convinced a susbstantial number of his fellow tribesmen and neighbors to rebel. During his confrontation with Moses and Aaron, Korach and his congregation were miraculously sucked into a deep pit, which *Pirkei Avot* states was thought of and created by G-d in the very first week of Creation. The Rebbe explains that Korach and his group were brought into the pit while still alive in order that they be granted the opportunity to repent and return to G-d, as did Korach's sons. This event happened on *Rosh Chodesh Sivan,* the begnning of this current month, and the Torah portion entitled "Korach,"

---

[140] *Nasso* has 176 paragraphs; the largest Psalm, 119, has 176 verses; the largest Talmudic tractate, *Bava Batra*, has 176 folios.

[141] Dr. Akiva G. Belk, "Elazar, Korach, Shuvah, Pride and Depression," *available at* http://www.jewishpath.org/ gematriaelazarkorachetc.html; http://www.safed-kabbalah. com/Arizal/Korach5761.htm

which recounts this story, is often read communally by the Jewish people during the last days of *Sivan*.

It is appropriate that Moses is also associated with the elephant, the largest of the land animals, because as noted in Week 4 and Week 23, Moses is also related to the eagle, the largest bird, and the Leviathan, the largest sea animal. Moses was, and will always be, the greatest of all prophets.

The lesson from *Pirkei Avot* for this week is from Rabbi Yishmael, who teaches that one who refrains from making legal ruling removes himself from enmity, theft and unnecessary oaths: but one that frivolously issues legal decisions is a fool, wicked and arrogant. (IV:7) Rabbi Yishmael also states that the only one who can judge on his own is G-d, and that an individual should not say, "Accept my view," for that is the right of the majority, not the individual's.

The teaching of Rabbi Yishmael is connected with the emphasis on unity and harmony linked to the month of *Sivan*, as well as to the humility necessary in order to properly fulfill the commandments of the Torah. We must do all that is in our power not to aggrandize ourselves at the Torah's expense, always remembering that only G-d is truly great.

Rabbi Yishmael's words are also a clear reference to the interactions between Moses and Korach. Korach was an enormously rich person, with a deep-seated enlarged view of himself. During his rebellion against Moses and Aaron, Korach's claim was based on a concept similar to the latter part of Rabbi Yishmael's words; that Moses and Aaron should follow the majority and not retain key positions for themselves. Moses explained that Korach's rebellion was ultimately against G-d Himself, who had chosen him and Aaron as the leaders of the Jewish people. As noted above, G-d does, and will, judge alone.

The combination of *sefirot* for this week results in *gevurah shebeyesod*. On this week, we must work with strength and discipline to maintain our solid foundation in our study of Torah and our fulfillment of *mitzvot*. The elephant represents this strong foundation. After all, who can move an elephant against its will?[142]

Finally, a lesson in self-improvement that we learn from the elephant is that even the largest animal realizes the infinite greatness and depth of *Hashem*.

---

[142] There also appears to be a connection between the elephant, *Pil* in Hebrew, and *Eliyahu HaNavi*. Both have the same *gematria*, 120; *See also* Talmud, *Brachot* 56B, where the description of a dream with an elephant follows the description of a dream with Pinchas, who is Elijah.

WEEK 38: TO BE STRONG AND COURAGEOUS IN ORDER TO DEFEND THE COMMON GOOD

> **The lion is saying,** "G-d shall go out as a mighty man, He shall arouse zeal, He shall cry, even roar, He shall prevail over His enemies." (Isaiah 42:13)
>
> **Rabbi Yonatan would say:** Whoever fulfills the Torah in poverty, will ultimately fulfill it in wealth; and whoever neglects the Torah in wealth, will ultimately neglect it in poverty.
>
> *Tiferet shebeYesod* (beauty and balance within the context of foundation and firmness)

And in the thirty-eighth week, at the end of the month of *Sivan*, comes the opportunity for the lion to declare in *Perek Shirah* that the Lord will come as a mighty warrior, and shall take revenge as a man of war. Triumphant, *Hashem* will roar and overcome His enemies. (Isaiah 42:13) This verse is connected with the month of *Sivan*, where all the people trembled at the voice of G-d presenting the Ten Commandments on Mount Sinai.

The lion's verse is also related to the tribe of Zevulun, who would go out to sea in search for trade. Our sages make a very interesting link between the idea of "going out to war" and "going out in order make a living," which as we know can be a kind of war. (*See* Week 20 regarding how the age of twenty is both the age to pursue a livelihood and to enlist for war).

The week of the lion is not only the last week of the month of *Sivan*, but is also the last week of spring. The next two months of the summer, *Tammuz* and *Av*, are quite intense, and are closely linked to the destruction of the Temple. Moreover, these months are also connected to the reconstruction of the Temple and the coming of *Mashiach*.

In this verse for week thirty-eight, *Hashem* Himself is referred to as a lion. It should be noted that the Temple is also often referred to as a lion (*Ariel*, which literally means "lion of G-d"). The lion is also the symbol of the tribe of Judah, from whom comes King David and *Mashiach*. There is a *Midrash* that further explores this lion theme: "The lion (Nebuchadnezzar, the Babylonian emperor) appeared during the lion (the month of *Av*) and destroyed *Ariel* (the Temple), so that the Lion (G-d) will appear during the lion (the month of *Av*) and rebuild *Ariel*."[143] Similarly, the lion's verse compares *Hashem* to a man at war, a roaring lion, who will defeat His enemies and redeem His people.

In the last week of *Sivan* we prepare spiritually, physically, and psychologically, for the intense period that is to come. The next months of *Tammuz* and *Av* can be ones of much pain, but also contain the spirit of redemption—it all depends on how we approach them. In order to succeed, we must connect with the spark of the lion of Judah, of David, and of *Mashiach*, which each of us carries inside. If we prepare well, taking into account everything we learned from Passover to *Lag Ba'Omer*, to *Shavuot*, we will

---

[143]   *Yalkut Shimoni*, Section 259

be strong as lions and, with G-d constantly on our side, we will have absolutely nothing to fear.

Thirty-eight is the *gematria* of the Hebrew word *Bul*, the Biblical name given to the month of *Cheshvan*. The Torah states that "in the month *Bul*, which is the eighth month, the house [of G-d] was finished throughout all the parts thereof, and according to all the fashion of it, and he [Solomon] built it in seven years."[144] On Week 23, in *Adar*, we had discussed the significance of the *gematria* of the word *Ziv*, the biblical name given to the month of *Iyar*. We mentioned how on *Iyar* the construction of Solomon's Temple began. Having fully experienced the redemption of *Adar* and *Nissan*, having worked on ourselves in *Iyar*, and experienced the revelation of the Torah in *Sivan*, our internal Temple should now feel completed. It is our duty to properly protect that Temple, and to bring about the reconstruction of *the* Temple in Jerusalem.

Thirty-eight is composed of the letters *chet* and *lamed*, which form the word *chol*, meaning sand, and reminds us of the blessing Abraham received that his offspring would be as numerous as the sand in the sea. *Chol* also means profane, connected to the destruction of our Temple, our exile, and the profanation of G-d's name that took place in the months that follow *Sivan*. *Chet* and *lamed* also form the word *lach*, which means wet or fresh. We leave *Sivan* and spring as a whole, fresh and full of water (a metaphor for Torah), and are now ready to face the summer heat.

---

144   Kings I, 6:38

The *Pirkei Avot* lesson for this week is from the teaching of Rabbi Yonatan (IV: 9): one who fulfills the Torah in poverty will fulfill it in wealth, but whoever neglects the Torah in wealth will come to neglect it in poverty. During this week we experience a similar concept. If we violate the Torah so close after we experienced its revelation in *Sivan*, it will be even harder to fulfill it in the potential poverty experienced during the months of *Tammuz* and *Av*. However, if we fulfill the Torah during those months of "poverty," we will transform them into months of tremendous spiritual, intellectual, and emotional enrichment, with the coming of *Moshiach*. In addition, our commitment to the Torah in the "spiritual poverty" of exile will be compensated with the ability to fulfill the Torah in the "spiritual wealth" of the Messianic era.

This week's *Pirkei Avot* is also closely linked to the tribe of Zevulun, given its wealth and ability to provide for the tribe of Issachar, who was devoted entirely to the study of Torah. Zevulun itself, although more professionally active than Issachar, also remained faithful to the Torah and devoted to its study.

The *sefirot* combination for this week results in *tiferet shebeyesod:* beauty and balance within foundation. During this week, we feel the beauty and balance of the Torah within us, and reinforce our Jewish foundations in order to face the difficult coming months.

A lesson in self-improvement that we draw from the lion is that we must be brave and willing to "go out" beyond our insulated worlds and comfort zones in order to help those around us.

WEEK 39: TO SEE THE WORLD IN A POSITIVE LIGHT IN ORDER TO ELEVATE IT

The bear is saying, "Let the wilderness and its cities lift up their voice, the village that Kedar inhabits; let the inhabitants of the rock sing, let them shout from the peaks of the mountains. Let them give glory to G-d and tell of His praise in the islands." (Isaiah 42:11-12)

Rabbi Meir would say: Engage minimally in business, and occupy yourself with Torah. Be humble before every man. If you neglect the Torah, there will be many more causes for neglect before you; if you toil much in Torah, there is much reward to give to you.

Netzach shebeYesod (victory and endurance within the context of foundation and firmness)

This week marks *Rosh Chodesh Tammuz* as well as *Gimmel Tammuz*, the date of the Lubavitcher Rebbe's passing and also the beginning of the liberation of the Sixth Lubavitcher Rebbe. *Tammuz* is represented by the tribe of Reuven, Jacob's firstborn.

The name Reuven comes from the word *reiyiah*, sight, and the month of *Tammuz* is related to the *tikkun*, the fixing, of our sense of sight. Reuven is also connected to *teshuvah* in general. The *Midrash* states about Reuven that he was the first to repent out of love, without first being chastised by *Hashem*.[145]

This month is also connected to the *tikkun* for the sin of the spies. Moses sent spies that journeyed throughout the Land of Israel during the entire month of *Tammuz* and, except for Joshua and Caleb, viewed the Land of Israel in a negative light.

Tammuz also is connected to several tragedies that occurred on the 17th day of this month. Among these tragedies is the destruction of the first tablets containing the Ten Commandments, as well as the breach of the walls of Jerusalem. However, *Tammuz* is also connected with the final redemption. In the future, when we ultimately repent and are redeemed, the 17th of *Tammuz* will no longer be a day of fasting and mourning, but rather a day of celebration.

The transformation and *teshuvah* of *Tammuz* parallels that of Reuven. Jacob took away Reuven's firstborn rights after a severe mistake he made involving one of his father's concubines. Reuven spent his entire life doing *teshuvah* for his sin. The Torah recognizes his repentance, still referring to Reuven as the firstborn son of Jacob long after the unfortunate event took place.

On the thirty-ninth week, the bear sings in *Perek Shirah*, asking all to raise their voice: the desert and the cities, the villages, and the wilderness of *Kedar*; everyone is to chant

---

[145] *Medrash Hamevuar*; http://torahweb.org/torah/2004/parsha/rwil_vayeshev.html

melodies and cry with joy: those that dwell among the rocks and on the top of the mountains as well as those in the islands. (Isaiah 42: 11-12)

The song of the bear alludes to the concept of looking at the world with good eyes, in a positive light. The bear sees that the deserts, the cities, the villages, the mountains and the islands, all have the great potential of praising G-d. This is how we should all see the world—everyone has this potential. We just need to open our eyes to see it.

One of the main accomplishments of the Seventh Rebbe, which actually began with the Sixth Rebbe, was to always see in each follower and in every Jew their enormous potential for good. That is how the Rebbe was able to form so many leaders and inspire so many people. The Rebbe was able to spread the light of Judaism and of Chassidism to the far corners of the world: cities as well as spiritual deserts, mountains and isolated islands.

Eliyahu HaNavi, who will announce the coming of *Mashiach*, is also associated with the bear. As explained in Week 12, the *Tanach* states that before Elijah ascended to heaven, Elisha asked him for a double portion of Elijah's own strength.[146] Soon afterwards, when Elisha purified the waters of a particular city, he was insulted by a few young men who would make their money transporting clean water from another location. Elisha's miracle had rendered their services useless. The youngsters starting instigating Elisha, calling him bald, which was meant to strike a contrast between him and Elijah, who had a head full of

---

[146]   2 Kings 2:9

hair. After the insult, Elisha cursed these youngsters, and two bears (an apparent reference to the double portion he had received from Elijah) came out of the wilderness and killed them.[147]

It is interesting to note that just as the bear's song makes explicit references to Arabia (*Kedar*), the Talmud contains various stories of how Elijah would disguise himself as an Arab when he would appear before *tzadikim*, either as a way to test or help them.

Thirty-nine is the number of the types of work prohibited on *Shabbat*. These prohibitions parallel the thirty-nine types of work performed in building the *Mishkan*, a miniature Temple where the Divine Presence resided. The *Mishkan* represents a microcosm of the world, and just as G-d rested on the seventh day during the creation of the world, the Jewish people rested on the same day when they were building the *Mishkan*.

The bear's song refers to distant and uninhabited places that have the potential of praising *Hashem*, thus making a home for *Hashem* in this world. The *Midrash Tanchumah* teaches that G-d's primary objective in creating the world was in order to make a home for Him in the lowly realms. That home is the *Mishkan*.

The letters that form the number thirty-nine, *lamed* and *tet*, spell out the word *tel*, which means mountain. The laws pertaining to *Shabbat* are known as "mountains on a

---

147   2 Kings 2:23-25

wire," because a vast number of prohibitions are deduced from just a few explicit verses in the Torah.

The *Pirkei Avot* of this week is expressed in the teachings of Rabbi Meir. The Talmud states that whoever saw Rabbi Meir studying, witnessed how he would take mountains and grind them into each other. He was also known for miracles, many of which involved *Eliyahu HaNavi*.

Rabbi Meir also represents the idea of *teshuvah*, return to G-d, and seeing the potential in people and in faraway places. He was himself a descendant of Roman converts. When a certain group of people mistreated and insulted him, he followed the advice of his wife Beruria, and instead of praying for their destruction, prayed that they do *teshuvah*, which they ultimately did.[148]

Rabbi Meir states that we should minimize our commercial activities in order to focus ourselves in Torah study. He advises us to be humble towards everyone. Furthermore, he teaches that if we waste Torah study time, we will find many obstacles against us, but if we toil greatly in its study, we will find abundant reward. Rabbi Meir's words are also connected to *Tammuz*, Reuven and the process of *teshuvah*, demanding that we humbly transform any lack of dedication to the Torah (which caused such obstacles and tragedies for our people), into full dedication and toil, leading ultimately to enormous reward.

This week, the combination of *sefirot* results in *netzach shebeyesod*. We must be persistent and determined to

---

148 Talmud *Brachot* 10a

maintain our foundation in Torah and *mitzvot*. We know that Joseph, who represents the *sefirah* of *yesod*, had to endure Potiphar's wife's constant attempts to seduce him, and yet Joseph was ultimately successful in resisting her. *Rashi* compares Potiphar's wife to a bear. There will always be bears trying to distract us from our central purpose. We must stand firm and strong like a bear, and not lose sight of our goal.

This week, we learn from the bear that wherever we find ourselves, we must attempt to speak of the Torah and elevate the place we are in as much as possible.

Week 40: To Fight for the Truth

> **The wolf is saying,** "For every matter of iniquity, for the ox, the donkey, the lamb, the garment, for every lost item which he says, 'This is it,' the matter of both of them shall come before the judge; he who the judge finds guilty shall pay double to the other." (Exodus 22:8)
>
> **Rabbi Eliezer the son of Yaakov would say:** He who fulfills one mitzvah, acquires for himself one angel-advocate; he who commits one transgression, acquires against himself one angel-accuser. Repentance and good deeds are as a shield against retribution.
>
> *Hod shebeYesod* (glory and gratefulness within the context of foundation and firmness)

In week forty, still in the beginning of the month of *Tammuz*, the wolf sings in *Perek Shirah* that for every matter of crime—upon the ox, donkey, sheep, clothes or any lost time for which there is a dispute—the cause of both parties shall come before the judge, and the one whom the judge finds guilty shall pay double to the other." (Exodus 22:8)

The song of the wolf has a very strong connection with Reuven. As explained in the previous week, Reuven had lost the double portion that was his right as a firstborn because of a mistake he made by moving the bed of one of Jacob's concubines. On another occasion, when Jacob refused to let his children take Benjamin to Egypt, Reuven said that if he personally did not bring Benjamin back, he would be willing to give up his two sons. This would amount to a double loss.

The wolf is the symbol of the tribe of Benjamin, who in turn, is also closely connected to the song of the wolf. After arriving in Egypt, Benjamin is accused of theft by the viceroy (Joseph). Of all of Jacob's children, Benjamin is also the one most connected with the Land of Israel, because he was the only one who was born there.

The wolf's song also contains a very interesting parallel with the conquest of the Land of Israel. *Rashi*'s first comment in the Torah explains why the Torah begins with the creation of the world and not with the first *mitzvah*, of blessing the new moon, which was given at the time of our departure from Egypt. *Rashi* explains that when the nations of the world accuse us of being "thieves," claiming that we are "stealing" the land, we will respond saying that the world and all that is in it belongs to G-d, and that it is He who determines what land to give to whom.

Forty is related to the intensification of firmness and stability of the number four. The number forty is also deeply related to the concept of internalizing G-d's eternal truth: the Torah. Forty is the number of days and nights that Moses spent in Mount Sinai to receive the Torah. (It should be noted that most of these days occurred during the month of *Tammuz*, including this very week). Forty is also the number of years the Jews wandered in the desert, the number of days and nights of the Flood, and the number of *seah* (unit of measurement) of water required for a kosher mikvah. In *Pirkei Avot*, the age of forty is associated with understanding—it takes forty years to truly understand his master's teaching. Moreover, pregnancy is forty weeks long (the time in which an angel teaches the fetus the entire Torah).

In *Perek Shirah*, the wolf sings of the verdict for a person who steals. It is known that the Flood only began after people began to steal. The Flood also served as a *mikvah* to purify the world.

This week, the lesson in *Pirkei Avot* is found in the words of Rabbi Eliezer the son of Yaakov, who teaches that he who does a mitzvah acquires for himself a defender, and he who commits one transgression, acquires for himself an accuser. Repentance and good deeds are like a shield against retribution (punishment). (IV: 11) *Pirkei Avot's* lesson is closely linked to thievery, a transgression that brings about an accuser. At the same time, it is also linked to the month of *Tammuz* and the *tikkun* of sight. It is important to look favorably upon the other and upon their possessions. Often jealousy is what leads to theft. We should also look favorably upon people, in order to serve as good defenders. We also see here the theme of *teshuvah*, closely connected with the tribe of Reuven.

The combination of *sefirot* results in *hod shebeyesod*, glory and gratefulness within the context of foundation and firmness. This week we should be thankful, dedicated, and grounded in our moral ways. The lesson in self-improvement we learn from the wolf is that we cannot give in to corruption. We must stand strong in order that justice and truth prevail over falsehood.

WEEK 41: NOT TO BECOME CORRUPT

> **The fox is saying,** "Woe to him that builds his house without justice and his chambers without lawfulness; that uses his friend's service without wages, and does not give him for his hire." (Jeremiah 22:13)
>
> **Rabbi Yochanan HaSandlar would say:** Every gathering that is for the sake of Heaven, will endure; that is not for the sake of Heaven, will not endure.
>
> **Yesod shebeYesod** (foundation and firmness within the context of foundation and firmness)

In the forty-first week, the fox in *Perek Shirah* warns against those who build without righteousness and justice. (Jeremiah 22:13) This week, beginning with the fast of the 17th of *Tammuz*, we begin the three weeks of mourning connected to the destruction of the Temple, the House of G-d. This destruction occurred due to the injustice and lawlessness of the Jews of that time.

This week also marks the Chassidic holiday of the 12th and 13th of *Tammuz*. This holiday, known as *Yud Beit-Yud Gimmel Tammuz*, celebrates the Sixth Lubavitcher Rebbe, Rabbi Yosef Yitzchak Schneersohn's birthday as well as the date in which he was freed from prison in Communist Russia. Among Chabad Chassidim, this day is called "*Chag HaGeulah*," the Festival of Redemption.[149]

---

[149] When each day of the year is given a combination of *sefirot*, the 12th of *Tammuz* falls on *gevurah shebeyesod shebeyesod*.

The fox is considered a symbol of the Temple's destruction, as depicted in the Talmud in the tractate of *Makkot*. The Talmud tells the story of how a group of rabbis were gathered soon after the destruction of the Temple and saw a fox enter the area of the Temple Mount where the holiest part of the Temple had stood. While all the other rabbis cry when they see the fox, Rabbi Akiva is able to see this event with optimism and in a positive light (characteristic related to the month of *Tammuz*), to such an extent that he starts to laugh. Rabbi Akiva then explains to them how the Torah makes the prophecy of Jerusalem's destruction dependent on the prophecy of its redemption. Now that the first prophecy was fulfilled, the second will be fulfilled as well. As he explains to the other rabbis the reasoning behind his laughter, Rabbi Akiva is able to truly comfort them. (*See* Conclusion)

At the time of *Yud Beit-Yud Gimmel Tammuz*, the Sixth Lubavitcher Rebbe challenged the entire Soviet empire at the time and won.[150] Despite his open defiance, refusal

---

The Rabbi Yosef Yitzchak was the sixth Rebbe, which parallels the sixth *sefirah*, *yesod*. Moreover, Yosef represents the *sefirah* of *yesod* while Yitzchak the *sefirah* of *gevurah*. It is worth noting that this book was completed on this date.

[150] Perhaps the most famous excerpt of his imprisonment was when the Communist interrogators tried to force the Rebbe to divulge certain information. When the Rebbe refused, they waved a gun at him and said:

"Do you see this little toy? This little toy has made a lot of people talk; it will make you talk as well."

The Rebbe answered very firmly, "That toy can only frighten people who have one world and many gods. A

to obey orders, and insistence of not giving up even an "inch" of his religiosity, the Previous Rebbe was eventually released from prison, and his death sentence was commuted. Years later, the Soviet Union itself, filled with injustice and G-dlessness, collapsed, along with the Berlin Wall. The Seventh Rebbe, Menachem Mendel Schneerson, predicted the fall of the Soviet Empire many years prior, when few thought that such a collapse was even possible.

The number forty-one spells the Hebrew word *em*, which means mother. This appears to be quite appropriate for the beginning of the three weeks of mourning, the second half of which takes place during the month of *Av*, which in Hebrew means father. In this historically difficult period for the Jewish people, it is important to remember that the difficulties presented to us by G-d are ultimately for our own good, just like a father and mother sometimes need to be strict with their child.

In Judaism, the mother is the *akeret habayit*, the anchor of the house—she is responsible for the home's values and general atmosphere. Similarly, the upkeep and moral atmosphere of the Temple, G-d's home, was primarily the responsibility of the *kohanim* (priests). Much of the extremely holy service of the priests paralleled house chores: the work involved in the daily sacrifices, the lighting of the Menorah, and tending to the upkeep of

---

person who has one G-d and two worlds is not afraid of your little toy." The Chassidic Approach to Joy, *available at:* http://www.sichosinenglish.org/books/the-chassidic-approach-to-joy/05.htm

the Temple were very similar to cooking, cleaning, and lighting candles for Shabat.

During the time of the Second Temple, the priestly class had become enormously corrupt. Even the position of the High Priest was open for sale to the highest bidder. The Temple itself could not stand due in great part to this lack of morality.

Rabbi Yochanan HaSandlar teaches in the *Pirkei Avot* for this week that an assembly that convenes for the sake of Heaven will be long lasting, but one that convenes not for the sake of Heaven will not. The teaching of Rabbi Yochanan is very similar to the above. He emphasizes the importance of not becoming corrupt or divided due to selfish motives. The firmness of the community comes from rock solid commitment to our principles and a desire to fulfill the will of G-d. The best example of this is the Sixth Rebbe of Lubavitch himself, whose efforts ensured Judaism's survival despite intense Communist oppression. On the other hand, when we do not follow the word of *Hashem*, the entire community suffers and our structures do not endure, as was the case during the destruction of the Temple.

The *sefirot* combination for this week is *yesod shebeyesod*: absolute firmness in our Jewish values. A lesson in self-improvement we learn from the fox is that we must not allow ourselves to be dragged down by dishonesty and thoughts of immediate gain. By walking in the path of Torah, we will certainly be more solid and secure.

Week 42: To Be Loyal and Pursue Justice

> **The hound is saying,** "Let the righteous rejoice in G-d; praise is befitting to the straight." (Psalms 33:1)
>
> **Rabbi Eliezer the son of Shamua would say:** The dignity of your student should be as precious to you as your own; the dignity of your colleague, as your awe of your master; and your awe of your master as your awe of Heaven.
>
> *Malchut shebeYesod* (kingship within the context of foundation and firmness)

In the forty-second week, now in the midst of the three weeks of mourning, the hound in *Perek Shirah* sings to the righteous to rejoice in the Lord, and that for the upright (*yesharim*) it is becoming to praise Him. (Psalm 33:1)

The hound represents uprightness, and often hunts after last week's animal, the fox, who represents corruption and injustice. The hound is also the quintessential example of loyalty. During this period, despite our outward signs of mourning, we also come to the realization that after so many centuries in exile and despite so many tragedies, like the hound, the Jewish people still managed to maintain its loyalty and faith in G-d. Furthermore, G-d also maintained His faith in us. Such loyalty and uprightness, both on the part of the Jewish people and on the part of G-d, is certainly worthy of recognition and praise.

The Talmud explains how the verse of the hound is also deeply connected to the Temple. The term "befitting" (*na'avah*), should be read as *naveh*, habitation, a reference of how the enemies of the Jewish people had no power over the Temple constructions performed by King David and Moses.[151] Similarly, it is important for us to remember that the world has no power over the "holy habitation" inside each one of us. Upon being released from prison, the Previous Rebbe was sent into exile by the Soviet regime. At the Leningrad train station, Rabbi Yosef Yitzchak Schneersohn parted with the following words, quoting his father: "This all the nations of the world must know: only our bodies were sent into exile and subjugated to alien rule; our souls were not given over into captivity and foreign rule . . . In any matter affecting the Jewish religion, the Torah, and its *mitzvot* and customs, we are not subject to the dictates of any power."[152]

Forty-two is the number of journeys of the Jewish people in the desert. During these journeys, G-d tested His people several times, yet we maintained our loyalty and proved ourselves worthy of His love. The Jewish people also tested G-d several times in the desert, yet G-d also did not give up hope in them.

Forty-two contains the letters *mem* and *beit*, which in Hebrew spells the word *bam*, which means "in them." The Ba'al Shem Tov teaches that the words "*vedibarta bam*," contained in the prayer of the *Shemah*, is a reference to the

---

151 Talmud, *Sotah* 9a.
152 "Daily Quote," *available at* http://www.chabad.org/dailystudy/hayomyom.asp?tDate=6/28/2007

forty-two personal journeys each individual undergoes in his or her life, which parallel the forty-two journeys of the Jewish people in the desert.

In *Pirkei Avot*, Rabbi Eliezer the son of Shamua teaches us that the honor of your student should be as precious to you as your own, while the honor of your colleague should be like that given to your teacher; the reverence for your teacher should be like the fear of Heaven. Here again there is a close connection with *Tammuz* and the ability to look deeper and see the great value and potential of each person, be it a student, a colleague, or a teacher. Interestingly, the hound itself is a perfect example of this teaching. Its devotion to its master is like that due to G-d!

Completing the cycle of *yesod*, this week's *sefirot* combination results is *malchut shebeyesod*, kingship within the context of foundation and firmness. This week, we maintain a solid foundation in our Judaism and use it to influence the world around us.

A lesson in self-improvement that we can extract from the hound is that just as it sings of being upright, and pursues the fox, we also must pursue justice at all costs, as stated in the verse in Deuteronomy: "*Tzedek Tzedek Tirdof*," "Justice, Justice you shall pursue."[153] We must always strive for justice.

---

[153] Deuteronomy 16:20

WEEK 43: TO PURSUE LOVE AND PEACE

The cat is saying, "If you rise up like a vulture, and place your nest among the stars, from there I shall bring you down, says G-d." (Obadiah 1:4) (. . .) And when the cat catches [the mouse], the cat says, "I have pursued my enemies and overtaken them, and I did not return until they were destroyed. (Psalms 18:38)

Rabbi Yehudah [Bar Ilai] would say: Be careful with your studies, for an error of learning is tantamount to a willful transgression.

Rabbi Shimon [Bar Yochai] would say: There are three crowns—the crown of Torah, the crown of priesthood and the crown of sovereignty—but the crown of good name surmounts them all.

Chesed shebeMalchut (kindness within the context of kingship)

Week forty-three is the week of *Rosh Chodesh Av*, when in *Perek Shirah* it is the turn of the cat to praise *Hashem*. At first, the cat sings that although the enemy may rise as high as the eagle and make its nest among the stars, G-d will bring it down. (Obadiah 1:4) After catching the mouse, the cat declares that it pursued its enemies and seized them, and did not return until they were destroyed. (Psalm 18:38) During this week we begin counting the Nine Days leading up to *Tisha b'Av*, a period of mourning over the destruction of the Temple that is even more intense (and requires greater hardships) than the rest of the Three Weeks.

The cat is like a miniature lion. On this month, we all have the potential to be like lions. *Mashiach* will be born in the month of *Av*, and will reign on earth like a lion. *Rosh Chodesh Av* is the *yahrzeit* of Aaron, one of the few *yahrzeit* dates mentioned explicitly in the Torah. Aaron was known for his incessant pursuit of peace.

The month of *Av* corresponds to the zodiac sign of Leo. The *Midrash Yalkut Shimoni*, quoted in Week 38, shows the clear relationship of the month of *Av* with the lion. This month is represented by the tribe of Shimon, who was known for its attribute of severe judgment. This month is also related to the *tikkun*, repair, of the sense of hearing. The name *Shimon* comes from the Hebrew word *Shmiah*, hearing, and this month is also connected to the *tikkun* of the sin that took place when the Children of Israel listened to the report of the spies.

It was in *Av* that the spies returned from the Land of Israel and described it to the people. Instead of focusing on Kalev and Joshua's positive account, the people focused on the negative account of the other ten spies and wept bitterly. Our sages teach us that because the Jewish People cried for no reason, *Hashem* would now give them a reason to cry for generations to come. The night the Jewish people cried was *Tisha B'Av*, the day in which both the First and Second Temples were destroyed.[154]

The relationship between the cat and the mouse in *Perek Shirah* can be interpreted (at least) in two different ways. First, throughout history, the Jews played the role of the

---

[154] Talmud, *Ta'anit* 29a

mouse, serving as prey for our enemies inside the nations in which we were exiled. For approximately the past two thousand years, we have been in the exile of Esau/Edom (Rome). However, in messianic times, these roles will be reversed. We will be the ones to pursue our enemies, specifically, the nation of Amalek, a descendant of Esau, who represents the height of immorality and G-dlessness.

The song of the cat comes from the prophet Obadiah, a convert from the nation of Edom, and whose entire prophecy is directed against it. Edom represents Rome and its descendants, and it was Rome which caused the destruction of the Second Temple. The prophet predicts that one day Edom will be punished for its actions.

The number forty-three is formed by the Hebrew letters *gimmel* and *mem*. These letters appear to reference the war of *Gog uMagog*, the two root letters of these words. According to Jewish tradition, *Gog uMagog* will be the final war before the coming of *Mashiach*. This war is believed to involve the descendants of Esau and Yishmael.

Mem and *gimmel* also form the Hebrew word *gam*, which means "also." This word appears prominently in the Psalm most connected to Aaron, whose *yahrzeit* is this week: "*Hineh Mah Tov uMah Naim Shevet Achim Gam Yachad . . .*" Behold how good and how pleasant it is for brothers *also* to dwell together! / As the good oil on the head runs down upon the beard, the beard of Aaron . . ."[155] Rav Ovadia Yosef asks why the word *gam* (also) is included in this verse, as it seems to be completely superfluous. He

---

[155]   Psalm 133

explains that when brothers sit together usually family problems come to the surface. Nevertheless, this *also* is for the good; we should also sit together despite such problems, and do our best to solve them.

There is also a similar connection here with the song of the cat, Aaron's *yahrzeit*, and the *tikkun* of the month of *Av*. Like the cat, Aaron also pursued enemies, but only did so in order to achieve peace between them and to bring them closer to the Torah. As Hillel states in *Pirkei Avot*, "Be of the disciples of Aaron, loving peace and *pursuing* peace, loving your fellow creatures and bringing them closer to Torah." This is how we transform the negative forces of this month into positive ones. As previously mentioned, the Temple was destroyed due to *Sinat Chinam*, baseless hatred, and will be rebuilt through *Ahavat Chinam*, baseless love.

This week in *Pirkei Avot*, Rabbi Yehudah Bar Ilai warns us to be cautious in our study because an inadvertent error (due to insufficient study) is considered a voluntary transgression. It is well known that the cause of the destruction of the First Temple was due to the lack of importance given to Torah study.

Moreover, Rabbi Yehudah is a perfect example of the possibility of peace between Jacob and Esau, the Jewish people and the Romans. Once Rabbi Yehudah encountered a Roman stranger, who had just experienced a shipwreck and was its only survivor. Despite not knowing who this stranger was, Rabbi Yehudah immediately gave the man of his own clothes. It was later discovered that this man was a powerful Roman legislator, and that due to Rabbi Yehudah's kindness he annulled all the harsh decrees that were about to be imposed on the Jewish people at that time.[156]

This week also includes an additional statement by Rabbi Shimon Bar Yochai, who teaches that there are three crowns: the crown of Torah, the crown of priesthood and the crown of the kingship, but that the crown of a good name surpasses them all. (IV: 13) The crowns mentioned by Rabbi Shimon are also all closely related to the major figures of this week and this month: *Aharon HaKohen* (priesthood) and *Mashiach* (kingship), as well Rabbi Shimon himself (Torah).

It is fascinating that additional words of Rabbi Shimon Bar Yochai are included along with Rabbi Yehudah's statements. Unlike Rabbi Yehudah, Rabbi Shimon initially did not get along well with the Romans. When Rabbi Yehudah once praised the Romans for building bridges, etc., Rabbi Shimon stated that he should not praise the Romans, because all that they do is for their own benefit. When the Roman emperor heard of this, Rabbi Yehudah was honored with a high position, while Rabbi Shimon was forced to flee and famously spent the next 12 years inside a cave with his son, Rabbi Elazar.

There is a tradition that Rabbi Shimon is a descendant of the Tribe of Shimon, the tribe of this month.[157] Rabbi Shimon's own life reflects a transition and *tikkun* of Shimon's strict justice. While in the cave, along with his son, he was concerned with pure spirituality. After leaving

---

[156] Marcus, p. 138

[157] Ryzman

the cave, he could not understand how people were spending so much time with material concerns, to the extent that everything that he and his son saw would be consumed by fire. He was therefore sent back to the cave, and stayed there for another year. When he came out of the cave the second time, he understood the value of being involved with the material world, which is related to his problems with the Roman way of doing things.

Rabbi Shimon's sayings in *Pirkei Avot* also appear to reflect this transition. Rabbi Shimon's previous sayings strictly focused on the importance of Torah over material things, while these additional sayings include the importance of other qualities other than Torah. It is quite appropriate that his sayings here are juxtaposed with Rabbi Yehuda's.

Rabbi Shimon Bar Yochai's additional words also seem to be literally complementing his saying in Week 16. There he mentions "three," but does not specify to what exactly three is referring. It is assumed that it means "three people." This time, he states, "there are three crowns." (It is interesting that both his sayings start with the word *shloshah*, three, and that the number he is most associated with is thirty-three, as *Lag Ba'Omer* is the 33rd day of the *omer*). This could also be read as "the three [mentioned previously] are the crowns (*shloshah, ketarim hem*). His previous saying can then be understood as follows: if a person has all three crowns "on his table," meaning he has the qualities of Torah, priesthood, and kingship, such a person should be praised by others and seen as a true example of a "Torah lifestyle" (i.e. given the crown of a "Good Name").

There is a well known story in which Rabbi Shimon Bar Yochai gave an interpretation of "*Hineh Mah Tov uMah Naim Shevet Achim Gam Yachad . . .*" and ended a drought. Again, Rashbi now understood the need for material concerns as well.

When each rabbi of *Pirkei Avot* represents a day of the *omer* count, Rabbi Shimon Bar Yochai's words span approximately the entire month of *Iyar*, the month of Rabbi Shimon's *yahrzeit* (as well as Rabbi Yehudah's). His first saying falls on 16th day of the *omer*, the 1st of *Iyar*, and his additional words are on the 43rd day of the *omer*, 28th of *Iyar*, *Yom Yerushalayim*. In terms of weeks, they span from the week after the Tenth of *Teveth*, to the week before *Tisha B'Av*.

This week, the combination of *sefirot* results in *chesed shebemalchut*, kindness within the context of kingship. Like Rabbi Yehudah Bar Ilai, we strive to do good deeds that have a direct impact on this material world. (This week would also represent the "eighth week," the "*Shavuot*" and "*Shivah Yemei Miluim*" of the cycle of *Yesod*)

Similarly, the lesson we can draw from the cat is that just as it chases after the mouse, we should be like Aaron and "pursue" those around us in a positive and friendly manner, to bring them closer to the path of unity, love, peace, and truth, all of which are quintessential "Torah values."

WEEK 44: TO RECOGNIZE OUR MISTAKES AND CHANGE

> **And the mouse says,** "I shall exalt you, G-d, for You have impoverished [uplifted] me, and You have not let my enemies rejoice over me." (Psalms 30.2) (. . .) And the mouse says [after being caught]: You are just for all that comes upon me, for You have acted truthfully, and I have been wicked." (Nehemiah 9:33)
>
> **Rabbi Nehora'i would say:** Exile yourself to a place of Torah; do not say that it will come after you, that your colleagues will help you retain it. Rely not on your own understanding.
>
> ***Gevurah shebeMalchut*** (discipline and judgment within the context of kingship)

The forty-fourth week of the Jewish calendar is marked by *Tisha B'Av*. In *Perek Shirah*, the mouse first thanks the Lord for elevating it, and for rejecting its enemies (Psalm 30:2). However, after it is caught by the cat, the mouse recognizes that G-d has been just and true regarding all that has happened, and that it had acted with iniquity. (Nehemiah 9:33)

The song of the mouse is closely related to Shimon and *Tisha B'Av*. Shimon, both the individual and the tribe, made serious mistakes. For example, Shimon was instrumental in the sale of Joseph, and the Tribe of Shimon, including its prince, openly rebelled against Moses. However, through repentance, Shimon will also be fully redeemed. Furthermore, just as the mouse is caught by the cat due to its own iniquities, so too was our Temple destroyed on *Tisha B'Av* due to our sins. The first step towards redemption is recognizing this fault of ours (it is said that every generation in which the Temple is not rebuilt, it is as if that generation destroyed it).

The letters that comprise the number forty-four, *mem* and *dalet*, spell the word *dam*, blood, as well as *mad*, from the verb *limdod*, "to measure." Historically, *Av* has been a month in which much blood has been spilled. However, once the Jewish people finally learn their lesson, measure their actions and improve, this will be a month of plenty of light and joy.

The same letters also spell the Hebrew word *dom*, to be silent. This word is often used in praise of how our greatest sages dealt with tragedy. Regarding Aaron, when he discovered that his two eldest sons had died, the Torah states "*yehidom Aharon*," Aaron was silent and did not complain. Our Chassidic masters explain that King David's approach to tragedy even surpassed Aaron. Even after experiencing great suffering, he states, "*l'man yezamerchah velo yidom*," I will sing to you and not be silent. There is much to gain from these approaches in learning how to properly observe *Tisha B'Av*.

The word *dom* also has a more positive side as well. When pursuing the enemies of the Jewish people, Joshua calls out to the sun, and commands it to be silent, "*Dom!*" By telling the sun to stop its song to G-d, Joshua causes the sun to literally stand still in its place. This gives the Jewish people enough time to finish pursuing their enemies before the beginning of the Sabbath.

In *Pirkei Avot* this week, the lesson comes from Rabbi Nehora'i, who advises us to exile ourselves to a place of Torah. He also cautions us not to rely on our own understanding, but rather to debate and discuss our ideas with colleagues. *Tisha B'Av* is generally about exile, but specifically about the exile to a place of Torah: Yavneh. It was through establishing Yavneh and bringing our sages there that Rabbi Yochanan Ben Zakkai was able to ensure the continuation of Judaism long after the Roman Empire had ceased existing.

Furthermore, as noted in *Pirkei Avot*, the suffering and destruction endured by the Jewish people during this week is indeed very difficult to understand. Therefore, it is extremely appropriate for Rabbi Nehora'i to teach us not to rely on our limited understanding, but rather to remain connected to the rest of our people.

The *sefirot* combination for this week results in *gevurah shebemalchut*, discipline and judgment within the context of kingship. This week, we work on our strength and determination to achieve goals in this material world, even in the face of many obstacles. Similar to the week of *Yom Kippur*, *gevurah shebechesed*, we also fast, although on this day we do not feel like angels—we feel more like the mouse. On *Yom Kippur*, one of the happiest days of the year, we fast for spiritual reasons. On *Tisha B'Av*, we fast out of a sense of mourning for the destruction of the Temple.

Tisha B'Av is also closely linked to the *sefirah* of *gevurah* since so many tragedies have occurred on this day, including the decree that the Jews would spend 40 years in the wilderness, as well as the destruction of both Temples. However, it is also connected to *sefirah malchut,* because it is exactly in the wake of such tragedy that *Mashiach* is born.

A lesson in self-improvement we can learn from the mouse is that G-d can raise us up at any given time. To leave a state of sadness, it is important to increase our prayers and direct them to G-d alone. Furthermore, it is important to understand that any fall we may experience, individually or as a people, is an opportunity to begin the process of *teshuvah.* Nevertheless, we must also keep in mind that judging oneself is only positive if it leads to better behavior, and not sadness. There is a fine line between temporarily feeling broken hearted over our sins, a regret that is positive, and sadness, which should be avoided at all costs. Broken-heartedness should lead to even greater joy, as will be further explained in the following week.

WEEK 45: TO RAISE OURSELVES UP THROUGH LOVE AND HUMILITY

> **The creeping creatures are saying**: "Let Israel rejoice in He Who made him; let the children of Zion be joyful in their King." (Psalms 149:2) Alternate version: "May the glory of G-d endure forever; may G-d rejoice in His works." (Psalms 104:31)
>
> **Rabbi Yannai would say:** We have no comprehension of the tranquility of the wicked, nor of the suffering of the righteous.
>
> *Tiferet shebeMalchut* (beauty and balance within the context of kingship)

The forty-fifth week is the week of *Tu B'Av*, and in *Perek Shirah* it is the turn of the creeping creatures to proclaim that Israel rejoice in its Creator and King; alternatively, they sing that the glory of G-d shall endure forever, and that He rejoice in His creations. (Psalm 149:2 and 104:31)

Tu B'Av is known to be the most romantic day on the Jewish calendar. It was at this time that the Tribes of Israel were once again allowed to intermarry among themselves. To celebrate this day, young Jewish women would dress in white, form a circle, and present themselves before the single men of the community that were in search of a bride. The Talmud teaches that each woman would speak of different qualities that they thought might make a good impression on a potential groom.[158] This is related to the *tikkun* of the sense of hearing connected to this month, which requires a constant focus on one's good points.

The main thrust of the song of the creeping creatures is joy, and according to the Talmud, *Tu B'Av*, along with *Yom Kippur*, was the happiest day of the year. The song specifically mentions the joy of Zion (Jerusalem), and *Tu B'Av* comes on the heels of *Tisha B'Av*, when Jerusalem was destroyed. It is important to understand that in many ways the joy of *Tu B'Av* can only come about through the sadness that we experienced on *Tisha B'Av*.

The creeping creatures are so numerous that their rate of reproduction serves as an example for the Jewish people. The Hebrew word in the Torah used to describe the extremely high rate in which we multiplied in Egypt is *yishretzu*, from the Hebrew word for creeping creature, *sheretz*.[159]

The number forty-five is the *gematria* of Adam, the first person created by G-d and the first to receive a soul mate, Eve. *Mem* and *heh* also spell the Hebrew word *mah*, meaning "what," and is closely associated with the humility, as in Moses' well known statement, "*Nachnu Mah*," we are what/nothing.

In *Pirkei Avot*, Rabbi Yannai states that we are not given the capacity to understand the serenity of the wicked or the affliction of the righteous. (IV: 15) Rabbi Yannai

---

158   Talmud, *Taanit* 31a

159   Exodus 1:7

speaks of serenity, such as is found during *Tu B'Av*, as well as suffering, such as in *Tisha B'Av*. Just as in last week's *Pirkei Avot* lesson, the thrust of this week's message is that we will never be able to fully understand His ways. All we can do is to have complete faith that everything He does is for the good.

This week, the *sefirot* combination results in *tiferet shebemalchut*, beauty and balance within the context of kingship. On *Tu B'Av*, balance and beauty connected to this physical world reigns supreme, just as in a Jewish wedding. In kabbalistic texts, it is well known that *Tiferet* is represented by Jacob, while *malchut* is represented by his wife, Rachel. *Tiferet* also means compassion, and this week is closely linked to mercy and consolation, as reflected in the *haftorah* readings for the seven weeks after *Tisha B'Av*.

The lesson in self-improvement we derive from the creeping creatures is that despite their humble condition (and perhaps exactly because of it), they are able to be truly happy, exalt and praise G-d's name, and be extraordinarily reproductive.

WEEK 46: TO KNOW OUR PLACE IN ORDER TO BE TRULY HAPPY

> **The prolific creeping creatures are saying**: "Your wife shall be like a fruitful vine in the recesses of your house; your children like olive shoots around your table." (Psalms 128:3)
>
> **Rabbi Matya the son of Charash would say:** Be first to greet every man. Be a tail to lions, rather than a head to foxes.
>
> *Netzach shebeMalchut* (victory and endurance within the context of kingship)

In week forty-six, the last week of the month of *Av*, in *Perek Shirah* the prolific creeping creatures state, "your wife shall be like a fruitful vine and your children as olive branches around your table." (Psalm 128: 3) This week also contains the *yahrzeit* of the Rebbe's father, Rabbi Levi Yitzchak Schneerson, on the 20th of *Av*.

In the week that follows that of *Tu B'Av*, *Perek Shirah* is still focused on marriage and reproduction. The continuation of this theme further emphasizes that love, marriage, and building a home together is not a one-time action or decision. That initial feeling that brought the couple together has to be worked on and improved throughout one's entire life, day by day, week by week, month by month, and year by year.

The *gematria* of forty-six is Levi. Levi and Shimon were individuals who both contained in them an overwhelming capacity for violence and radical behavior, especially when they acted together. The two were responsible for the killing of the inhabitants of the city of *Shchem*, and were the main actors in the kidnapping and sale of Joseph. The tribe of Levi was able to transform these extreme qualities into positive traits. They used their zealousness in acting on behalf of G-d, and became a tribe consisting solely of priests. Ultimately, Shimon will also use its enormous strength and potential only for the good.

In *Pirkei Avot* this week, Rabbi Matya the son of Charash teaches that we should be the first to greet another, and that it is better to be the tail of a lion than the head of a fox. (IV: 15) It is amazing to note that this lesson is contained exactly in the last week of the month of *Av*, whose zodiac sign is Leo, and is just a week away from being the week of *Rosh Chodesh*, which literally means the "head of the month."

In the past, Shimon, and his tribe as a whole, led actions that were "fox-like." However, the *Tanach* also recounts that the tribe also ultimately agreed to act as the tail of a "lion," the tribe of Judah. After the passing of Joshua, when it came time for the tribes to conquer the remaining parts of the Land of Israel, Judah was chosen to act first. Judah then approached Shimon and asked that it follow it in battle. Judah said, "Come up with me into my lot, and we will fight against the Canaanites, and I will also go with you into your lot."[160]

---

[160]   Book of Judges 1:3

The *Bnei Yissachar* explains that this statement has a much deeper meaning, and is connected to the redemption of Passover, which occurred in the month of *Nissan* (Judah) and the future redemption connected to *Mashiach*, born on *Tisha B'Av* (Shimon). On Passover, we keep an egg on the *Seder* plate to remind us of the destruction that took place in *Av*. In the final redemption, even though it will be one of unprecedented miracles, we will still remember the redemption from Egypt that took place in *Nissan*.

Similarly, despite enormous Soviet pressure and oppression, Rabbi Levi Yitzchak was very firm in his values and refused to associate himself with the "fox-like" Communist leadership. His extreme piety and stringency when it came to the *kashrut* of the *matzah* he mass-produced for Passover is a great example of his tremendous resolve. His refusal to give in to Communist demands caused him to be exiled to Siberia, where he passed away on this week of the Jewish calendar. It is known that the lion brings its tail to its head, while the fox brings its head to its tail.[161] While today, the father of the Rebbe is still held in tremendous esteem as a great leader, rabbi, and scholar, Soviet Communism is a completely outdated and bankrupt concept.

This week, the combination of *sefirot* results in *netzach shebemalchut*, victory and endurance within the context of kingship. We must be persistent in our attempt to connect ourselves to the King of kings and reveal Him in this material world.

---

[161]   *Midrash Shmuel*

The lesson in self-improvement we derive from the prolific creeping creatures is that the humility that we achieved during this month of judgment must be used productively: to grow and reproduce, just as the vine and the olive tree.

The snake is saying, "G-d supports all the fallen, and straightens all the bent." (Psalms 145:14)

Rabbi Yaakov would say: This world is comparable to the antechamber before the World to Come. Prepare yourself in the antechamber, so that you may enter the banquet hall.

He would also say: A single moment of repentance and good deeds in this world is greater than all of the World to Come. And a single moment of bliss in the World to Come is greater than all of the present world.

Hod shebeMalchut (glory and gratefulness within the context of kingship)

This week marks *Rosh Chodesh Elul*. *Elul's* main characteristic is *teshuvah*, repentance. The Alter Rebbe explains that the King (G-d) spends most of the year inside his palace, where it is more difficult to reach him. During the month of *Elul*, the King goes out to the field to speak to His people and to listen to their pleas. During this time, He greets everyone with a smiling countenance. In *Elul*, we can have greater direct contact with G-d by increasing our Torah studies, prayer and repentance, as well as good deeds.

During this month, we have the opportunity to be extremely close to G-d. Through *teshuvah* and asking for forgiveness, we can properly prepare ourselves for *Rosh*

Hashanah. Elul is represented by the tribe of Gad. Gad was a very powerful and courageous tribe. Its name literally means "luck," and indicates that the Jewish people are completely above luck and chance—everything depends on our *teshuvah*.[162]

How appropriate then it is that the animal to sing this week in *Perek Shirah* is the snake, who declares that G-d supports all the fallen, and straightens all bent. (Psalm 145:14) The snake, from the story of Creation and beyond, has always been associated with sin and the evil inclination. Its verse perfectly embodies the spirit of *teshuvah* with which we begin the month of *Elul*.

The number forty-seven is the *gematria* of the name *Yoel* (Joel).[163] The Book of Joel contains many parallels to the month of *Elul*. Like several other books of the prophets, the book speaks profoundly about the need for repentance. Joel specifically refers to the need for *teshuvah* before the "great day" of judgment. The book also describes the Jewish people's closeness to G-d, and makes many mentions to the sound of the *shofar*. During almost the entire month of *Elul*, we blow the *shofar* every day after prayer as a preparation for the Day of Judgment, *Rosh Hashanah*.

In *Pirkei Avot* this week, Rabbi Yaakov states that this world is like an antechamber for the World to Come; one must prepare oneself in the antechamber in order to

---

162   Ryzman, p. 195
163   This week also marks the *yahrzeit* of Rabbi Yoel Teitelbaum, the Satmar Rebbe, on the 26th of Av.

enter the banquet hall. He also states that one moment of repentance and good deeds in this world is better than the entire life of the world to come. Similarly, a single moment of pleasure in the World to Come is better than all the life of this world. (IV: 16-17) This teaching is perfectly suitable for *Rosh Chodesh Elul*, when the Jewish people begin the process of *teshuvah*. Similarly, just as the purpose of this world is only to serve as an ante-room for the World to Come, the month of *Elul* also serves as a preparation for *Rosh Hashanah* and *Yom Kippur*.

This week, the combination of *sefirot* results in *hod shebemalchut*, glory and gratefulness within the context of kingship. It is time to bring our service of *Hashem* to fruition in a tangible and real way.

A lesson in self-improvement that we extract from the snake is that even if we fall to the lowest possible levels, we can still repent and be forgiven and uplifted by G-d.

WEEK 48: TO FIGHT COLDNESS WITH WARMTH

The scorpion is saying, "G-d is good to all, and His mercy is upon all of His handiwork." (Psalms 145:9)

Rabbi Shimon the son of Elazar would say: Do not appease your friend at the height of his anger; do not comfort him while his dead still lies before him; do not ask him about his vow the moment he makes it; and do not endeavor to see him at the time of his degradation.

Yesod shebeMalchut (foundation and firmness within the context of kingship)

In week forty-eight, which includes the second day of *Rosh Chodesh Elul*, the scorpion in *Perek Shirah* sings of how G-d is good to all and is merciful to all His creations. (Psalm 145:9) The scorpion carries a heavy load of transgression and sin, and therefore thanks G-d for His mercy towards it.

Spiritually speaking, the scorpion's venom is worse than that of the snake. The snake's venom is hot, representing passion and desire for forbidden things; however, the scorpion's venom is cold, symbolizing indifference. It is much easier to redirect passion for what is forbidden towards something positive than it is to attempt to "redirect" indifference.

Nevertheless, it is possible to "treat" indifference as well, through the study of Torah. We see this in the purification process of the *metzorah*, someone who had been inflicted with a form of spiritual "leprosy/psoriasis" due to slander or other related sins and/or problematic social behaviors. The Torah concludes this section by stating, *"zot Torat hametzorah,"* "this is the Torah of the *metzorah.*" The Alter Rebbe asks why verse uses the word "Torah," when instead is should have simply stated "this is the purification of the *metzorah.*" The answer is that the Torah *is* the *metzorah*'s purification.

The number forty-eight is the number of qualities listed in *Pirkei Avot* necessary in order to acquire the Torah. It is also the number of male prophets and the number Levitical cities explicitly mentioned in the Torah. All of these three categories have at least one thing in common: they each represent the Torah itself.

The Hebrew letters for the number forty-eight is *mem* and *chet*, which spell the word *mo'ach*, brain. The intellect is the main conduit to receiving and internalizing the Torah, but it is also usually associated with coolness. However, by inverting these two letters, one spells the word *cham*, which means hot. Perhaps this is another hint as to how to combat coldness and indifference. At times one might need to let go of one's intellect, even if only temporarily, in order to divert feelings of indifference and convert them into a heated desire for Torah and *mitzvot*.

The *Pirkei Avot* lesson this week is contained in the teachings of Rabbi Shimon the son of Elazar. He advises us not to appease our neighbor at the time of his anger, not to console a mourner while his dead lies before him, not to ask about the details of a vow at the time it is made, and not to seek someone at the time of his degradation. (IV:

18) Rabbi Shimon's words are the inverse of the scorpion's song, as it describes situations in which a person is affected and overly "heated" by their emotions. At such times, any attempt to interfere, even for the sake of helping out that person, would most likely prove to be counterproductive. In the situations described by Rabbi Shimon, it is better to coldly use our intellect and to distance ourselves from the situation for now. In this sense, the cold qualities of the scorpion can be used for the good.

The words of Rabbi Shimon also describe part of the process *teshuvah* during *Elul*. At first, in the heat of *Rosh Chodesh Elul*, we might think that we can repent from all sins and transform ourselves in a single moment. While this certainly is possible, usually the most effective *teshuvah* is the one that is experienced over a longer period of time. That is why we gradually perform *teshuvah* over the course of the entire month of *Elul*, in order to remain firm in our resolve all the way to *Rosh Hashanah* and *Yom Kippur*.

This *sefirot* combination for this week results in *yesod shebemalchut*. During this week, we intensify our Jewish foundation to do *teshuvah*, thereby further establishing G-d's kingship in this world.

Finally, the lesson in self-improvement we learn from the scorpion is that we have the ability and the responsibility to help those individuals who are distanced from the Torah and to show them the warmth and the beauty of Judaism.

WEEK 49: TO BRING MORE LIGHT IN ORDER TO EXTINGUISH DARKNESS ALTOGETHER

> **The snail is saying,** "Like the snail that melts away, a stillborn of a mole that does not see the sun." (Psalms 58:9)
>
> **Shmuel the Small would say:** "When your enemy falls, do not rejoice; when he stumbles, let your heart not be gladdened. Lest G-d see, and it will displeasing in His eyes, and He will turn His wrath from him [to you]" (Proverbs 24:17-18).
>
> *Malchut shebeMalchut* (kingship within the context of kingship)

In week forty-nine, as we approach the middle of the month of *Elul*, the snail in *Perek Shirah* declares that the enemies of *Hashem* will melt and will be like a stillborn that does not see the sun. (Psalm 58:9) The snail seems to be in a position that is even worse than that of the snake and the scorpion; it is literally fading and melting away. This verse is also deeply connected to the month of *Elul* when through our *teshuvah* we melt away our inner feelings of darkness and sadness and connect directly to G-d's light.

The song of the snail comes from a Psalm in which King David refers to the ability to reduce the evil inclination to nothing, as he himself was able to accomplish. This statement is very appropriate for this week, given that it is on day forty-nine (or week forty-nine in this case) that we complete the Counting of the *Omer*. With the end of week forty-nine, we conclude the work of self-improvement of the emotional *sefirot* for this year. After climbing step by step, week after week, we hopefully significantly diminished the evil inclination within us.

As noted above, the number forty-nine represents the number of days of the *omer* count, as well as the number of years until the Jubilee. Forty-nine is the culmination of the entire *omer* count, and represents completion, seven times seven.

The lesson from *Pirkei Avot* for this week is in the words of Shmuel *HaKatan* ("the Small"), who teaches us not to rejoice when our enemy falls, lest G-d dislike it, and turn away His wrath from him (onto us). (Chapter IV: 19; Proverbs 24:17-18) The teaching of Shmuel is connected to how we ought to behave in the face of the fall of our greatest enemy—our evil inclination. Shmuel *HaKatan*, was so named because of his great humility. We must seek always to be humble, especially in these days of *Elul*.

And completing the cycle, this week the *sefirot* combination results in *malchut shebemalchut*, which represents completely majestic behavior still connected to this material world. *Malchut* is also called the "poor" *sefirah*, in that it has nothing of its own—it simply reflects the emanations of the other *sefirot*. In that sense, it is very humble, like Shmuel *HaKatan*.

The lesson for self-improvement derived from the snail is that we must bring the light of the Torah to all those who are currently in spiritual darkness.

Week 50: To Know That There Are No Limits to Our Growth and Closeness to G-d

> **The ant is saying,** "Go to the ant, you sluggard; consider her ways and be wise." (Proverbs 6:6)
>
> **Elisha the son of Avuyah would say:** One who learns Torah in his childhood, what is this comparable to? To ink inscribed on fresh paper. One who learns Torah in his old age, what is this comparable to? To ink inscribed on erased paper.
>
> *Chochmah* (wisdom)

Weeks fifty to fifty-two represent the holiday of *Shavuot*, in which we are given an even higher level of the intellectual *sefirot* than the level originally given to us on Passover. These three weeks are also connected with the "Passover" weeks of the coming year, representing the intellectual *sefirot* granted prior to the Counting of the *Omer*. The intellectual *sefirot* are *chochmah* (wisdom), *binah* (understanding) and *da'at/keter* (knowledge/crown). This first week is connected to the *sefirah* of *chochmah*.

On week fifty, which contains the Chassidic holiday of *Chai Elul*, in *Perek Shirah* it is the ant's turn to sing. It tells those that are lazy to study its ways and gain wisdom. (Proverbs 6:6) *Chai Elul* is the birthday of the Ba'al Shem Tov as well as that of the Alter Rebbe. The Ba'al Shem Tov was the founder of the Chassidic movement, and the one who revealed deep secrets of the Torah that enabled every

Jew to serve *Hashem* on a higher level. The Alter Rebbe, who considered himself the spiritual grandson of the Ba'al Shem Tov, was the founder of Chabad Chassidism. The name Chabad is an acronym for the three intellectual *sefirot, chochmah, binah* and *da'at*, often translated as wisdom, understanding, and knowledge. The main goal of Chabad Chassidism is to bring light and Chassidic warmth to the intellect, the coldest part of the human being. As mentioned in Week 12, Chassidism lights a certain fire inside the person, a kind of wake up call for us to serve *Hashem* more appropriately and be more diligent, like the ant.[164]

The number fifty represents the festival of *Shavuot* as well as the Jubilee year. Fifty, like the number eight, symbolizes something extraordinary, beyond nature and beyond human comprehension. The ant is an example of an animal that does not appear to conform to logical parameters. Its force appears to be above comprehension, since it is able to carry loads that are dozens of times its own weight. The ant sings of how we can acquire wisdom, *chochmah*, by following its own example and behavior. To the extent that we are connected to *Hashem*, we are also capable of doing things that at first glance appear to be impossible, because G-d's power is completely beyond nature. When we connect to the immense *teshuvah* that results from the teachings of the Ba'al Shem Tov and the Alter Rebbe, as well as the many great miracles that took place during their lives, the power and energy we receive on *Chai Elul* itself is also something that exceeds our comprehension.

---

[164] *Hayom Yom*, 17th of *Av*, p. 79a

In *Pirkei Avot*, Elisha the son of Avuyah states that those who learn Torah when young are compared to ink written on new paper, while those that learn it in their old age resemble ink written on paper that has been erased. (IV: 20) This first interaction with the Torah, both by a child and by an older person is linked to *sefirah* of *chochmah*. *Chochmah* represents the first contact with the wisdom, that feeling we have when an idea first lights up in our minds.

The Talmud refers to Elisha the son of Avuyah as *Acher*, "The Other," because he was excommunicated by the rabbis of the time. His actions and behavior were incredibly disrespectful and evil in G-d's eyes, to the point that a heavenly voice declared that everyone should do *teshuvah*, except for Elisha the son of Avuyah.[165] It is not mere coincidence that *Acher* falls exactly in the week of *Chai Elul*. The Chassidic way is always to try to find the good side of people and situations, and to bring closer even those furthest away and help them do *teshuvah*. This was previously explained in Week 12 as well, the week of the 19th of *Kislev*, the *Rosh Hashanah* of Chassidism, in which the raven sings. The Rebbe of Lubavitch, based on an interpretation of the *Arizal*, explains that G-d would have accepted even *Acher's* repentance.[166]

Furthermore, the teaching of Elisha the son of Avuyah, which appears to be negative, can also be taken in an extremely positive way. The word used for old, *zaken*, also means wise, and stands for "*zeh shekanah chochmah*," one

---

[165] *Talmud Yerushalmi, Chagigah* 77B
[166] Marcus, p. 151

who has acquired wisdom.[167] The word used for erased *machuk*, is spelled the same as *mechok*, which means from a *chok*, a law of the Torah that is beyond human comprehension. With these two concepts in mind, the second part of the teaching of Elisha the son of Avuyah can be understood in the following sense: a sage who studies the Torah resembles the ink written on paper absorbed as a law that is beyond human comprehension. A true sage accepts all of the Torah, even the parts that are more comprehensible to the human mind, as if it were all a *chok*, something beyond understanding. This in fact was exactly the initial mistake that *Acher* made that led him astray. He was somewhat arrogant and thought that he could understand everything with his intellect. When faced with a particular situation that went beyond his logical grasp, he became a heretic. The Ba'al Shem Tov always extolled the beauty of the faith of simple Jews who lacked great understanding. These Jews accepted the Torah as if it were all a *chok*.

Moreover, the Alter Rebbe teaches that the word *chok* is also connected to the word *chakuk*, meaning carved or etched. When a person begins to study Torah, he or she connects to the Torah, but both the person and the Torah are still separate entities, such as the ink and the paper. However, once a human being matures and studies like a sage, the person and the Torah become a single entity—the Torah is carved in the heart of the person, and there is no way to erase it any longer. This concept can also be found in the Talmud, in the tractate of *Shvuot*, which states that when a person begins to study the Torah it is called the

---

[167]   Talmud, *Kedushin* 32b

Torah of *Hashem*. After studying, that Torah is now called *Toratoh* (his Torah), since the Torah is now an intrinsic part of that person.

Acher's lesson is also connected to the ant. As much as the ant has the wonderful qualities noted above, it is also capable of having a not very positive characteristic: feelings of arrogance and superiority. We see that in its own song, it calls others lazy while praising its own qualities. In many ways, arrogance is even considered worse than sin. About someone arrogant, G-d says that "He and I cannot live together." This is something very serious, and something Chassidism also came to fix. There is a well known saying by one of the most extraordinary of all Chabad *chassidim*, Reb Hillel Paritcher. He said that before he became a *chassid*, he considered himself a *tzadik*. However, once he began to study the *Tanya* (the main writing of the Alter Rebbe), he thought to himself: "*Halevai* [I hope I can become] a *beinoni* (an intermediate Jew)!" The *Alter Rebbe* himself emphasized the importance of humility in a *ma'amar* (Chassidic discourse) he recited soon after his release from prison on the 19th of *Kislev*. In this *ma'amar*, entitled *Katonti* (I became small), the Alter Rebbe explains that we must realize that any accomplishment we achieve is due to the grace shown to us by G-d. Acknowledging this Divine assistance should make us even more grateful, small, and humble. Every time we get closer to G-d we must feel even smaller in relation to Him. This correct response to blessings we receive is exemplified by Jacob after he fled from Laban.

At the end of the first chapter of the *Tanya*, the Alter Rebbe explains that impurity, *kelipah*, is linked to the four natural elements: fire, water, air and earth. The Alter Rebbe explains that fire is connected to anger and arrogance (the ant). Water represents the desire for physical pleasure (the snake). Air is connected to indifference and sarcasm (the scorpion). Earth represents sadness and laziness (the snail). During the first four weeks connected to the month of *Elul*, we do *teshuvah* for our sins related to each one of these elements and animals.[168]

In the Talmudic tractate of *Chullin*, Rabbi Akiva states the following:

> How manifold are Thy works, O Lord! Thou hast creatures that live in the sea and Thou hast creatures that live upon the dry land; if those of the sea were to come up upon the dry land they would straightway die, and if those of the dry land were to go down into the sea they would straightway die. Thou hast creatures that live in fire and Thou hast creatures that live in the air; if those of the fire were to come up into the air they would straightway die, and if those of the air were to go down into the fire they would straightway die. How manifold are Thy works, O Lord![169]

Rabbi Akiva's statement is connected to the four natural elements mentioned above. In fact, he seems to be teaching

---

168 *See also* the writings regarding the month of *Elul* of Rabbi Chaim Yosef David Azulay, the *Chidah*.
169 *Chullin* 127A

how to deal with these different types of *kelipah*: take them out of their natural habitat.

As mentioned above, this week is connected to *Shavuot* and to the *sefirah* of *chochmah*. This week would also represent the "eighth week," of *Shavuot* and "*Shivah Yemei Miluim*" of the cycle of *malchut*.

The great "gift" of self-improvement that we can receive from the ant is that there are no limits to our closeness to *Hashem*, and that like the ant we can serve as an example for people who wish to attain higher levels in their Judaism.

WEEK 51: TO UNDERSTAND THAT WE ARE ALL ONE SOUL

The weasel is saying, "Let every soul praise G-d, Halleluyah!" (Psalms 150:6)

Rabbi Yossi the son of Yehudah of *Kfar HaBavli* would say: One who learns Torah from youngsters, whom is he comparable to? To one who eats unripe grapes and drinks [unfermented] wine from the press. One who learns Torah from the old, whom is he comparable to? To one who eats ripened grapes and drinks aged wine.

Said Rabbi Meir: Look not at the vessel, but at what it contains. There are new vessels that are filled with old wine, and old vessels that do not even contain new wine.

Binah (understanding)

In the fifty-first week, still in the month of *Elul*, it is the weasel (*Chuldah*) who proclaims that all live beings should praise the Lord, *Haleluyah*! (Psalm 150:6). This is a reference to the power of repentance in the month of *Elul* and also to the messianic age when all beings, even the lowest, will openly praise *Hashem*. Week 51 also includes the 25th of *Elul*, the day in which the world was created (on *Rosh Hashanah*, man was created, *See* Week 52), and is therefore connected with the concept that all living things should praise G-d, the Creator and Master of the Universe.

Chuldah is also the name of one of the seven prophetesses mentioned in the *Tanach*. She was the last to prophesy before the beginning of the Babylonian exile. Her words related to the fall of the Davidic dynasty in the kingdom Judah. The dynasty was extremely corrupt, and the prophecy of Chuldah is very powerful and incriminating.

The weasel represents corruption and decay, both in nature and in civilization. *Chuldah* comes from the word *Chaled*, which means decadent. Interestingly, the Talmud states that the weasel is the only land animal that has no correspondent in the sea.[170] In the first time that the world became corrupt, G-d brought upon the Flood. The weasel, who cannot live in water and does not have any sea animal that corresponds to it, reminds us of this unfortunate time in the history of humanity and the world as a whole.

The weasel beautifully describes the redemption from this decaying state, as well as how to achieve it. Whereas before, due to its decadence, the whole world was destroyed as a single entity, the weasel urges us all to praise G-d together as a single entity. In the song of the weasel, the word used for living being is *neshamah*, which literally means breath, as well as soul. In this verse, the word is used in the singular, even though it is referring to all beings. The explanation for this is that the weasel understands that we are all ultimately a single soul, a part of G-d.

As mentioned above, *neshamah* also means breath. Breath itself represents life, as well as the most basic connection we have with *Hashem*. Through our breath we are

---

[170] *Bechorot* 8A

connected to *Hashem* and the world constantly, in a way that is beyond our comprehension. In *Elul*, we recognize this constant connection with G-d. As also mentioned previously, we know that in *Elul*, "the King is in the field," ready to hear our requests. *Elul* is also a good time to go to the field or any other secluded place to breathe, meditate, and talk to *Hashem*.

In this week, the lesson from *Pirkei Avot* comes from Rabbi Yossi the son of Yehudah of *Kfar HaBavli*, who teaches that to learn Torah from the young is like eating unripe grapes and drinking [unfermented] wine out of the press, but to learn from older masters is like eating ripe grapes and drinking old wine. Rabbi Meir adds to this statement, saying that one should not just look at the vessel, but what is inside. There are new containers full of old wine and old vessels that do not even contain new wine. (IV: 20) Rabbi Yossi compares the Torah to wine, which affects us in ways that are beyond our intellect. Also, with age, a person acquires knowledge and experiences that go beyond his or her previous intellectual capacity.

The wine comparison made by Rabbi Yossi is also related to the *sefirah* of *binah*, the second intellectual *sefirah*. After the "light bulb moment" at the time an idea is conceived, that idea then needs to be developed and properly understood intellectually, just like the fermentation of wine. Rabbi Yossi teaches us that it is not ideal to learn from those who have not had time to properly process their Torah ideas, even though Rabbi Meir explains that this is not necessarily related to the teacher's physical age.

As in the previous week, here too there is a way to understand Rabbi Yossi's lesson in a purely positive way. The word for young, *ketanim*, literally means small, but can also be understood as humble, such as in the Shmuel *HaKatan* (the Small), who teaches the *Pirkei Avot* lesson for week forty-nine. The Hebrew word used for grapes, *anavim*, is phonetically practically the same as the word humble in Hebrew, *anav*. The Hebrew word used for unripe is *kehot*, which is also the name of Moses and Aaron's grandfather, Kehot. Finally, the term used for "out of the winepress" is *migitoh*, which, with a bit of poetic license, can be read as a *m'yegiatoh*, which means "from one's own efforts." Wine is a metaphor of the most mysterious secrets of the Torah. A humble person teaches these secrets in a way in which the student deduces the most hidden secrets of the Torah through his own efforts. This is much more valuable than simply receiving all of one's knowledge "on a silver platter."

One could then read the above verse as follows: "One who learns Torah from humble ones is like studying under Kehot, i.e., Moses and Aaron, and learning the deep secrets of the Torah through one's own efforts. This is closely connected to *Elul* and *Rosh Hashanah*, when we humbly strive to correct our behavior and connect with G-d.

As mentioned above, this week is connected to *Shavuot* and to the *sefirah* of *binah*. A "gift" of self-improvement we receive from the weasel is that any person, no matter their level, can connect directly to *Hashem* in a simple and natural way, without the need for intermediaries, just like the very act of breathing. We must also remember to realize that we are all one.

WEEK 52: TO CROWN G-D AS OUR KING

The dogs are saying: "Come, let us worship and bow down; let us kneel before G-d our Maker." (Psalms 95:6)

Rabbi Elazar HaKapar would say: Envy, lust and honor drive a man from the world.

He would also say: Those who are born will die, and the dead will live. The living will be judged, to learn, to teach and to comprehend that He is G-d, He is the former, He is the creator, He is the comprehender, He is the judge, He is the witness, He is the plaintiff, and He will judge. Blessed is He, for before Him there is no wrong, no forgetting, no favoritism, and no taking of bribes; know, that everything is according to the reckoning. Let not your heart convince you that the grave is your escape; for against your will you are formed, against your will you are born, against your will you live, against your will you die, and against your will you are destined to give a judgment and accounting before the king, king of all kings, the Holy One, blessed be He.

Daat/Keter (knowledge/crown)

Finally, we come to week fifty-two, when the dogs cry out for all to worship and prostrate themselves before G-d our Maker. (Psalm 95:6) This week coincides with *Rosh Hashanah* of the following year. On *Rosh Hashanah*, man was created. The question then arises why do we celebrate *Rosh Hashanah* on this date, and not on the 25th of *Elul*?

The *Midrash* also relates that when Adam was created even his heel (the lowest and least sensitive part of his body), outshone the sun, so holy was he. In fact, he was so full of light that all of the animals came and bowed down to him, believing that he was their creator. But Adam told them, "Come let us bow down together and worship the One Who created us all." This was his function and purpose—to bring all of the world to the service of *Hashem*.[171]

The words of the dogs in *Perek Shirah* are Adam's exact words on the day of *Rosh Hashanah*, recalling the desire for all of Creation to bow before G-d and worship Him. It also describes the main purpose of *Rosh Hashanah*: crowning *Hashem*, our Creator, as our King. What a remarkable conclusion for this awe-inspiring text.

The song of the dogs echoes that of the rooster, as we start the yearly cycle over again. *Rosh Hashanah* and *Yom Kippur* are the two times of year when Jews kneel and completely bow before G-d during prayers. By lowering our heads all the way to the ground, we submit our intellect to the Divine King, who is infinitely greater than us and beyond our comprehension. The dog has this same characteristic, as the word for dog in Hebrew, *kelev*, means *kuloh lev*, it is "all heart"—its heart completely dominates its intellect. In our daily lives, it is a basic principle in Chabad Chassidism that the intellect must always rule over the heart. However,

---

[171] http://beta.chabad.org/library/article_cdo/aid/97517/jewish/The-Significance-of-Being-Alone.htm

when we stand before *Hashem*, our Father, King and Judge, we know that our intellect is nothing compared to Him.

In Kabbalah, the dog also represents the concept of *kelipah*, impurity. The very image of Satan, also known as the Angel of Death, is that of a dog with many eyes. The dog is all heart, and it is specifically by way of our emotions that the evil inclination attacks. The conclusion of *Perek Shirah* contains an explanation given by an angel to Rabbi Yeshaya, a student of Rabbi Chanina Ben Dosa, as to the reason for the inclusion of the dog in *Perek Shirah*. The angel explains that the dogs behaved very well and remained silent during the Jewish people's departure from Egypt. The angel also mentions how the dog's feces are used in tanning leather for *tefillin* and other holy writings. As with the redemption from Egypt, in the final redemption and the messianic era, even the deepest impurities will be nullified, and will be elevated for the fulfillment of Torah and *mitzvot*.

The number fifty-two has the *gematria* of the Hebrew word *kelev* (dog) and also the word *Behemah* (animal), which also represents a form of *kelipah*. Moreover, the number fifty-two is the number of one of the names of G-d, B"N, which is connected to the kabbalistic concept of raising the divine sparks that are stuck in the *kelippot*. When we finished raising all these sparks, G-d finally send our *Mashiach*. Fifty-two is also the *gematria* of *Eliyahu* (Elijah), the name of the prophet who will announce *Mashiach*'s arrival.

Week fifty-two represents the total transformation of the dog, from being associated with impurity to holiness, marking the time of the coming of *Mashiach*, announced by *Eliyahu HaNavi*. The Talmud on *Bava Kama* 60b states that, "When dogs 'cry' the Angel of Death has come to town. When they 'laugh' Elijah the Prophet has come."

We already see today, just how much dogs themselves have changed. They are no longer usually associated with impurity. Instead, they are man's loyal companions, and demonstrate enormous positive, healing behaviors.

The letters *nun* and *beit* together form the word *ben*, which means son. There is a verse from the Book of the Prophets saying that before the great final day, G-d will send Elijah, who will bring back the hearts of parents through their children.

Rosh Hashanah is a day of judgment, and we relate to G-d as our King. However, it is also a day in which we relate to *Hashem* as His children. Children are an important theme in the Torah readings of *Rosh Hashanah*. We read of how Sarah was barren for 90 years until she gave birth to Isaac. We also read of a similar story regarding Chanah.[172] Both of these events took place on *Rosh Hashanah*. The story we read about Hagar, Abraham's maidservant, is also about saving the life of her son, Yishmael. On the second day of *Rosh Hashanah*, we read about the sacrifice of Isaac, and the *haftorah* is about Rachel weeping for her children, and of Ephraim, described as *Hashem's* dear and beloved son. Moreover, perhaps the story most associated with the

---

[172] The very last day of this week, the last day of the entire cycle, is the 6th of Tishrei, *yahrzeit* of Rebbetzin Chanah Schneerson, the mother of the Rebbe.

blowing of the *shofar* is about a lost prince who after many years even forgets his mother tongue, yet when he sees his father the King, he calls out in a deep and loud cry.

Fifty-two is also the *gematria* of the word "*bakol*," which means "in everything." The Torah states that by the end of Abraham's life he had been blessed with "*bakol*." There are many interpretations of what *bakol* means (especially given the fact that Isaac was blessed with "*mikol*" ("from everything") and Jacob with "*kol*" (everything)). Nevertheless, one of the main interpretations of this verse is that Abraham was blessed with a daughter. This is also appropriate for this last week, as we complete "everything" in the year, and begin again.[173]

When the letters of the word "*bakol*" are spelled out, their numerical value is the same as the *gematria* of the word "*shofar*."[174] This appears to be another connection between Week 52 and Week 1.

This week in *Pirkei Avot*, Rabbi Elazar HaKapar teaches that envy, lust and the pursuit of honor take a man out of the world. (IV:21) Rabbi Elazar's statement captures the idea that we must be in control of our emotions. Ultimately, feelings of envy, lust and pursuit of honor are irrational, given that it is *Hashem* who runs the world and that everything He does and commands is for our own good.

---

[173] *Noam Elimelech*; Rabbi Yitchak Ginsburgh

[174] <u>Vedibarta Bam—And You Shall Speak of Them</u>, Volume I—Bereishit; Chayei Sarah, *available at*: http://www. sichosinenglish.org/books/vedibarta-bam/005.htm

There is also a more positive way to understand this teaching. If we direct these desires toward G-d, in "holy" envy (also known as the envy of scholars), desire to be close to G-d, and to honor Him, our relationship with G-d will be so strong that it will take us out of the concealment and illusion that is this world. As mentioned previously, the Hebrew word for world is *olam*, which comes from the word *ehelem*, which means illusion and concealment.

He also states as follows:

> Those who are born are destined to die, those who are dead are destined to live again (in another version to be resurrected), and those who live (again) are destined to be judged. To know, to make it known and to have knowledge that He is G-d, He is the Maker, He is the Creator, He is the Comprehender, He is the Judge, He is the Witness, He is the Litigant, and He will judge. Blessed be He, before whom there is no iniquity, no forgetfulness, no favoritism or bribery, and know that everything is done according to the reckoning. Let not your evil inclination convince you that the tomb is a place of refuge for you, for you were created against your will, against your will you were given birth, against your will you live, against your will you will die, and against your will you are destined to provide accounts before the Supreme King of kings, the Holy One, blessed be He." (IV:22)

This second part of Rabbi Elazar's teaching is a perfect description of what *Rosh Hashanah* is all about. With these words, we recommence the yearly cycle, as well as life's cycle in general.

Rabbi Elazar HaKapar's lesson is closely connected with the judgment of *Rosh Hashanah*, as well as with the *sefirah* of *da'at*, the application of knowledge to the reality of everyday living. Notice how the word *da'at* (knowledge) appears repeatedly in Rabbi Elazar's words: "to know, to make known and to have knowledge" in Hebrew are written as *leidah*, *lehodiah*, *le'ivadah*, all verbs that have the *da'at* as their root.

This week is connected to *Shavuot* and the sefirah of *da'at*, also referred to as *keter*, crown. As mentioned previously, during the week of *Rosh Hashanah*, we crown G-d as our King. We must understand that we are nothing compared to Him. He alone decides, judges and creates. He is G-d, King of Kings, Blessed and One. There is nothing besides Him.

A lesson we can derive from the dogs is that it is our duty to reach out to those who are suffering and distant from Judaism, to raise them so that they too can praise their Creator.

Conclusion

This guide showed a connection between the Counting of the *Omer* and the weeks of the year. Through *Perek Shirah*, *Pirkei Avot*, the numbers, and the *sefirot*, this work sought to lead the reader on a path of self-analysis and annual development, so that we can be happier, more humble and grateful, constantly praising G-d, and finding the positive side of everything.

Rabbi Akiva is perhaps the person who best represents all of the above qualities, as well as the concepts and texts mentioned. He was the one who was most impacted by the Counting of the *Omer*, given that it was during these days that 24,000 of his students passed away because they did not show enough respect towards one another. This fault of theirs was especially grave in light of Rabbi Akiva's main teaching, "*VeAhavtah LeRe'echah Kamochah Zeh Klal Gadol BaTorah,*" "To love your neighbor as yourself is *the* great [guiding] principle of the Torah.".

Rabbi Akiva's connection to *Pirkei Avot* is also quite strong. Despite losing his students, Rabbi Akiva did not give up hope and sought out to teach at least another five disciples: Rabbi Meir, Rabbi Yehudah, Rabbi Yossi, Rabbi Shimon Bar Yochai and Rabbi Elazar Ben Shamua. Consequently, the teachings of these five students turned out to be the basis for large part of our tradition, including *Pirkei Avot* itself.

The connection of Rabbi Akiva to the *sefirot* and to Kabbalah is also very clear. Rabbi Akiva is the rabbi that entered the *Pardes*, along with three other rabbis mentioned in *Pirkei Avot*: Ben Azzai, Ben Zoma, and *Acher*. Pardes literally means "orchard," but is also a reference to a state of intense spiritual elevation, as well as to the four levels of Torah knowledge: *Peshat* (simple/ meaning), *Remez* (implied/hinted), *Derush* (interpreted), and *Sod* (secret). During this intense spiritual encounter, Ben Azzai died, Ben Zoma became crazy, and *Acher* a heretic. Only Rabbi Akiva entered in peace and left in peace.[175] As previously mentioned, it is also Rabbi Akiva who teaches in *Pirkei Avot* that, "Beloved is man, since he was created in the image [of G-d], and it is an additional love bestowed upon him that he was made aware that he was created in the image [of G-d]." As also previously mentioned, our understanding of the *sefirot* is based on this notion.

It is also striking to note that several of the stories and teachings of Rabbi Akiva include animals that reflect teachings found in *Perek Shirah*.[176] It is no coincidence that there are opinions that claim that it was Rabbi Akiva himself who authored it. Below are a few examples of these parallels:

When the Romans decreed that the study of Torah be prohibited under penalty of death, Rabbi Akiva continued

---

[175] Talmud *Chagigah* 14b; It is interesting to note that the word diaspora, has the same letters as the word *Pardes*.

[176] Rabbi Akiva is a descendant of Yael, who killed Siserah during the battle led by Devorah, and who is praised in her song. Yael is also the Hebrew name of an animal: the mountain goat.

to study and to teach. When asked whether he feared the Roman decree, Rabbi Akiva gave the following example: Once the fox (animal of the week of the 17th day of *Tammuz* in *Perek Shirah*, which represents the destruction of the Temple) was walking by a creek when it saw a group of fish (who represent the month of *Adar*, Week 24, of Purim, and the ability to overcome material concerns even under great pressure). The fox asked the fish why they were all crowded in one spot, and the fish answered that they were hiding from the nets of fishermen. The fox then suggested to the fish that they should come to the dry land and stay with it. The fish responded by stating that they were not safe in the water, their natural habitat, outside the water would certainly lead to their death! Torah is our lifeline, just like water for fish.

In another fascinating parable found in the Talmud, at the end of tractate of *Makkot*, Rabbi Akiva again is linked to the fox, as well as to the destruction of the Temple. Once he was heading to Jerusalem with Rabban Gamliel, Rabbi Elazar ben Azaria and Rabbi Yehoshua, when they saw the mount where the Temple recently stood. When they saw a fox come out of where once was the Holy of Holies, the most sacred part of the Temple, they all tore their garments. Each one of them began to cry with the exception of Rabbi Akiva, who began to laugh. They asked him, "Why are you laughing?" Rabbi Akiva then answered their question with another question, and asked why they were all crying. The responded: "This place is so sacred that we know that anyone who would come near it would die. Now that a mere fox enters is, should we not cry?" Rabbi Akiva then said to them: "That's exactly why I am laughing." Rabbi Akiva then explained to them how the

Torah makes the prophecy of Zachariah dependent on the prophecy of Uriah, and then continued: "According to Uriah, it is written: 'Due to your guilt, Zion will be plowed like a field, Jerusalem will be in ruins, and the Temple Mount will become a heap of stones lost in the forest.' According to Zacharias, we learn that, 'Older men and women still sit in the streets of Jerusalem [when it is redeemed].'" Rabbi Akiva then concluded: "Now that the prophecy of Uriah has taken place, it is certain that the prophecy of Zachariah will take place as well." After hearing these words, the sages replied, "Akiva, you have truly comforted us!"

There is also another classic parable with Rabbi Akiva that illustrates the concept that everything that G-d does is for the good. This story involves Rabbi Akiva, a rooster, a donkey, a cat, and a lion. Rabbi Akiva was traveling when he arrived in a certain city. Although he was refused accommodation for the night, he famously stated, "Everything G-d does is for the good," and went to spend the night in the countryside. He was accompanied by a rooster, a donkey and a lamp. The wind came and blew out the lamp, a cat came and ate the rooster and a lion came and ate the donkey! Despite all these apparent mishaps, Rabbi Akiva repeated, "Everything that G-d does is for the good." That night, an army invaded and took all the inhabitants of the city captive. Rabbi Akiva then said to his disciples: "Did I not explain to you that everything G-d does is for the good? For if the lamp had not been put out by the wind, I would have been imprisoned by the enemy, if the donkey had brayed or the rooster crowed, the army would have found my hiding place, and I would have been captured!"

There is a Chassidic saying that one should not ask questions regarding a story, but at least one needs to be asked: Rabbi Akiva had a rooster that would wake him at midnight? Roosters do not usually crow that early. Apparently there is a kind of black rooster that does crow at midnight, but perhaps the real explanation and message here is that Rabbi Akiva's rooster was like him, able to see the light in the darkest hour of the night!

Despite only making *teshuvah* (returning to G-d) and beginning his study at the age of forty, Rabbi Akiva transformed himself into one of the greatest rabbis of all times. At the moment of his death as a martyr, as he was being excruciatingly tortured, he praised and glorified G-d, with the *Shemah Yisrael* on his lips.

Rabbi Akiva serves as an example to be followed during our annual journey. By perfecting our Divine image reflected in the *sefirot*, and learning from our sages, from numbers, and even from animals, we are assured that we will finally discover our song—the song of the soul, of Israel, of humanity, and of nature.

After the journey, when we awaken on *Rosh Hashanah* of the following year, we will hear the sound of the *shofar* in a way that is both more intimate and more conscious. G-d willing, in the merit of our efforts, we shall soon hear the *shofar* blast of Elijah the Prophet. This blast will announce, at last, the coming of *Mashiach*, who shall teach us to sing in unison, in an even more elevated manner, with much health, happiness, and peace.

APPENDIX I

The Jewish calendar actually has two beginnings, one in *Tishrei*, on *Rosh Hashanah*, the head of the year, and the other in *Nissan*, on *Rosh Chodesh Nissan*, the head of "the head of the months." There is even a debate in the *Mishnah* regarding which of these days is linked to Creation (because, as mentioned above, *Rosh Hashanah* actually celebrates the creation of man, on the sixth day, the creation of the world would have been five days prior, either on the 25th of *Elul* (as is the final ruling) or the 25th of *Adar*). Both in the months of *Nissan* and *Tishrei*, *Tachanun*, supplication prayers, are not said.

There are also various important parallels and contrasts in both these sequences. For example, both Passover and *Sukkot* fall on the 15th day of the 1st or 7th month, depending from which month the counting begins. Similarly, *Tu B'Av* and *Tu B'Shvat* fall on the 15th day of the 5th or 11th month, depending on which sequence is followed.

Interestingly, there is a custom to use the twelve days preceding *Tishrei*, from the eighteenth of *Elul* (*Chai Elul*) to *Erev Rosh Hashanah* to atone for the twelve months of the year, with *Chai Elul* representing *Tishrei* and *Erev Rosh Hashanah* representing *Elul*. In contrast, in the thirteen days from *Rosh Chodesh Nissan* to the thirteenth of *Nissan*, it is the custom to read the offerings brought by the princes of the tribes during in honor of the inauguration of the *Mishkan*, the Tabernacle. Each tribe brought their sacrifices on a different day. As explained previously, each tribe represents a different month, and the sequence of tribes' offerings goes according to the months of the year, beginning with Judah (*Nissan*) and ending with Naftali (*Adar I*) and Levi (*Adar II*).

It is also fascinating that the Alter Rebbe's birthday is on *Chai Elul*, the first of the twelve days, representing *Tishrei*, while the birthday of the grandson he raised, the Tzemach Tzedek, is on *Erev Rosh Hashanah*, the last of the twelve days, representing *Elul* itself. Furthermore, the Tzemach Tzedek's *yahrzeit* is also on the last day of the reading of the princes, the thirteenth of *Nissan*. The *yahrzeit* of the Rebbe Rashab, the Tzemach Tzedek's own grandson, is on the second day of *Nissan*, at the very beginning of the reading of the princes.

The duality between *Tishrei* and *Nissan* appears to relate to the contrast of the role of *Hashem* portrayed primarily as the One that creates us, judges and forgives us, and of *Hashem* as the One that redeems us, collectively and individually, and gives us the Torah. The duality is found also in the very first commentary of Rashi in the Torah. He asks why the Torah, which is primarily a Book of Laws, begin with the creation of the world, when it would seem more appropriate for it to begin with the first *mitzvah* given to the Jewish people, that of *Rosh Chodesh Nissan*.

In Kabbalah, another difference between *Tishrei* and the ensuing "winter months" and *Nissan* and the accompanying "summer months" (both of which have twenty-six weeks) is that *Tishrei* represents the concept of *Ohr Chozer* (reflective light), while *Nissan* represents *Ohr Yashar* (direct light). On *Tishrei*, we initiate our return to G-d, and G-d responds accordingly—that is why the month is spelled with the last three letters of the Hebrew alphabet, in descending order, mirroring/reflecting the first three letters in ascending order. On *Nissan*, G-d is the one that initiates the relationship, taking us out of bondage, independently of (or even despite) whether or not we merit it. This contrast is connected to the kabbalistic concepts of *Ita'aruta de L'tata* (arousal from below) and *Ita'aruta de L'Eila* (arousal from above), and which of the two come first.

It is interesting to note that in the "winter months," from *Tishrei* to *Adar*, the animals in *Perek Shirah* comprise of birds, flying insects, and water animals, while those from *Nissan* to *Elul* are all land animals. From *Tishrei* on, we must first ascend to G-d, and in turn He descends to us. From *Nissan* on, *Hashem* first descends to us, and only then do we ascend to Him.

This duality in the Jewish calendar is reflected in the Jewish people itself and in their two prototypical leaders: Judah and Joseph. As mentioned above, Judah represents *Nissan*. *Tishrei* is represented by Ephraim, the son of Joseph (his other son, Menashe represents the following month, *Cheshvan*).

The tension, balance, and contrast between Judah and Joseph is very apparent in the way the Torah places the very parallel stories of Joseph and Judah side by side,[177] as well as in the depiction of their direct confrontation, in

---

[177] Genesis, Ch. 37-39

the Torah portion of *Vayigash*.[178] Even the names of these two tribes are similar, because Joseph sometimes is called "*Yehosef*," carrying the first three letters of G-d's name, *Hashem*, just like Judah.

This balance and tension has continued throughout our history, most notably with King David and King Shaul, the two kingdoms of Judah and Israel (also called Ephraim in the Torah), and even eventually with the coming of two *Mashiachs, ben David* and *ben Yosef*, also known as *Mashiach ben Ephraim*.

Rabbi Moshe Wolfsohn explains that this division is reflected even in the current differences between Chassidic and Lithuanian/non-Chassidic. Similar differences seem to exist between Ashkenazim and Sephardim, and *baalei teshuvah* (those who return to G-d, acknowledging their mistakes) and *tzadikim gemurim* (righteous one, who never sinned in the first place). Joseph is the prototype of the *tzadik gamur*, while Judah of the *baal teshuvah*.

The prophet Ezekiel's vision of the Holy Chariot, *Hashem's* holy throne, has a lion on the right (the symbol of Judah) and an ox on the left (the symbol of Joseph). The same prophet Ezekiel, in the *haftorah* reading for *Vayigash*, is told by G-d to collect one stick for Judah and one for Ephraim, and to join them together, symbolizing that in future *Yosef* and *Yehudah* will become completely united.[179]

---

178 Genesis, 44:18

179 Ezekiel 37:15; *See* Matis Weinberg, <u>Patterns in Time, Volume 8: Chanukah</u>, Feldheim Publishers, New York, 1992

The Jewish calendar also contains another duality and synthesis: its days are counted in accordance with the cycles of the sun *and* the moon. While the West's calendar (based on the Roman one) is purely solar, and the Islamic calendar is purely lunar, the Jewish calendar has aspects of both. Each month in the Jewish calendar follows the moon, yet, as mentioned in Week 22, the Jewish year often contains two *Adar* months. This way, Passover always occurs in the spring, and all other months correspond to particular seasons accordingly. Here also, Joseph appears primarily associated with the year as a whole (countering Esau), while Judah appears to be primarily connected to the lunar months (countering Yishmael).

Appendix II

Perek Shirah also has a connection to the day itself. If we divide the day into 52 parts, in a typical winter day, each animal listed in *Perek Shirah* sings for approximately 20 minutes, from sunrise until midnight. Thus, the day begins with the rooster's crow at sunrise; the donkey's (33rd animal) song is during sunset; and the dogs end their song at midnight.

Interestingly, the donkey and the dog are specifically mentioned in the Talmud, in the tractate of *Brachot*, as determinants of time (the braying of the donkey takes place during the first watch of the night while the dogs bark at midnight). The rooster is also mentioned in several places in the Torah as a marker of time, announcing the beginning of the day, as we say every day in the morning blessings: "Blessed are you G-d our Lord King of the Universe who gives the rooster understanding to distinguish between day and night."

Each kind of animal is also connected with a different time for the daily prayers. The birds sing from sunrise (first allowable time for *Shacharit*, the morning prayer) until noon (the last permissible time). The insects and the water animals sing from *Minchah Gedolah* (first time for *Minchah*, the afternoon prayer) to before *Minchah Ketanah* (the second time for this prayer). The farm animals sing from *Minchah Ketanah* until sunset (the latest time for the afternoon prayer). The wild animals, and all those remaining sing from nightfall (the first allowable time for *Ma'ariv*, the prayer of the night) until midnight (the last allowable time). (*See* Table I below for details on the schedules attached to each type of animal)

It is also incredible to think that the day itself reflects the year. We rise in the morning with the crow of the rooster, just as we spiritually arise with the blowing of the *shofar* on *Rosh Hashanah*, acknowledging G-d as our King, from the very moment we awake, reciting *Modeh Ani Lefanechah Melech* . . . "I acknowledge/give thanks before you Living and Eternal King, for You have mercifully restored my soul, great is Your faithfulness." Soon after, in the morning prayers, we recognize all the material and spiritual blessings that G-d has given us, from the very crow of the rooster, to the clothes we wear, and the opportunities given to perform *mitzvot*.

Later, come the morning prayers (*Shacharit*), which are normally done while one is still fasting, like on *Yom Kippur*. Some have the custom to eat a bit in order to better focus on prayer, just as it is a *mitzvah* to eat on the eve of this sacred day. As on *Yom Kippur*, in the morning prayers we focus purely on our spiritual side.

Afterwards, we study Torah and eat breakfast in a state of joy, just as on *Sukkot*. Soon we go out and start our day by bringing the joy of being Jewish and being connected to the Torah to all, just as on *Hoshanah Rabbah*, *Shemini Atzeret* and *Simchat Torah*.

After completing our morning spiritual activities, we start our physical labor of elevating the world around us, just such as *Rosh Chodesh Cheshvan* and the rest of that month. Once we distance ourselves a bit from the beginning of our day and start becoming fully immersed in our worldly affairs, we might begin to forget some of the sanctity with which we started the day. At this point, it is important to have *gevurah* and also make sure to include some moments of light, such as in *Chanukah*.

The parallels between the day and the year continue until bedtime, when we make a spiritual inventory of our entire day, returning to G-d and preparing for the next day, just as in the month of *Elul*.

Finally, we lie down to go to sleep, bowing like on *Rosh Hashanah*, accepting G-d as our King, understanding that against our will we were born and against our will we will die. In the morning, we are like new creations.

TABLE I

Important dates taking place in week of year	Important date during *omer* count and time of day	Animal in *Perek Shirah*	#	Rabbi in *Pirkei Avot* and thrust of his teaching	*Sefirot*
Rosh Hashanah	*Pessach* **Netz Hachamah** (sunrise)	Rooster, (Introduction and 7 verses) (first bird)	1	Introduction and 14 rabbis (7 pairs)—acquiring a master.	*Chesed shebeChesed*
Yom Kippur	*Chol haMoed*	Hen	2	Shimon ben Raban Gamliel—"silence" of the body	*Gevurah shebeChesed*
Sukkot	*Chol haMoed*	Dove	3	Rabban Shimon ben Gamliel—justice, truth and peace	*Tiferet shebeChesed*
Shemini Atzeret	*Chol haMoed*	Eagle	4	Rabbi Yehudah HaNassí—an eye that sees, and Ear that hears, and all your deeds are written in a Book	*Netzach shebeChesed*
Rosh Chodesh Cheshvan	*Chol haMoed*	Crane	5	Rabban Gamliel ben Rabbi Yehudah HaNassí—combine Torah study with work	*Hod shebeChesed*
First Week of *Cheshvan* (*Potential 3rd Temple Holiday*)[179]	*Chol haMoed*	Songbird	6	Rabban Yochanan ben Zakai—an individual that learned much Torah should not feel that he or she deserves special recognition	*Yesod shebeChesed*

---

[179] There is a parallel between *Kislev* and *Cheshvan*. The *Mishkan* was first completed in *Kislev*, but then inaugurated in *Nissan*. *Kislev* was, so to speak, deprived of a holiday. *Hashem* repaid *Kislev*, with the rededication of the Temple in the times of the Hasmoneans, as well as the holiday forever established at that time: *Chanukah*. Similarly, the first Temple was completed by King Solomon in *Cheshvan*. However, King Solomon only inaugurated it in *Tishrei*. *Cheshvan* was then also deprived of

Second Week of *Cheshvan* (3rd *Temple*)	Seventh day of *Pessach*	Swallow	7	Rabbi Eliezer—the honor of your neighbor should be as precious in your eyes as your own, and do not become easily irritated	*Malchut shebeChesed*
Third Week of *Cheshvan* (3rd *Temple*)	Last Day of *Pessach*	Swift	8	Rabbi Yehoshua—an evil eye, an evil inclination, and hatred of one's fellow takes a man out of this world	*Chesed shebeGevurah*
Fourth Week of *Cheshvan* or *Rosh Chodesh Kislev*	*Isru Chag* **Latest time to recite the *Shemah***	Stormy Petrel	9	Rabbi Yossi—the possessions of your neighbor should be as dear to you as your own	*Gevurah shebeGevurah*
Rosh Chodesh Kislev or 1st week		Bat	10	Rabbi Shimon—be careful in reciting the ***Shemah* and the *Shmoneh Esreh***. Do not make of your prayer a routine act	*Tiferet shebeGevurah*
Yud Kislev	*Erev Yom HaShoah* **Latest proper time to recite the *Shmoneh Esreh***	Stork	11	Rabbi Elazar—know what to answer the heretic and be diligent in your Torah study.	*Netzach shebeGevurah*
Yud Tet Kislev	*Yom HaShoah*	Raven	12	Rabbi Tarfon—the day is short, the work is great, the workers are lazy, the reward is big, and the Owner is pressing.	*Hod shebeGevurah*

a holiday, but it will be repaid with the inauguration of the Third Temple. The First Temple was completed in *Cheshvan*, inaugurated on the 8th of *Tishrei*, and the festivities lasted until the 22nd day of that month. It therefore appears likely that the future Third Temple holiday will extend from the 8th to the 22nd day of *Cheshvan*.

Chanukah		Starling	13	Akaviah ben Mahalalel—know from where you come and to where you are going, and before Whom you will be judged.	*Yesod shebeGevurah*
Chanukah/Rosh Chodesh Tevet	Erev Rosh Chodesh Iyar	Domestic Goose	14	Rabbi Chaninah, *Segan Kohen Gadol*—pray for the welfare of the government, for if it were not for the fear of it . . .	*Malchut shebeGevurah*
10th of *Teveth*	Rosh Chodesh Iyar	Wild Goose	15	Rabbi Chaninah ben Teradion—if two people are sitting together and do not exchange words of Torah . . .	*Chesed shebeTiferet*
Third Week of Tevet	Rosh Chodesh Iyar	Ducks	16	Rabbi Shimon [Bar Yochai]—Three people that ate together and did not say words of Torah . . .	*Gevurah shebeTiferet*
Fourth Week of Tevet	**Chatzot (midday—latest time for morning prayers**	Bee-Eater **(Last bird)**	17	Rabbi Chaninah ben Chachinai—one who is awake at night or travels on the road, and turns his heart to idleness . . .	*Tiferet shebeTiferet*
Rosh Chodesh Shvat	**Minchah Gedolah (earliest time for Minchah)**	Grasshopper **(first insect)**	18	Rabbi Nechuniah—one who takes upon oneself the yoke of Torah, the yoke of making a living and of government are removed from him	*Netzach shebeTiferet*
Yud Shvat	Yom HaZikaron	Locust	19	Rabbi Chalaftah—ten men that are gathered and occupy themselves in Torah . . .	*Hod shebeTiferet*

Tu B'Shvat	*Yom Ha'Atzma'ut*	Spider	20	Rabbi Elazar de Bartota—give to Him what is His, for you and all that is yours is His.	*Yesod shebeTiferet*
Fourth Week of *Shvat*		Fly	21	Rabbi Yaakov—whoever is travelling on the road while studying and interrupts to exclaim how beautiful is this tree . . .	*Malchut shebeTiferet*
Rosh Chodesh Adar		Sea Monsters	22	Rabbi Dostai, ben Yanai—one who forgets their Torah knowledge . . .	*Chesed shebeNetzach*
First Week of *Adar*		Leviathan	23	Rabbi Chaninah ben Dossah—one whose fear of sin is greater than his wisdom, his wisdom will endure . . .	*Gevurah shebeNetzach*
Purim		Fish	24	Rabbi Dossah ben Harkinas—the sleep of the morning, wine of the afternoon, the talk of children, and meeting places of the ignorant . . .	*Tiferet shebeNetzach*
Third Week of *Adar*		Frog	25	Rabbi Elazar, the Modahite—one who profanes sacred objects, degrades the festivals, humiliates other in public . . .	*Netzach shebeNetzach*
Rosh Chodesh Nissan	**Minchah Ketanah**	Sheep and Goat (**first farm animal**)	26	Rabbi Yishmael—be submissive to the head, and courteous to the young, and receive every person with joy.	*Hod shebeNetzach*
First Week of *Nissan*		Cow	27	Rabbi Akiva—jest and frivolity accustom a person to lust . . . everything is prepared for the banquet	*Yesod shebeNetzach*

First Day of Pessach	Erev Pessach Sheni	Pig and Rabbit	28	Rabbi Elazar ben Azariah—without Torah there is no common decency . . . without flour there is no Torah . . .	Malchut shebeNetzach
Pessach	Pessach Sheni **Plag Haminchah**	Beast of Burden **(first animal used for carrying)**	29	Rabbi Elazar ben Chismah—the laws of bird sacrifices and menstrual periods are essential . . .	Chesed shebeHod
Fourth Week of Nissan		Camel	30	Ben Zomah—Who is wise? One that learns from everyone	Gevurah shebeHod
Rosh Chodesh Iyar/ 5 de Iyar	**Candle Lighting**	Horse	31	Ben Azai—run to pursue a mitzvah, and flee from transgression. A mitzvah attracts another mitzvah . . .	Tiferet shebeHod
Second Week of Iyar		Mule	32	Rabbi Levitas of Yavneh—be extremely humble, because the hope of mortal man is worms . . .	Netzach shebeHod
Pessach Sheini/ Lag Ba'Omer	Lag Ba'Omer **Shkiah (sunset)**	Donkey	33	Rabbi Yochanan ben Berokah—whoever profanes the Divine Name in secret will be punished in public . . .	Hod shebeHod
Fourth Week of Iyar	**Tzeit Hakochovim (nightfall)**	Ox **(last farm animal, and last animal used for carrying)**	34	Rabbi Yishmael the son of Rabbi Yossi—one who studies Torah in order to teach is given the opportunity to learn and teach; one that studies Torah in order to practice . . .	Yesod shebeHod
Rosh Chodesh Sivan/ Yom Yerushalayim		Wild Animals	35	Rabbi Tzadok—do not separate yourself from the community . . . do not make the Torah into a crown to glorify yourself	Malchut shebeHod

Shavuot		Gazelle	36	Rabbi Yossi—one that honors the Torah will be honored by men . . .	Chesed shebe Yesod
Third Week of Sivan		Elephant	37	Rabbi Yishmael—one who refrains from serving as a judge avoid hatred, theft and false oaths.	Gevurah shebe Yesod
Fourth Week of Sivan		Lion	38	Rabbi Yonatan—whoever fulfills the Torah in poverty will ultimately fulfill it in wealth . . .	Tiferet shebe Yesod
Rosh Chodesh Tammuz/ 3rd of Tammuz		Bear	39	Rabbi Meir—engage minimally in business, and occupy yourself with Torah . . .	Netzach shebe Yesod
Second Week of Tammuz		Wolf	40	Rabbi Eliezer—one who fulfills one mitzvah acquires an advocate for himself . . .	Hod shebe Yesod
12th and 13th of Tammuz/ 17th of Tammuz		Fox	41	Rabbi Yochanan HaSandlar—every gathering that is for the sake of Heaven will endure . . .	Yesod shebe Yesod
Fourth Week of Tammuz	Erev Yom Yerushalayim	Hound	42	Rabbi Eliezer ben Shammuah—the honor of your student should be as precious to you as your own . . .	Malchut shebe Yesod
Rosh Chodesh Av	Yom Yerushalayim	Cat	43	Rabbi Yehudah—be careful in your studies, for an error in learning it tantamount to a willful sin.	Chesed shebeMalchut
Tisha B'Av	Erev Rosh Chodesh Sivan **End of the first watch of the night**	Mouse **(last house animal)**	44	Rabbi Nehorai—exile yourself to a place of Torah; do not say that it will come after you . . . rely not on your own understanding.	Gevurah shebeMalchut

Tu B'Av	*Rosh Chodesh Sivan*	Creeping Creatures	45	Rabbi Yanai—we cannot comprehend the tranquility of the wicked or the suffering of the righteous . . .	*Tiferet shebeMalchut*
Third Week of *Av*		Prolific Creeping Creatures	46	Rabbi Matiah ben Charash—be first to greet every man. Be a tail to lions, rather than a head to foxes.	*Netzach shebeMalchut*
Rosh Chodesh Elul	*Yemei Hagbalah*	Snake	47	Rabbi Yaakov—this world is like an antechamber for the World to Come . . .	*Hod shebeMalchut*
First Week of *Elul*	*Yemei Hagbalah*	Scorpion	48	Rabbi Shimon ben Elazar—do not attempt to appease your friend at the moment of his anger . . .	*Yesod shebeMalchut*
Second Week of *Elul*	*Yemei Hagbalah*	Snail	49	Shmuel the Small—when your enemy falls, do not rejoice . . .	*Malchut shebeMalchut*
Chai Elul	*Shavuot*	Ant	50	Elishah ben Avuyah—one who learns Torah in his childhood, to what is he compared? To ink on fresh paper . . .	*Shavuot— Chochmah*
Fourth Week of *Elul/Slichot*	*Shavuot*	Weasel	51	Rabbi Yossi ben Yehudah of Kfar Bavli—one who learns Torah from youngsters . . .	*Shavuot— Binah*
Slichot/Rosh Hashanah	*Isru Chag/Pessach* **Chatzot** (midnight)	Dogs **(last animals)**	52	Rabbi Elazar HaKappar—envy, lust, and honor take a man out of the world . . . Those who are born will die, and the dead will live [again] . . .	*Shavuot— Da'at/ Keter*

265

Explanation for the Week of Purim:

By looking at the above table, one can see that, for the most part, the weeks in which there are holidays in the Jewish calendar match important days during the Counting of the *Omer* (such as holidays and *Rosh Chodesh*, or the eve of such dates). The only major exceptions to this appear to be the weeks that include the weeks with holidays that fall during the Counting of the *Omer* itself (such as the week of *Yom Ha'Atzmaut, Yom Yerushalayim*, and *Shavuot*) and Purim. It is understandable that the weeks of the first set of holidays would not be able to have matches, since the very days of each of these holidays are matched with other weeks. However, why Purim does not appear to have a parallel during the Counting of the *Omer* appears to be somewhat of a conundrum.

A likely explanation is that the week of Purim actually matches *Yom Ha'Atzmaut* as well. The story of Purim somewhat parallels that of *Yom Ha'Atzmaut*. On Purim, a leader of Amalek got enormous power, and tried to annihilate us completely. We survived, and were victorious in miraculous ways that seemed natural. G-d was "Hidden." In the next generation, the Jewish people were permitted to return to their land. On *Yom Ha'Atzmaut*, history seemed to repeat itself. At the time of the Holocaust, a leader of Amalek gained enormous power and tried to annihilate us completely. We survived, many of us in miraculous ways, but G-d seemed to be completely "Hidden." Some years later, the United Nations recognized our right to the Land of Israel; we won a War of Independence; and established a Jewish government in our land.

Before Purim, there is a day of fasting, *Ta'anit Esther*. Before *Yom Ha'Atzmaut* there is also a solemn day, *Yom HaZikaron*, the day they remember the soldiers who died in recent wars, as well as victims of terrorism. *Ta'anit Esther* also commemorates the Jewish people fast before they went to war against their enemies at the time.

The *Mishnah* in the tractate of *Megillah* explains that one can read the *Megillah* from the 11th of *Adar* until the 15th. Our rabbis instituted that the *Megillah* could be read earlier (or later) in the countryside, for people who could not easily assemble on the 14th of *Adar*. The difference between the 11th and the 15th of *Adar* is 4 days. This is the very difference between day 20 of the *omer* (*Yom Ha'Atzmaut*) and the 24th day of the *omer*, which would match the week of Purim. It is very interesting to note that in Israel today *Yom Ha'Atzmaut* is often not celebrated on the 5th of *Iyar*. To prevent any violation of Shabbat, our rabbis instituted that we commemorate *Yom HaZikaron* and *Yom Ha'Atzmaut* on different dates, just like the reading of the *Megillah* was often done on different dates. For example, in year 5771, because the 4th of *Iyar* fell on a Sunday, *Yom HaZikaron* was commemorated on Monday the 5th, and *Yom Ha'Atzmaut* on Tuesday, the 6th of *Iyar*. Theoretically, if *Yom HaZikaron* fell on a Thursday, and *Yom Ha'Atzmaut* on Friday, these holidays could be postponed and celebrated on the following Monday and Tuesday, four days later. *Yom Ha'Atzmaut* would then fall on the 24th day of the *omer*, corresponding to week 24 of the year, the week of Purim. So far, the custom now has been to celebrate *Yom HaZikaron* and *Yom Ha'Atzmaut* a day earlier instead.

Table II: Cycles of 50 Years, with Historical Events Taking Place Mostly in Years 31-34 and 51-52; Leadership of Chassidic Movement and Chabad

1. Chassidic Movement	1	1666	Shabtai Tzvi disgrace, not long after Chimelnicky massacres.	Fellowship of Hidden Tzadikim
Turning Point	33	1698	Birth of the Ba'al Shem Tov	Fellowship of Hidden Tzadikim
2. Chassidic and Lithuanian Systems	52/ 2	1717 (1720)	Birth of Rebbe Elimelech of Lizhensk, brother of Reb Zushya of Anipoli (Birth of the Vilna Gaon)	Ba'al Shem Tov (1716-1760)
Turning Point	31-34	1746-1749	Birth of the Alter Rebbe (*Elul* 1745) and Rav Chayim of Volozhin	Ba'al Shem Tov (1716-1760)
3. Second Generation Chassidic Movement	51/1	1766	Birth of Yaakov Yitzchak Rabinowicz, the "Yid haKodesh"	Magid of Mezeritch (1761-1772), Leadership Divided
Turning Point	31-33	1796-1798	Birth of the Ruzhiner Rebbe; Publication of the Tanya; *Yud Tet Kislev*	Alter Rebbe (1798-1812)
4. Jewish Emancipation	52/2	1815	Pope forbids giving more rights to the Jews, and they lose the few rights they had received.	Mitteler Rebbe (1813-1827)
Turning Point	33-34	1848-1849	Revolutions in Europe give Jews complete civil rights in many countries.	Tzemach Tzedek (1827-1866)
5. Zionism	51/1	1866	Birth of Rabbi Avraham Yitzchak Kook (*Elul* 1865)	Rebbe Maharash (1866-1882[180\])
Turning Point	31-34	1896-1899	Publication of "The Jewish State." WZO and Jewish Colonial Trust established	Rebbe Rashab (1893-1920)

The Rebbe Maharash passed away at the young age of 48, when the Rebbe Rashab was only 21 years old. The Rebbe Rashab officially became Rebbe at the age of 32.

6. Israel's Independence	52/2	1917	World War I; Balfour Declaration. Beginning of British Mandate	Rebbe Rayatz (1920-1950)
Turning Point	32-34	1947-1949	War of Independence, Declaration of State, shortly after the Holocaust	The Rebbe (1950-1994)
7. Modern Israel	52/2	1967	Six Day War, *Yom Yerushalayim*	The Rebbe (1950-1994)
Turning Point	31-34	1996-1999	Benjamin Netanyahu is prime minister after surprise victory.	Brotherhood of Chassidim

TABLE III: DATES OF THE WEEKS OF THE "ANNUAL OMER COUNT" (5772-5780)

Starting from *Adar* (or *Adar II* in case of a leap year) the dates are always the same

	5772	5773	5774	5775	5776	5777	5778	5779	5780
Days of the Week	Sunday-Saturday	Wednesday-Tuesday	Wednesday-Tuesday	Sunday-Saturday	Sunday-Saturday	Wednesday-Tuesday	Sunday-Saturday	Sunday-Saturday	Friday-Thursday
1	26 Elul-3 Tishrei	25 Elul-2 Tishrei	29 Elul-6 Tishrei	26 Elul-3 Tishrei	29 Elul-6 Tishrei	25 Elul-2 Tishrei	26 Elul-3 Tishrei	29 Elul-6 Tishrei	27 Elul-4 Tishrei
2	4-10 Tishrei	3-9 Tishrei	7-13 Tishrei	4-10 Tishrei	7-13 Tishrei	3-9 Tishrei	4-10 Tishrei	7-13 Tishrei	5-11 Tishrei
3	11-17 Tishrei	10-16 Tishrei	14-20 Tishrei	11-17 Tishrei	14-20 Tishrei	10-16 Tishrei	11-17 Tishrei	14-20 Tishrei	12-18 Tishrei
4	18-24 Tishrei	17-23 Tishrei	21-27 Tishrei	18-24 Tishrei	21-27 Tishrei	17-23 Tishrei	18-24 Tishrei	21-27 Tishrei	19-25 Tishrei
5	25 Tishrei-1 Cheshvan	24-30 Tishrei (Rosh Chodesh Cheshvan)	28 Tishrei-4 Cheshvan	25 Tishrei-1 Cheshvan	28 Tishrei-4 Cheshvan	24-30 Tishrei (Rosh Chodesh Cheshvan)	25 Tishrei-1 Cheshvan	28 Tishrei-4 Cheshvan	26 Tishrei-2 Cheshvan
6	2-8 Cheshvan	1-7 Cheshvan	5-11 Cheshvan	2-8 Cheshvan	5-11 Cheshvan	1-7 Cheshvan	2-8 Cheshvan	5-11 Cheshvan	3-9 Cheshvan
7	9-15 Cheshvan	8-14 Cheshvan	12-18 Cheshvan	9-15 Cheshvan	12-18 Cheshvan	8-14 Cheshvan	9-15 Cheshvan	12-18 Cheshvan	10-16 Cheshvan
8	16-22 Cheshvan	15-21 Cheshvan	19-25 Cheshvan	16-22 Cheshvan	19-25 Cheshvan	15-21 Cheshvan	16-22 Cheshvan	19-25 Cheshvan	17-23 Cheshvan
9	23-29 Cheshvan	22-28 Cheshvan	26 Cheshvan-2 Kislev	23-29 Cheshvan	26 Cheshvan-2 Kislev	22-28 Cheshvan	23-29 Cheshvan	26 Cheshvan-2 Kislev	24-30 Cheshvan (Rosh Chodesh Kislev)
10	1-7 Kislev	29 Cheshvan-6 Kislev	3-9 Kislev	1-7 Kislev	3-9 Kislev	29 Cheshvan-6 Kislev	1-7 Kislev	3-9 Kislev	1-7 Kislev
11	8-14 Kislev	7-13 Kislev	10-16 Kislev	8-14 Kislev	10-16 Kislev	7-13 Kislev	8-14 Kislev	10-16 Kislev	8-14 Kislev
12	15-21 Kislev	14-20 Kislev	17-23 Kislev	15-21 Kislev	17-23 Kislev	14-20 Kislev	15-21 Kislev	17-23 Kislev	15-21 Kislev

13	22-28 Kislev	21-27 Kislev	24-30 Kislev (Rosh Chodesh Tevet)	22-28 Kislev	24-30 Kislev (Rosh Chodesh Tevet)	21-27 Kislev	22-28 Kislev	24-30 Kislev (Rosh Chodesh Tevet)	22-28 Kislev
14	29 Kislev-5 Tevet	28 Kislev-5 Tevet	1 Tevet-7 Tevet	29 Kislev-5 Tevet	1 Tevet-7 Tevet	28 Kislev-5 Tevet	29 Kislev-5 Tevet	1 Tevet-7 Tevet	29 Kislev-5 Tevet
15	6-12 Tevet	6-12 Tevet	8-14 Tevet	6-12 Tevet	8-14 Tevet	6-12 Tevet	6-12 Tevet	8-14 Tevet	6-12 Tevet
16	13-19 Tevet	13-19 Tevet	15-21 Tevet	13-19 Tevet	15-21 Tevet	13-19 Tevet	13-19 Tevet	15-21 Tevet	13-19 Tevet
17	20-26 Tevet	20-26 Tevet	22-28 Tevet	20-26 Tevet	22-28 Tevet	20-26 Tevet	20-26 Tevet	22-28 Tevet	20-26 Tevet
18	27 Tevet-4 Shevat	27 Tevet-4 Shevat	29 Tevet-6 Shevat	27 Tevet-4 Shevat	29 Tevet-6 Shevat	27 Tevet-4 Shevat	27 Tevet-4 Shevat	29 Tevet-6 Shevat	27 Tevet-4 Shevat
19	5 Shevat-11 Shevat	5 Shevat-11 Shevat	7 Shevat-13 Shevat	5 Shevat-11 Shevat	7 Shevat-13 Shevat	5 Shevat-11 Shevat	5 Shevat-11 Shevat	7 Shevat-13 Shevat	5 Shevat-11 Shevat
20	12-18 Shevat	12-18 Shevat	14-20 Shevat	12-18 Shevat	14-20 Shevat	12-18 Shevat	12-18 Shevat	14-20 Shevat	12-18 Shevat
21	19-25 Shevat	19-25 Shevat	21-27 Shevat	19-25 Shevat	21-27 Shevat	19-25 Shevat	19-25 Shevat	21-27 Shevat	19-25 Shevat
22	26 Shevat-2 Adar	26 Shevat-2 Adar	28 Shevat-4 Adar I	26 Shevat-2 Adar	28 Shevat-4 Adar I	26 Shevat-2 Adar	26 Shevat-2 Adar	28 Shevat-4 Adar I	26 Shevat-2 Adar
(23)			5-11 Adar I		5-11 Adar I			5-11 Adar I	
(24)			12-18 Adar I		12-18 Adar I			12-18 Adar I	
(25)			19-25 Adar I		19-25 Adar I			19-25 Adar I	
(22)			26 Adar I-2 Adar II		26 Adar I-2 Adar II			26 Adar I-2 Adar II	
23	3-9 Adar (II)								
24	10-16 Adar (II)								
25	17-23 Adar (II)								
26	24 Adar (II)-1 Nissan								
27	2-8 Nissan								
28	9-15 Nissan								
29	16-22 Nissan								
30	23-29 Nissan								
31	30 Nissan (Rosh Chodesh Iyar)-6 Iyar								

32	7-13 Iyar
33	14-20 Iyar
34	21-27 Iyar
35	28 Iyar-5 Sivan
36	6-12 Sivan
37	13-19 Sivan
38	20-26 Sivan
39	27 Sivan-3 *Tammuz*
40	4-10 *Tammuz*
41	11-17 *Tammuz*
42	18-24 *Tammuz*
43	25 *Tammuz*-2 Av
44	3 Av-9 Av
45	10-16 Av
46	17-23 Av
47	24-30 Av (Rosh Chodesh Elul)
48	1-7 Elul
49	8-14 Elul
50	15-21 Elul
51	22-28 Elul
52	29 Elul-6 Tishrei

5774 Calendar with Numbers for Each Week and Sefirot for Each Day

September 2013

Sunday	Monday	Tuesday	Wednesday	Thursday	Friday	Saturday
1	2	3	4 (WEEK 1) 29th of Elul 5773 Erev Rosh Hashana *Chesed* *shebeChesed* *shebeChesed*	5 1st of Tishrei Rosh Hashana *Gevurah* *shebeChesed* *shebeChesed*	6 2nd of Tishrei Rosh Hashana II *Tiferet* *shebeChesed* *shebeChesed*	7 3rd of Tishrei *Netzach* *shebeChesed* *shebeChesed*
8 4th of Tishrei Tzom Gedaliah *Hod* *shebeChesed* *shebeChesed*	9 5th of Tishrei *Yesod* *shebeChesed* *shebeChesed*	10 6th of Tishrei *Malchut* *shebeChesed* *shebeChesed*	11 (WEEK 2) 7th of Tishrei *Chesed* *shebeGevurah* *shebeChesed*	12 8th of Tishrei *Gevurah* *shebeGevurah* *shebeChesed*	13 9th of Tishrei Erev Yom Kippur *Tiferet* *shebeGevurah* *shebeChesed*	14 10th of Tishrei Yom Kippur *Netzach* *shebeGevurah* *shebeChesed*
15 11th of Tishrei *Hod* *shebeGevurah* *shebeChesed*	16 12th of Tishrei *Yesod* *shebeGevurah* *shebeChesed*	17 13th of Tishrei *Malchut* *shebeGevurah* *shebeChesed*	18 (WEEK 3) 14th of Tishrei Erev Sukkot *Chesed* *shebeTiferet* *shebeChesed*	19 15th of Tishrei Sukkot I *Gevurah* *shebeTiferet* *shebeChesed*	20 16th of Tishrei Sukkot II *Tiferet* *shebeTiferet* *shebeChesed*	21 17th of Tishrei Sukkot III *Netzach* *shebeTiferet* *shebeChesed*
22 18th of Tishrei Sukkot IV *Hod* *shebeTiferet* *shebeChesed*	23 19th of Tishrei Sukkot V *Yesod* *shebeTiferet* *shebeChesed*	24 20th of Tishrei Sukkot VI *Malchut* *shebeTiferet* *shebeChesed*	25 (WEEK 4) 21st of Tishrei Sukkot VII (Hoshana Raba) *Chesed* *shebeNetzach* *shebeChesed*	26 22nd of Tishrei Shmini Atzeret *Gevurah* *shebeNetzach* *shebeChesed*	27 23rd of Tishrei Simchat Torah *Tiferet* *shebeNetzach* *shebeChesed*	28 24th of Tishrei *Netzach* *shebeNetzach* *shebeChesed*
29 25th of Tishrei *Hod* *shebeNetzach* *shebeChesed*	30 26th of Tishrei *Yesod* *shebeNetzach* *shebeChesed*					

October 2013

Sunday	Monday	Tuesday	Wednesday	Thursday	Friday	Saturday
		1 27th of Tishrei *Malchut* *shebeNetzach* *shebeChesed*	2 (WEEK 5) 28th of Tishrei *Chesed* *shebeHod* *shebeChesed*	3 29th of Tishrei *Gevurah* *shebeHod* *shebeChesed*	4 30th of Tishrei Rosh Chodesh Cheshvan *Tiferet* *shebeHod* *shebeChesed*	5 1st of Cheshvan Rosh Chodesh Cheshvan *Netzach* *shebeHod* *shebeChesed*
6 2nd of Cheshvan *Hod* *shebeHod* *shebeChesed*	7 3rd of Cheshvan *Yesod* *shebeHod* *shebeChesed*	8 4th of Cheshvan *Malchut* *shebeHod* *shebeChesed*	9 (WEEK 6) 5th of Cheshvan *Chesed* *shebeYesod* *shebeChesed*	10 6th of Cheshvan *Gevurah* *shebeYesod* *shebeChesed*	11 7th of Cheshvan *Tiferet* *shebeYesod* *shebeChesed*	12 8th of Cheshvan *shebeYesod* *shebeChesed*
13 9th of Cheshvan *Hod* *shebeYesod* *shebeChesed*	14 10th of Cheshvan *Yesod* *shebeYesod* *shebeChesed*	15 11th of Cheshvan *Malchut* *shebeYesod* *shebeChesed*	16 (WEEK 7) 12th of Cheshvan *Chesed* *shebeMalchut* *shebeChesed*	17 13th of Cheshvan *Gevurah* *shebeMalchut* *shebeChesed*	18 14th of Cheshvan *Tiferet* *shebeMalchut* *shebeChesed*	19 15th of Cheshvan *Netzach* *shebeMalchut* *shebeChesed*
20 16th of Cheshvan *Hod* *shebeMalchut* *shebeChesed*	21 17th of Cheshvan *Yesod* *shebeMalchut* *shebeChesed*	22 18th of Cheshvan *Malchut* *shebeMalchut* *shebeChesed*	23 (WEEK 8) 19th of Cheshvan *Chesed* *shebeChesed* *shebeGevurah*	24 20th of Cheshvan *Gevurah* *shebeChesed* *shebeGevurah*	25 21st of Cheshvan *Tiferet* *shebeChesed* *shebeGevurah*	26 22nd of Cheshvan *Netzach* *shebeChesed* *shebeGevurah*
27 23rd of Cheshvan *Hod* *shebeChesed* *shebeGevurah*	28 24th of Cheshvan *Yesod* *shebeChesed* *shebeGevurah*	29 25th of Cheshvan *Malchut* *shebeChesed* *shebeGevurah*	30 (WEEK 9) 26th of Cheshvan *Chesed* *shebeGevurah* *shebeGevurah*	31 27th of Cheshvan *Gevurah* *shebeGevurah* *shebeGevurah*		

November 2013

Sunday	Monday	Tuesday	Wednesday	Thursday	Friday	Saturday
					1 28th of Cheshvan *Tiferet* *shebeGevurah* *shebeGevurah*	**2** 29th of Cheshvan *Netzach* *shebeGevurah* *shebeGevurah*
3 30th of Cheshvan Rosh Chodesh Kislev *Hod* *shebeGevurah* *shebeGevurah*	**4** 1st of Kislev Rosh Chodesh Kislev *Yesod* *shebeGevurah* *shebeGevurah*	**5** 2nd of Kislev *Malchut* *shebeGevurah* *shebeGevurah*	**6 (WEEK 10)** 3rd of Kislev *Chesed* *shebeTiferet* *shebeGevurah*	**7** 4th of Kislev *Gevurah* *shebeTiferet* *shebeGevurah*	**8** 5th of Kislev *Tiferet* *shebeTiferet* *shebeGevurah*	**9** 6th of Kislev *Netzach* *shebeTiferet* *shebeGevurah*
10 7th of Kislev *Hod* *shebeTiferet* *shebeGevurah*	**11** 8th of Kislev *Yesod* *shebeTiferet* *shebeGevurah*	**12** 9th of Kislev *Malchut* *shebeTiferet* *shebeGevurah*	**13 (WEEK 11)** 10th of Kislev *Chesed* *shebeNetzach* *shebeGevurah*	**14** 11th of Kislev *Gevurah* *shebeNetzach* *shebeGevurah*	**15** 12th of Kislev *Tiferet* *shebeNetzach* *shebeGevurah*	**16** 13th of Kislev *Netzach* *shebeNetzach* *shebeGevurah*
17 14th of Kislev *shebeNetzach* *shebeGevurah*	**18** 15th of Kislev *Yesod* *shebeNetzach* *shebeGevurah*	**19** 16th of Kislev *Malchut* *shebeNetzach* *shebeGevurah*	**20 (WEEK 12)** 17th of Kislev *Chesed* *shebeHod* *shebeGevurah*	**21** 18th of Kislev *Gevurah* *shebeHod* *shebeGevurah*	**22** 19th of Kislev *Tiferet* *shebeHod* *shebeGevurah*	**23** 20th of Kislev *Netzach* *shebeHod* *shebeGevurah*
24 21st of Kislev *Hod* *shebeHod* *shebeGevurah*	**25** 22nd of Kislev *Yesod* *shebeHod* *shebeGevurah*	**26** 23rd of Kislev *Malchut* *shebeHod* *shebeGevurah*	**27 (WEEK 13)** 24th of Kislev Chanukah *Chesed* *shebeYesod* *shebeGevurah*	**28** 25th of Kislev Chanukah *Gevurah* *shebeYesod* *shebeGevurah*	**29** 26th of Kislev Chanukah *Tiferet* *shebeYesod* *shebeGevurah*	**30** 27th of Kislev Chanukah *Netzach* *shebeYesod* *shebeGevurah*

December 2013

Sunday	Monday	Tuesday	Wednesday	Thursday	Friday	Saturday
1 28th of Kislev Chanukah *Hod* *shebeYesod* *shebeGevurah*	2 29th of Kislev Chanukah *Yesod* *shebeYesod* *shebeGevurah*	3 30th of Kislev Rosh Chodesh Tevet Chanukah *Malchut* *shebeYesod* *shebeGevurah*	4 (WEEK 14) 1st of Tevet Rosh Chodesh Tevet Chanukah *Chesed* *shebeMalchut* *shebeGevurah*	5 2nd of Tevet Chanukah: 8th Day *Gevurah* *shebeMalchut* *shebeGevurah*	6 3rd of Tevet *Tiferet* *shebeMalchut* *shebeGevurah*	7 4th of Tevet *Netzach* *shebeMalchut* *shebeGevurah*
8 5th of Tevet *Hod* *shebeMalchut* *shebeGevurah*	9 6th of Tevet *Yesod* *shebeMalchut* *shebeGevurah*	10 7th of Tevet *Malchut* *shebeMalchut* *shebeGevurah*	11 (WEEK 15) 8th of Tevet *Chesed* *shebeChesed* *shebe Tiferet*	12 9th of Tevet *Gevurah* *shebeChesed* *shebe Tiferet*	13 10th of Tevet Asara B'Tevet *Tiferet* *shebeChesed* *shebe Tiferet*	14 11th of Tevet *Netzach* *shebeChesed* *shebe Tiferet*
15 12th of Tevet *Hod* *shebeChesed* *shebe Tiferet*	16 13th of Tevet *Yesod* *shebeChesed* *shebe Tiferet*	17 14th of Tevet *Malchut* *shebeChesed* *shebe Tiferet*	18 (WEEK 16) 15th of Tevet *Chesed* *shebeGevurah* *shebe Tiferet*	19 16th of Tevet *Gevurah* *shebeGevurah* *shebe Tiferet*	20 17th of Tevet *Tiferet* *shebeGevurah* *shebe Tiferet*	21 18th of Tevet *Netzach* *shebeGevurah* *shebe Tiferet*
22 19th of Tevet *Hod* *shebeGevurah* *shebe Tiferet*	23 20th of Tevet *Yesod* *shebeGevurah* *shebe Tiferet*	24 21st of Tevet *Malchut* *shebeGevurah* *shebe Tiferet*	25 (WEEK 17) 22nd of Tevet *Chesed* *shebe Tiferet* *shebe Tiferet*	26 23rd of Tevet *Gevurah* *shebe Tiferet* *shebe Tiferet*	27 24th of Tevet *Tiferet* *shebe Tiferet* *shebe Tiferet*	28 25th of Tevet *Netzach* *shebe Tiferet* *shebe Tiferet*
29 26th of Tevet *Hod* *shebe Tiferet* *shebe Tiferet*	30 27th of Tevet *Yesod* *shebe Tiferet* *shebe Tiferet*	31 28th of Tevet *Malchut* *shebe Tiferet* *shebe Tiferet*				

January 2014

Sunday	Monday	Tuesday	Wednesday	Thursday	Friday	Saturday
			1 (WEEK 18) 29th of Tevet *Chesed shebeNetzach shebe Tiferet*	**2** 1st of Sh'vat Rosh Chodesh Sh'vat *Gevurah shebeNetzach shebe Tiferet*	**3** 2nd of Sh'vat *Tiferet shebeNetzach shebe Tiferet*	**4** 3rd of Sh'vat *Netzach shebeNetzach shebe Tiferet*
5 4th of Sh'vat *Hod shebeNetzach shebe Tiferet*	**6** 5th of Sh'vat *Yesod shebeNetzach shebe Tiferet*	**7** 6th of Sh'vat *Malchut shebeNetzach shebe Tiferet*	**8 (WEEK 19)** 7th of Sh'vat *Chesed shebeHod shebe Tiferet*	**9** 8th of Sh'vat *Gevurah shebeHod shebe Tiferet*	**10** 9th of Sh'vat *Tiferet shebeHod shebe Tiferet*	**11** 10th of Sh'vat *Netzach shebeHod shebe Tiferet*
12 11th of Sh'vat *Hod shebeHod shebe Tiferet*	**13** 12th of Sh'vat *Yesod shebeHod shebe Tiferet*	**14** 13th of Sh'vat *Malchut shebeHod shebe Tiferet*	**15 (WEEK 20)** 14th of Sh'vat *Chesed shebeYesod shebe Tiferet*	**16** 15th of Sh'vat Tu BiShvat *Gevurah shebeYesod shebe Tiferet*	**17** 16th of Sh'vat *Tiferet shebeYesod shebe Tiferet*	**18** 17th of Sh'vat *Netzach shebeYesod shebe Tiferet*
19 18th of Sh'vat *Hod shebeYesod shebe Tiferet*	**20** 19th of Sh'vat *Yesod shebeYesod shebe Tiferet*	**21** 20th of Sh'vat *Malchut shebeYesod shebe Tiferet*	**22 (WEEK 21)** 21st of Sh'vat *Chesed shebeMalchut shebe Tiferet*	**23** 22nd of Sh'vat *Gevurah shebeMalchut shebe Tiferet*	**24** 23rd of Sh'vat *Tiferet shebeMalchut shebe Tiferet*	**25** 24th of Sh'vat *Netzach shebeMalchut shebe Tiferet*
26 25th of Sh'vat *Hod shebeMalchut shebe Tiferet*	**27** 26th of Sh'vat *Yesod shebeMalchut shebe Tiferet*	**28** 27th of Sh'vat *Malchut shebeMalchut shebe Tiferet*	**29 (WEEK 22)** 28th of Sh'vat *Chesed shebeChesed shebeNetzach*	**30** 29th of Sh'vat *Gevurah shebeChesed shebeNetzach*	**31** 30th of Sh'vat Rosh Chodesh Adar I *Tiferet shebeChesed shebeNetzach*	

February 2014

Sunday	Monday	Tuesday	Wednesday	Thursday	Friday	Saturday
						1 1st of Adar I Rosh Chodesh Adar I *Netzach* *shebeChesed* *shebeNetzach*
2 2nd of Adar I *Hod* *shebeChesed* *shebeNetzach*	**3** 3rd of Adar I *Yesod* *shebeChesed* *shebeNetzach*	**4** 4th of Adar I *Malchut* *shebeChesed* *shebeNetzach*	**5 (WEEK 23)** 5th of Adar I *Chesed* *shebeGevurah* *shebeNetzach*	**6** 6th of Adar I *Gevurah* *shebeGevurah* *shebeNetzach*	**7** 7th of Adar I *Tiferet* *shebeGevurah* *shebeNetzach*	**8** 8th of Adar I *Netzach* *shebeGevurah* *shebeNetzach*
9 9th of Adar I *Hod* *shebeGevurah* *shebeNetzach*	**10** 10th of Adar I *Yesod* *shebeGevurah* *shebeNetzach*	**11** 11th of Adar I *Malchut* *shebeGevurah* *shebeNetzach*	**12 (WEEK 24)** 12th of Adar I *Chesed* *shebeTiferet* *shebeNetzach*	**13** 13th of Adar I *Gevurah* *shebeTiferet* *shebeNetzach*	**14** 14th of Adar I Purim Katan *Tiferet* *shebeTiferet* *shebeNetzach*	**15** 15th of Adar I *Netzach* *shebeTiferet* *shebeNetzach*
16 16th of Adar I *Hod* *shebeTiferet* *shebeNetzach*	**17** 17th of Adar I *Yesod* *shebeTiferet* *shebeNetzach*	**18** 18th of Adar I *Malchut* *shebeTiferet* *shebeNetzach*	**19 (WEEK 25)** 19th of Adar I *Chesed* *shebeNetzach* *shebeNetzach*	**20** 20th of Adar I *Gevurah* *shebeNetzach* *shebeNetzach*	**21** 21st of Adar I *Tiferet* *shebeNetzach* *shebeNetzach*	**22** 22nd of Adar I *Netzach* *shebeNetzach* *shebeNetzach*
23 23rd of Adar I *Hod* *shebeNetzach* *shebeNetzach*	**24** 24th of Adar I *Yesod* *shebeNetzach* *shebeNetzach*	**25** 25th of Adar I *Malchut* *shebeNetzach* *shebeNetzach*	**26 (WEEK 22)** 26th of Adar I *Chesed* *shebeChesed* *shebeNetzach*	**27** 27th of Adar I *Gevurah* *shebeChesed* *shebeNetzach*	**28** 28th of Adar I *Tiferet* *shebeChesed* *shebeNetzach*	

March 2014

Sunday	Monday	Tuesday	Wednesday	Thursday	Friday	Saturday
						1 29th of Adar I *Netzach* *shebeChesed* *shebeNetzach*
2 30th of Adar I Rosh Chodesh Adar II *Hod* *shebeChesed* *shebeNetzach*	**3** 1st of Adar II Rosh Chodesh Adar II *Yesod* *shebeChesed* *shebeNetzach*	**4** 2nd of Adar II *Malchut* *shebeChesed* *shebeNetzach*	**5 (WEEK 23)** 3rd of Adar II *Chesed* *shebeGevurah* *shebeNetzach*	**6** 4th of Adar II *Gevurah* *shebeGevurah* *shebeNetzach*	**7** 5th of Adar II *Tiferet* *shebeGevurah* *shebeNetzach*	**8** 6th of Adar II *Netzach* *shebeGevurah* *shebeNetzach*
9 7th of Adar II *Hod* *shebeGevurah* *shebeNetzach*	**10** 8th of Adar II *Yesod* *shebeGevurah* *shebeNetzach*	**11** 9th of Adar II *Malchut* *shebeGevurah* *shebeNetzach*	**12 (WEEK 24)** 10th of Adar II *Chesed* *shebeTiferet* *shebeNetzach*	**13** 11th of Adar II Ta'anit Esther *Gevurah* *shebeTiferet* *shebeNetzach*	**14** 12th of Adar II *Tiferet* *shebeTiferet* *shebeNetzach*	**15** 13th of Adar II Erev Purim *Netzach* *shebeTiferet* *shebeNetzach*
16 14th of Adar II Purim *Hod* *shebeTiferet* *shebeNetzach*	**17** 15th of Adar II Shushan Purim *Yesod* *shebeTiferet* *shebeNetzach*	**18** 16th of Adar II *Malchut* *shebeTiferet* *shebeNetzach*	**19 (WEEK 25)** 17th of Adar II *Chesed* *shebeNetzach* *shebeNetzach*	**20** 18th of Adar II *Gevurah* *shebeNetzach* *shebeNetzach*	**21** 19th of Adar II *Tiferet* *shebeNetzach* *shebeNetzach*	**22** 20th of Adar II *Netzach* *shebeNetzach* *shebeNetzach*
23 21st of Adar II *Hod* *shebeNetzach* *shebeNetzach*	**24** 22nd of Adar II *Yesod* *shebeNetzach* *shebeNetzach*	**25** 23rd of Adar II *Malchut* *shebeNetzach* *shebeNetzach*	**26 (WEEK 26)** 24th of Adar II *Chesed* *shebeHod* *shebeNetzach*	**27** 25th of Adar II *Gevurah* *shebeHod* *shebeNetzach*	**28** 26th of Adar II *Tiferet* *shebeHod* *shebeNetzach*	**29** 27th of Adar II *Netzach* *shebeHod* *shebeNetzach*
30 28th of Adar II *Hod* *shebeHod* *shebeNetzach*	**31** 29th of Adar II *Yesod* *shebeHod* *shebeNetzach*					

April 2014

Sunday	Monday	Tuesday	Wednesday	Thursday	Friday	Saturday
		1 1st of Nisan Rosh Chodesh Nisan *Malchut shebeHod shebeNetzach*	2 (WEEK 27) 2nd of Nisan *Chesed shebeYesod shebeNetzach*	3 3rd of Nisan *Gevurah shebeYesod shebeNetzach*	4 4th of Nisan *Tiferet shebeYesod shebeNetzach*	5 5th of Nisan *Netzach shebeYesod shebeNetzach*
6 6th of Nisan *Hod shebeYesod shebeNetzach*	7 7th of Nisan *Yesod shebeYesod shebeNetzach*	8 8th of Nisan *Malchut shebeYesod shebeNetzach*	9 (WEEK 28) 9th of Nisan *Chesed shebe Malchut shebeNetzach*	10 10th of Nisan *Gevurah shebe Malchut shebeNetzach*	11 11th of Nisan *Tiferet shebe Malchut shebeNetzach*	12 12th of Nisan *Netzach shebe Malchut shebeNetzach*
13 13th of Nisan *Hod shebe Malchut shebeNetzach*	14 14th of Nisan Ta'anit Bechorot Erev Pesach *Yesod shebe Malchut shebeNetzach*	15 15th of Nisan Pesach I *Malchut shebe Malchut shebeNetzach*	16 (WEEK 29) 16th of Nisan Pesach II 1st of the Omer *Chesed shebeChesed shebeHod*	17 17th of Nisan Pesach III 2nd of the Omer *Gevurah shebeChesed shebeHod*	18 18th of Nisan Pesach IV 3rd of the Omer *Tiferet shebeChesed shebeHod*	19 19th of Nisan Pesach V 4th of the Omer *Netzach shebeChesed shebeHod*
20 20th of Nisan Pesach VI 5th of the Omer *Hod shebeChesed shebeHod*	21 21st of Nisan Pesach VII 6th of the Omer *Yesod shebeChesed shebeHod*	22 22nd of Nisan Pesach VIII 7th of the Omer *Malchut shebeChesed shebeHod*	23 (WEEK 30) 23rd of Nisan 8th of the Omer *Chesed shebeGevurah shebeHod*	24 24th of Nisan 9th of the Omer *Gevurah shebeGevurah shebeHod*	25 25th of Nisan 10th of the Omer *Tiferet shebeGevurah shebeHod*	26 26th of Nisan 11th of the Omer *Netzach shebeGevurah shebeHod*
27 27th of Nisan 12th of the Omer *Hod shebeGevurah shebeHod*	28 28th of Nisan Yom HaShoah 13th of the Omer *Yesod shebeGevurah shebeHod*	29 29th of Nisan 14th of the Omer *Malchut shebeGevurah shebeHod*	30 (WEEK 31) 30th of Nisan Rosh Chodesh Iyar 15th of the Omer *Chesed shebeTiferet shebeHod*			

May 2014

Sunday	Monday	Tuesday	Wednesday	Thursday	Friday	Saturday
				1 1st of Iyar Rosh Chodesh Iyar 16th of the Omer *Gevurah shebeTiferet shebeHod*	**2** 2nd of Iyar 17th of the Omer *Tiferet shebeTiferet shebeHod*	**3** 3rd of Iyar 18th of the Omer *Netzach shebeTiferet shebeHod*
4 4th of Iyar 19th of the Omer *Hod shebeTiferet shebeHod*	**5** 5th of Iyar Yom HaZikaron 20th of the Omer *Yesod shebeTiferet shebeHod*	**6** 6th of Iyar Yom HaAtzma'ut 21st of the Omer *Malchut shebeTiferet shebeHod*	**7 (WEEK 32)** 7th of Iyar 22nd of the Omer *Chesed shebeNetzach shebeHod*	**8** 8th of Iyar 23rd of the Omer *Gevurah shebeNetzach shebeHod*	**9** 9th of Iyar 24th of the Omer *Tiferet shebeNetzach shebeHod*	**10** 10th of Iyar 25th of the Omer *Netzach shebeNetzach shebeHod*
11 11th of Iyar 26th of the Omer *Hod shebeNetzach shebeHod*	**12** 12th of Iyar 27th of the Omer *Yesod shebeNetzach shebeHod*	**13** 13th of Iyar 28th of the Omer *Malchut shebeNetzach shebeHod*	**14 (WEEK 33)** 14th of Iyar Pesach Sheni 29th of the Omer *Chesed shebeHod shebeHod*	**15** 15th of Iyar 30th of the Omer *Gevurah shebeHod shebeHod*	**16** 16th of Iyar 31st of the Omer *Tiferet shebeHod shebeHod*	**17** 17th of Iyar 32nd of the Omer *Netzach shebeHod shebeHod*
18 18th of Iyar Lag B'Omer 33rd of the Omer *Hod shebeHod shebeHod*	**19** 19th of Iyar 34th of the Omer *Yesod shebeHod shebeHod*	**20** 20th of Iyar 35th of the Omer *Malchut shebeHod shebeHod*	**21 (WEEK 34)** 21st of Iyar 36th of the Omer *Chesed shebeYesod shebeHod*	**22** 22nd of Iyar 37th of the Omer *Gevurah shebeYesod shebeHod*	**23** 23rd of Iyar 38th of the Omer *Tiferet shebeYesod shebeHod*	**24** 24th of Iyar 39th of the Omer *Netzach shebeYesod shebeHod*
25 25th of Iyar 40th of the Omer *Hod shebeYesod shebeHod*	**26** 26th of Iyar 41st of the Omer *Yesod shebeYesod shebeHod*	**27** 27th of Iyar 42nd of the Omer *Malchut shebeYesod shebeHod*	**28 (WEEK 35)** 28th of Iyar Yom Yerushalayim 43rd of the Omer *Chesed shebeMalchut shebeHod*	**29** 29th of Iyar 44th of the Omer *Gevurah shebeMalchut shebeHod*	**30** 1st of Sivan Rosh Chodesh Sivan 45th of the Omer *Tiferet shebeMalchut shebeHod*	**31** 2nd of Sivan 46th of the Omer *Netzach shebeMalchut shebeHod*

June 2014

Sunday	Monday	Tuesday	Wednesday	Thursday	Friday	Saturday
1 3rd of Sivan 47th of the Omer *Hod shebeMalchut shebeHod*	**2** 4th of Sivan 48th of the Omer *Yesod shebeMalchut shebeHod*	**3** 5th of Sivan Erev Shavuot 49th of the Omer *Malchut shebeMalchut shebeHod*	**4 (WEEK 36)** 6th of Sivan Shavuot I *Chesed shebeChesed shebeYesod*	**5** 7th of Sivan Shavuot II *Gevurah shebeChesed shebeYesod*	**6** 8th of Sivan *Tiferet shebeChesed shebeYesod*	**7** 9th of Sivan *Netzach shebeChesed shebeYesod*
8 10th of Sivan *Hod shebeChesed shebeYesod*	**9** 11th of Sivan *Yesod shebeChesed shebeYesod*	**10** 12th of Sivan *Malchut shebeChesed shebeYesod*	**11 (WEEK 37)** 13th of Sivan *Chesed shebeGevurah shebeYesod*	**12** 14th of Sivan *Gevurah shebeGevurah shebeYesod*	**13** 15th of Sivan *Tiferet shebeGevurah shebeYesod*	**14** 16th of Sivan *Netzach shebeGevurah shebeYesod*
15 17th of Sivan *Hod shebeGevurah shebeYesod*	**16** 18th of Sivan *Yesod shebeGevurah shebeYesod*	**17** 19th of Sivan *Malchut shebeGevurah shebeYesod*	**18 (WEEK 38)** 20th of Sivan *Chesed shebeTiferet shebeYesod*	**19** 21st of Sivan *Gevurah shebeTiferet shebeYesod*	**20** 22nd of Sivan *Tiferet shebeTiferet shebeYesod*	**21** 23rd of Sivan *Netzach shebeTiferet shebeYesod*
22 24th of Sivan *Hod shebeTiferet shebeYesod*	**23** 25th of Sivan *Yesod shebeTiferet shebeYesod*	**24** 26th of Sivan *Malchut shebeTiferet shebeYesod*	**25 (WEEK 39)** 27th of Sivan *Chesed shebeNetzach shebeYesod*	**26** 28th of Sivan *Gevurah shebeNetzach shebeYesod*	**27** 29th of Sivan *Tiferet shebeNetzach shebeYesod*	**28** 30th of Sivan Rosh Chodesh Tamuz *Netzach shebeNetzach shebeYesod*
29 1st of Tamuz Rosh Chodesh Tamuz *Hod shebeNetzach shebeYesod*	**30** 2nd of Tamuz *Yesod shebeNetzach shebeYesod*					

July 2014

Sunday	Monday	Tuesday	Wednesday	Thursday	Friday	Saturday
		1 3rd of Tamuz *Malchut* *shebeNetzach* *shebeYesod*	**2 (WEEK 40)** 4th of Tamuz *Chesed* *shebeHod* *shebeYesod*	**3** 5th of Tamuz *Gevurah* *shebeHod* *shebeYesod*	**4** 6th of Tamuz *Tiferet* *shebeHod* *shebeYesod*	**5** 7th of Tamuz *Netzach* *shebeHod* *shebeYesod*
6 8th of Tamuz *Hod* *shebeHod* *shebeYesod*	**7** 9th of Tamuz *Yesod* *shebeHod* *shebeYesod*	**8** 10th of Tamuz *Malchut* *shebeHod* *shebeYesod*	**9 (WEEK 41)** 11th of Tamuz *Chesed* *shebeYesod* *shebeYesod*	**10** 12th of Tamuz *Gevurah* *shebeYesod* *shebeYesod*	**11** 13th of Tamuz *Tiferet* *shebeYesod* *shebeYesod*	**12** 14th of Tamuz *Netzach* *shebeYesod* *shebeYesod*
13 15th of Tamuz *Hod* *shebeYesod* *shebeYesod*	**14** 16th of Tamuz *Yesod* *shebeYesod* *shebeYesod*	**15** 17th of Tamuz Tzom Tammuz *Malchut* *shebeYesod* *shebeYesod*	**16 (WEEK 42)** 18th of Tamuz *Chesed* *shebeMalchut* *shebeYesod*	**17** 19th of Tamuz *Gevurah* *shebeMalchut* *shebeYesod*	**18** 20th of Tamuz *Tiferet* *shebeMalchut* *shebeYesod*	**19** 21st of Tamuz *Netzach* *shebeMalchut* *shebeYesod*
20 22nd of Tamuz *Hod* *shebeMalchut* *shebeYesod*	**21** 23rd of Tamuz *Yesod* *shebeMalchut* *shebeYesod*	**22** 24th of Tamuz *Malchut* *shebeMalchut* *shebeYesod*	**23 (WEEK 43)** 25th of Tamuz *Chesed* *shebeChesed* *shebeMalchut*	**24** 26th of Tamuz *Gevurah* *shebeChesed* *shebeMalchut*	**25** 27th of Tamuz *Tiferet* *shebeChesed* *shebeMalchut*	**26** 28th of Tamuz *Netzach* *shebeChesed* *shebeMalchut*
27 29th of Tamuz *Hod* *shebeChesed* *shebeMalchut*	**28** 1st of Av Rosh Chodesh Av *Yesod* *shebeChesed* *shebeMalchut*	**29** 2nd of Av *Malchut* *shebeChesed* *shebeMalchut*	**30 (WEEK 44)** 3rd of Av *Chesed* *shebeGevurah* *shebeMalchut*	**31** 4th of Av *Gevurah* *shebeGevurah* *shebeMalchut*		

August 2014

Sunday	Monday	Tuesday	Wednesday	Thursday	Friday	Saturday
					1 5th of Av *Tiferet* *shebeGevurah* *shebeMalchut*	2 6th of Av *Netzach* *shebeGevurah* *shebeMalchut*
3 7th of Av *Hod* *shebeGevurah* *shebeMalchut*	4 8th of Av Erev Tish'a B'Av *Yesod* *shebeGevurah* *shebeMalchut*	5 9th of Av Tish'a B'Av *Malchut* *shebe Gevurah* *shebeMalchut*	6 (WEEK 45) 10th of Av *Chesed* *shebeTiferet* *shebeMalchut*	7 11th of Av *Gevurah* *shebeTiferet* *shebeMalchut*	8 12th of Av *Tiferet* *shebeTiferet* *shebeMalchut*	9 13th of Av *Netzach* *shebeTiferet* *shebeMalchut*
10 14th of Av *Hod* *shebeTiferet* *shebeMalchut*	11 15th of Av *Yesod* *shebeTiferet* *shebeMalchut*	12 16th of Av *Malchut* *shebeTiferet* *shebeMalchut*	13 (WEEK 46) 17th of Av *Chesed* *shebeNetzach* *shebeMalchut*	14 18th of Av *Gevurah* *shebeNetzach* *shebeMalchut*	15 19th of Av *Tiferet* *shebeNetzach* *shebeMalchut*	16 20th of Av *Netzach* *shebeNetzach* *shebeMalchut*
17 21st of Av *Hod* *shebeNetzach* *shebeMalchut*	18 22nd of Av *shebeNetzach* *shebeMalchut*	19 23rd of Av *shebeNetzach* *shebeMalchut*	20 (WEEK 47) 24th of Av *Chesed* *shebeHod* *shebeMalchut*	21 25th of Av *Gevurah* *shebeHod* *shebeMalchut*	22 26th of Av *Tiferet* *shebeHod* *shebeMalchut*	23 27th of Av *Netzach* *shebeHod* *shebeMalchut*
24 28th of Av *Hod* *shebeHod* *shebeMalchut*	25 29th of Av *Yesod* *shebeHod* *shebeMalchut*	26 30th of Av Rosh Chodesh Elul *Malchut* *shebeHod* *shebeMalchut*	27 (WEEK 48) 1st of Elul Rosh Chodesh Elul *Chesed* *shebeYesod* *shebeMalchut*	28 2nd of Elul *Gevurah* *shebeYesod* *shebeMalchut*	29 3rd of Elul *Tiferet* *shebeYesod* *shebeMalchut*	30 4th of Elul *Netzach* *shebeYesod* *shebeMalchut*
31 5th of Elul *Hod* *shebeYesod* *shebeMalchut*						

September 2014

Sunday	Monday	Tuesday	Wednesday	Thursday	Friday	Saturday
	1 6th of Elul *Yesod shebe Yesod shebeMalchut*	2 7th of Elul *Malchut shebe Yesod shebeMalchut*	3 (WEEK 49) 8th of Elul *Chesed shebeMalchut shebeMalchut*	4 9th of Elul *Gevurah shebeMalchut shebeMalchut*	5 10th of Elul *Tiferet shebeMalchut shebeMalchut*	6 11th of Elul *Netzach shebeMalchut shebeMalchut*
7 12th of Elul *Hod shebeMalchut shebeMalchut*	8 13th of Elul *Yesod shebeMalchut shebeMalchut*	9 14th of Elul *Malchut shebeMalchut shebeMalchut*	10 (WEEK 50) 15th of Elul *Chochmah*	11 16th of Elul *Chochmah*	12 17th of Elul *Chochmah*	13 18th of Elul *Chochmah*
14 19th of Elul *Chochmah*	15 20th of Elul *Chochmah*	16 21st of Elul *Chochmah*	17 (WEEK 51) 22nd of Elul *Binah*	18 23rd of Elul *Binah*	19 24th of Elul *Binah*	20 25th of Elul *Binah*
21 26th of Elul *Binah*	22 27th of Elul *Binah*	23 28th of Elul *Binah*	24 (WEEK 52) 29th of Elul Erev Rosh Hashana *Da'at/Keter*	25 1st of Tishrei, 5775 Rosh Hashana *Da'at/Keter*	26 2nd of Tishrei, 5775 Rosh Hashana II; *Da'at/ Keter*	27 3rd of Tishrei, 5775 *Da'at/Keter*
28 4th of Tishrei, 5775 *Da'at/Keter*	29 5th of Tishrei, 5775 *Da'at/Keter*	30 6th of Tishrei, 5775 *Da'at/Keter*				

SUMMARIZED BIBLIOGRAPHY

ARUSH, Rabbi Shalom. *The Garden of Emuna*; translated by Rabbi Lazer Brody, 3rd edition, Jerusalem, Chut Shel Chessed Institutions, 2008.

Inner.org: Authentic Jewish Mysticism and Thought Based on the Teachings of Harav Yitzchak Ginsburgh. Available at: <http://www.inner.org/hebrew_calendar/index.php> and <http://www.inner.org/powers/powers.htm> Acessed on: 14 Jun. 2012.

JACOBSON, Rabbi Simon. *A Spiritual Guide to the Counting of the Omer: Forty-Nine Steps to Personal Refinement According to Jewish Tradition*, N.Y., Vaad Hanochos Hatimim, 1996.

MARCUS, Rabbi Yosef. *Pirkei Avot: Ethics of the Fathers*, N.Y., Kehot Publication Society, 2009.

RYZMAN, Zvi. *The Wisdom in the Hebrew Months*; adapted and translated by Rabbi Yehuda Heimowitz, N.Y., Mesorah Publications, Ltd, 2009.

SCHNEERSOHN, The Rebbe, Rabbi Yosef Y. *Hayom Yom . . . From Day to Day*, compiled by The Rebbe, Rabbi Menachem M. Schneerson, revised edition, N.Y., Kehot Publication Society, 2005.

SLIFKIN, Rabbi Nosson. *The Torah Universe: Nature's Song*, Southfield, MI, Targum Press, 2001.

WINEBERG, Rabbi Yosef. *Lessons in Tanya,* 2nd Edition, N.Y., Kehot Publication Society, 2001.

English translations of Hebrew texts come primarily from Chabad.org, except for the translation of *Perek Shirah,* which is Rabbi Nosson Slifkin's.